The Interpreter's Daughter

The Interpreter's Daughter

TERESA LIM

MICHAEL  JOSEPH

PENGUIN MICHAEL JOSEPH

UK | USA | Canada | Ireland | Australia
India | New Zealand | South Africa

Penguin Michael Joseph is part of the Penguin Random House group of companies
whose addresses can be found at global.penguinrandomhouse.com

First published by Michael Joseph 2022

001

Research supported by the National Heritage Board of Singapore. The views expressed here are
solely those of the author in her private capacity and do not in any way represent the views of
the National Heritage Board and/or any government agencies.

Picture credits: Map and family tree: © Ian Moores. Integrated images: p. 14 © The British Library Board
(Source: 0 11102.b.20, p.21; 0 11102.b.20, p.25); p. 85 © The British Library Board (Source: 0 16126.d.1(14));
p. 86 © The British Library Board (Source: 0 16126.d.1(55)); all other images author's own. Inset:
p. 1 (top image) © The British Library Board (Source: 0 16126.d.1(55)); (bottom image)
© The British Library Board (Source: 0 16126.d.1(14)); p.2 (Cantonment Road) from Wikipedia, Zairon:
https://commons.wikimedia.org/wiki/File:Singapore_Cantonment_Road.jpg. No changes made;
p. 4 (registration form) with kind permission of University Archives, University of Hong Kong;
(smudged signature) with kind permission of Susan Tsang; p. 7 (street scene) with kind permission of
Dr Ho Nai-Kiong; bottom photograph with kind permission of Lianhe Zaobao.
All other images author's own.

Every effort has been made to trace copyright holders and to obtain their permission for the use of
copyright material. The publisher apologizes for any errors or omissions and would be grateful
to be notified of any corrections that should be incorporated in future editions of this book.

Set in 13.5/16pt Garamond MT Std
Typeset by Jouve (UK), Milton Keynes
Printed and bound in Great Britain by Clays Ltd, Elcograf S.p.A.

The authorized representative in the EEA is Penguin Random House Ireland,
Morrison Chambers, 32 Nassau Street, Dublin D02 YH68

A CIP catalogue record for this book is available from the British Library

HB ISBN: 978–0–241–54440–2
OM PAPERBACK ISBN: 978–0–241–54441–9

www.greenpenguin.co.uk

For Nick and Violet

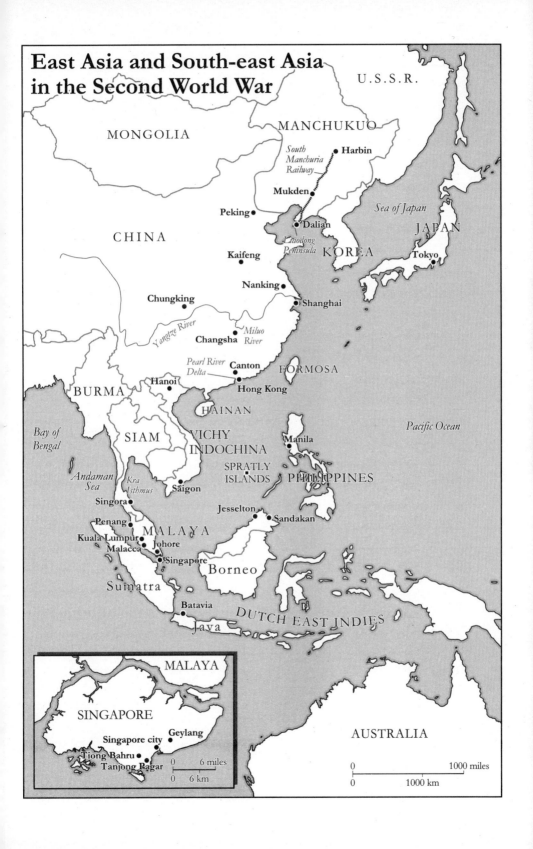

East Asia and South-east Asia in the Second World War

MONGOLIA

U.S.S.R.

MANCHUKUO

South Manchuria Railway

Harbin

Mukden

Peking

Dalian

Sea of Japan

JAPAN

CHINA

Kaifeng

Liaodong Peninsula

KOREA

Tokyo

Chungking

Nanking

Shanghai

Yangtze River

Changsha

Miluo River

Pearl River Delta

Canton

FORMOSA

Hanoi

Hong Kong

BURMA

HAINAN

Pacific Ocean

Bay of Bengal

SIAM

VICHY INDOCHINA

Manila

Andaman Sea

Kra Isthmus

Saigon

SPRATLY ISLANDS

PHILIPPINES

Singora

Penang

Jesselton

Sandakan

Kuala Lumpur

MALAYA

Malacca

Johore

Singapore

Borneo

Sumatra

Batavia

DUTCH EAST INDIES

Java

MALAYA

SINGAPORE

Geylang

Singapore city

Tiong Bahru

Tanjong Pagar

0   6 miles

0   6 km

AUSTRALIA

0   1000 miles

0   1000 km

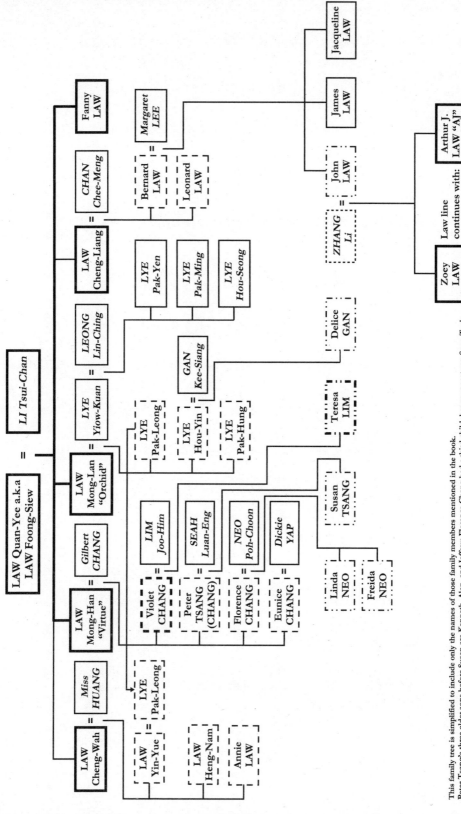

This family tree is simplified to include only the names of those family members mentioned in the book.
Peter Tsang's three older sons before Susan are Kenneth, Alan, and Jeffrey; Florence Chang had a third child, her youngest son Soon Teck.

Author's Note

Chinese spellings: Nearly all place names are Romanized according to the Wade–Giles system in use during my great-grandfather's time. Exceptions are when there are more familiar forms, e.g. Canton province instead of Kwangtung province or Dalian instead of Ta-lien, or when places are mentioned in a current context. Dynasty names seem less confusing if left in Pinyin. The names of my ancestors in the family genealogy were translated into Pinyin, and I have left them as they are.

Chinese surnames: A reminder that Chinese names traditionally start with the surname first, followed by the given names, usually two. I have hyphenated the given names, e.g. Law Quan-Yee.

Names and terms which were commonly used in the past have been left unchanged for authenticity. I have adopted the same approach when quoting from books written before some of their terminology became offensive to many.

Singapore Chilli Crab

Buy two mud crabs live and quarter.

Pound to a paste a thumb-piece of ginger, two fistfuls of shallot, four cloves of garlic, a pair of red, red chillies.

Heat lard in a wok, add mixture, stir till spicy smells erupt.

Turn up the heat and fry the crabs quickly. Throw in a bowlful of water, a spoonful of sugar, a splash of soy sauce, fiery chilli oil and enough ketchup to make the colours come alive – as red and angry as the cooked crab, as fierce as longing or regret.

Thicken with beaten egg. Serve.

Introduction

One cold morning in 1992, on the very last day of February, I arrived to live in Britain for the first time with my husband, who is English, and our three-year-old son. London was as grey and damp as everyone said it would be.

We had left a country full of smiling people, where the air was warm and where our Malaysian housekeeper had knitted a farewell jumper for our son in a colour as bright and optimistic as the sky above our heads: a pure cerulean. It was out of place in London where navy ruled the playground and where, if you were lucky, the early spring sky was dull white with cloud.

We moved into a north-facing house in south London that had recently been burgled of most of its furniture and where the boiler had stopped working. I was in my late thirties, no longer culturally nimble. Everything was surprising or seemed difficult.

I thought that I spoke and understood English – my education in Singapore had been entirely in English – but it wasn't English in its rich diversity of regional accents and colloquialisms. I couldn't understand the Mancunian telephonist at British Gas or the plumbers who came to fix the boiler. It took a while to recognize 'Aw-rite?' as a greeting.

The nursery-school friend and his mother who came to lunch ('We *love* Chinese food') found my fried rice, with its lashings of treacly oyster sauce, impossible to eat. When I dropped off our son at his classmate's birthday party, the children whispered audibly to each other: 'That's Victor's mother. She's *Chinese*.'

This was our home now and I wanted to belong. Determined at least to appear more western culturally, I forced every protesting sinew in my body to do as it was bid the first time that I found myself in a swimming-pool changing room with our son. Not looking at anyone, trying to appear as nonchalant as possible, I stripped off completely in front of the other mothers and children while I swapped a wet swimsuit for knickers and bra, T-shirt and jeans. I had heard that this was what European women did. Oops, wrong European country. The entire changing room fell silent.

You don't get to understand a country straight away even when you're fluent in the language.

At the parties that we went to in London they could have been speaking Swahili for all I knew: recently arrived, my mind drew a huge blank around Westminster gossip, the latest English comedians, the latest English bands, the latest English television. There was very little interest in Southeast Asia. As if the region could be any less pertinent, at a dinner in Dulwich a young English solicitor one along on the table placement was surprised to discover that Singapore was once a British colony. 'Really?' she asked.

The chill and anxiety of those early years were warmed and eased by emails from cousins who had also married men from strange, cool climates. There was Freida in Australia, Linda in Germany and Delice in Sweden, their names, like mine, the vestige of a European empire.

They sent recipes like curls of sultry air straight into my cold study, carrying the memory of colour and heat, replicating the smells and tastes that we longed for, of *laksas* and *gorengs* bright orange with warmth and promise.

I decided that this could be a great format for a cookbook. We could call it 'Four Cousins' and it would show how we ate our way out of missing home by adapting our Singaporean dishes to what we could buy from the *Isemarkt* of Hamburg, the *marknad* of Stockholm, and the farmers' markets and supermarkets of Fremantle and south London. But my cousins were less than enthusiastic. '*Thirty* recipes each? You're mad!'

I wasn't ready to give up. I desperately needed occupation, the comfort of activity beyond the everyday when the everyday was reminding me that I was far from home. Here was a project that could keep me close to everything familiar. Perhaps I could win my cousins over if, first, I wrote a preface on the person whose blood we share? Our cookbook would then be more of an extended family essay. Linda, Freida and I have the same grandmother; her younger sister was Delice's grandmother. We are therefore first and second cousins with our maternal great-grandfather in common.

We knew almost nothing about him, only that he had left China for Singapore when he was seventeen and had loved his daughters as much as his sons, a remarkable quirk for a Chinese man of his era. It would be worth finding out more but his children were no longer alive and his grandchildren, my uncles and my aunts, had not much more than the odd recollection.

My mother remembered the most. She was the oldest of the grandchildren who had lived with him and I knew her stories. I had asked for them again and again as I was growing up, an only child left at home with the cook all day; to me, my mother's childhood seemed entrancing, crowded with the company of younger siblings and cousins, full of games and pranks.

They were only anecdotes, but my mother also had a photograph. I did not know it at the time, but this one clue would take me, over several years, to libraries and archives in Britain and Asia and allow me to follow our great-grandfather's voyage from Canton to Singapore while I reflected on my own transfer to another exotic place, London.

I discovered that I was just one in a long line of emigrants in my family. These stretched back far beyond my great-grandfather, forced out of their homes by past exigencies (whereas I had travelled comfortably to Britain in peaceful times).

It became clear that to find out more about my great-grandfather, I would also have to navigate long-ago famines and the forgotten wars of East Asia – driven by imperialism – that had such an impact on his family. Few of us escape from what makes history, even if it happens far from where we are. My family had felt securely distant from the pressures building up around the world, but these would shatter on their doorstep.

My preface grew over many years to take me to another unexpected place: when I set off to look for our great-grandfather, I had no idea the search would end with our great-aunt. It is our great-grandfather's youngest daughter who is at the heart of this story.

I was unaware of her till I was eight years old, home from school one day full of a theatrical classmate's tragic and violent descriptions of her family's ordeal in Singapore during the Second World War. Did we have anything similar? I had asked my mother hopefully. She had said yes, there was misfortune involving her aunt, my great-aunt, but she wouldn't say much more. What she did tell me was so spare and matter-of-fact that it put me off completely. I felt let down. This was never going to impress my new, blood-thirsty friend.

It was only years later, seeing this great-aunt in a photograph for the first time, young and beautiful, that I became curious again about her.

This time, no longer a child, I pressed my mother with questions and there were answers, but also prevarications. I began to get the sense that this was never going to be a story fully told. What was missing was the flesh and blood of the woman in the picture.

She began to fill out as I looked into my great-grandfather's history. She was his youngest child and she had dreamed that she could break free of the centuries of tradition that had confined and weighed on Chinese women. She believed that she could transform herself with an English name and an English education. She had enrolled herself at an English primary school at the age of seventeen and went on to university in Hong Kong in 1932, the only woman to go directly from Singapore. She did not foresee that larger forces can sometimes bear upon us to interfere with our plans.

She chose an English name for herself that is engraved on her tombstone – Fanny Law – though when she died she was still chained to Chinese tradition. But by then she had built a bridge between the orthodox and the modern for the later generations of women in her family, and they never looked back.

And yet Fanny's nieces and nephews – my uncles and my aunts – never wanted to talk about her. I would learn from them that the stories families leave out have the power to redefine what they keep in. With my family these were not secrets intentionally withheld, but truths too painful to confront.

It was detective work, serendipity and the kindness of strangers that guided me to Fanny's ordinary, extraordinary life and her world of sworn spinsters, ghost husbands and the working-class feminists of nineteenth-century south China. There were such happy chances in my research that they made me think, more than once, that Fanny wanted to be heard – though I would have to wait till the end of writing this book to find the piece of puzzle that was missing.

Reclaiming Fanny's story made me realize that to remember is to perform a kind of magic: the simple act of remembering, even momentary or cursory, awards respect to a life however brief or unfulfilled, mundane or wretched, to acknowledge the fact that every individual existence is profound.

And context is nearly everything. We cannot fully understand lives without it. To recover my great-aunt's past, we have first to know her family, the times and circumstances in which they lived, the momentous conflicts that would lead to the Second World War in Singapore and ultimately to family tragedy.

A cliché quickly attached itself to me: no story is just one story and of course Fanny's had begun long before she was born. Other histories wanted inspection first (including even a little of my own). There was her father – our great-grandfather – the migrant to Singapore, the starting point of this memoir, of whom the only certain piece of information I had was on a photograph. At the start, all that I had was the photograph.

Before she grew forgetful, my mother had copies of a cherished picture made for those in it who were still alive. She kept her original for me. It is mounted in a card folder with the name of the studio stamped at the bottom in Chinese characters. She has written down the place and the date: 'Hong Kong, 1935'. It will have to be where I begin.

Half a century has passed since my great-grandfather sailed from China to the southern seas or Nanyang, to an island in the tropics where rats grew as big as cats and centipedes wriggled and multiplied in the rafters to fall in clumps on the unwary. He has grown old, lost when without his ebony opium pipe. He longs to go home to die.

He has gathered up his daughters and nearly all his grand-children (his sons have had to remain behind) to sail with him by steamship from Singapore to Hong Kong. He wants them close on his final journey home.

The plan is to spend a few days sightseeing in Hong Kong before taking the train from Kowloon to Canton. From there they will travel to the village where he was born to say their final goodbyes.

In Hong Kong, he has an idea. They should mark this moment with a photograph. Someone spots a studio called Source of Beauty (inspired by the owner's wife, perhaps; more likely by his mistress) and they bustle noisily through the door, bearing with them like a gift an old man with a walking stick. The older women loudly negotiate the cost of a family portrait as the children scatter about the shop. If they distract the proprietor just enough, he may give way on the price.

The photographer recognizes instantly from their unfashionable clothes and accents that they are Cantonese from the Nanyang, emigrants to Malaya, but he doesn't turn his nose up at them. This is 1935. Hong Kong is finally collapsing from the aftershocks of the Great Depression while, too close to home, the Japanese are again aggressive in China. Business has slowed right down.

He gives a long inward sigh and deals deftly with the inquisitive young men and their endless questions about his camera, the pesky children nearly knocking over the lights, the background din of the young ladies' constant high-pitched chat.

'Watch my hand, watch, watch, watch!' and poof! after a cloud of flash powder, there they are, my family, captured forever: my mother on the far right in a cardigan, my aunties young and fresh in demure Chinese shifts; my uncles surprisingly handsome in their borrowed linen jackets; and the older women with their carefully arranged expressions of resigned expectation. The young children now appear angelic.

They are all positioned respectfully around an old man, their fading star – my mother's grandfather, my great-grandfather, a former interpreter in the administration of the British Straits Settlements. He is seated on a rattan chair, small and frail in a padded Chinese gown and silk shoes. His legs are crossed, his hands are on his lap. He is still a commanding presence though his eyes are nearly empty, drained by experience and an opium habit.

His eldest daughter, my grandmother, is behind him in a light-coloured cheongsam, her dark hair scraped back severely to reveal her magnificent forehead, as pale and implacable as a chalk cliff. To her right is her youngest sister Fanny, twenty-eight years old, their father's favourite child.

My great-aunt Fanny is looking directly at the camera, her short black hair swept softly away from her oval face. Her dark silk dress is flecked with a pattern of what look oddly like tiny slices of watermelon. You can just glimpse a slim gold watch on her left wrist. Her eyes are luminous; her face is expressive. There is entreaty in the slight tilt of her head. You can see why I found her compelling though our family wanted to forget her.

We are all sub-texts of history, which cannot be erased. Sometimes it offers merely a digression. Sometimes, it rewrites the stories of our lives.

If I had to make a guess, I'd say that the old man in the photograph, our great-grandfather, looks about seventy. Sometimes you must leap into the unknown and hope to fly.

Working back from the date of the picture then takes me to 1865 for the year when he was born. It was in a place called 'New District' – Sun Wui[1] – though it was given its name in AD 420 when China had gone through another of its periodic ruptures: the Eastern Jin dynasty had just ended, and a new, short-lived kingdom hardly justifying its own name busied itself drawing up new prefectural boundaries.

The year 1865 was peaceful enough, though the decade before had been turbulent with a second Opium War and a disastrous Taiping Rebellion. My great-grandfather would have been born to unreserved rejoicing in his village of Leong Kai. He was the first son of his nuclear family and a new male member for the Law clan that had, for centuries, lived in the Canton Delta.

The Canton or Pearl River Delta is an extraordinary place, so vast that one imagines it to be the work of nature over millennia. It is in fact manmade.

It started out as a wide and shallow bay fed by many rivers that flooded regularly. The people who lived there channelled the floods by building dykes along the riverbanks. Between the tenth and seventeenth centuries, from the Song to the Ming Dynasties, more than 1,000 kilometres of these were raised.[2] These dykes forced the rivers, turned sluggish as they moved through flattening land, to flow a little further before dumping their load of silt into the estuary. Sandbars began to form naturally, downstream of these. Farmers added rock and alluvium to expand them, and planted legumes to anchor them. Over two thousand years, the patient tending of countless sandbars by countless pairs of hands gradually merged together a delta bigger than Puerto Rico, 10,000 square kilometres in size.[3]

The people of this delta evolved to become exquisite agriculturalists. They wasted nothing. They managed their land so carefully that they could crop rice twice, even three times a year.[4] Later, they would produce nearly 15 per cent of the world's raw silk.[5]

But the delta's very breadth and fertility would be its undoing. It drew in refugees from famine and war. At first it could absorb everyone. Later, it could not.

At the start of the nineteenth century, China was richer than either Britain or France,[6] to which it exported enormous quantities of porcelain, tea and silk. It acquired miraculous New World crops – tapioca, peanut, sorghum – that could grow where nothing else would. With abundant food and foreign exchange, more people lived and more people lived longer. The population of China doubled from 150 million people to 300 million over the course of the eighteenth century. By 1850, fifteen years before my great-grandfather was born, it had swelled to 430 million.[7]

But land that could be cultivated was finite. A once full and contented population turned hungry and discontented. China's foreign Manchu rulers struggled to cope. Their Qing government, bloated by past prosperity and riven with corruption, was besieged from abroad by Western imperialists wanting access to China's market. Now they had also to contend with large-scale internal unrest.

The worst of these was, ironically, named 'Great Peace' or 'Taiping'. It began in 1850 just north of the Canton Delta to become what historians call the 'deadliest civil war in all of human history'.[8] It ended in 1864, killing 30 million people as it spread northwards towards Peking. Villages were burned and vast tracts of farmland laid waste in the violence between the rebels and the Emperor's armies.

'What is your village going to be like, Grandfather?'

In 1935, the fourteen of them are squeezed around a table for ten in a restaurant in Hong Kong at the end of a day spent sightseeing. Food is important to the Cantonese. You eat something special together – suckling pig, roast duck, barbecued pork – to mark an event. It is the ritual of those whose genes carry the experience of starvation. In a day or so they will board the train for Canton to find their way to Sun Wui and their grandfather's ancestral village of Leong Kai. From there on they will be in the company of extended family. Hong Kong is the last time that they will be on their own together.

'It is the most beautiful place in the world,' he replies as he puts his chopsticks down across his bowl of rice. He has worked and slept all these years like every emigrant abroad, dreaming of the day he would go back to the place to which his connection was umbilical. Whenever he closes his eyes, he can see its innumerable rice-fields shimmering together, like a green and silver sea.

This was a place of primary colours.

In early summer, lychees ripened in the trees to swag whole villages in red; in autumn, persimmons glowed orange. In winter, globes of mandarins lit up on their branches like small suns, and in spring, little yellow plums were plentiful.

These colours were reflected in the water that was everywhere. The people of the delta had judged over the centuries that their ecosystem worked best if they sculpted out the land and filled nearly half of it with water,[9] on which floated images of the blue sky and the fruit and the trees that grew around them on the dykes.

'We had ponds so full of fish, you could put your hand in and pick one up,' he says. It is the sort of boast an old man makes and his grandchildren ignore as they fight over the last pieces of roast pork, though one of them pauses long enough to ask, 'Then why did you leave?'

Sometime between the middle of the sixteenth and nineteenth centuries, the Earth's northern hemisphere went through a cooling period now known as the Little Ice Age. In

Europe this ended in 1850,[10] but in China it carried on into the 1890s, bringing freezing winters and cool summers.[11] Weather patterns became irregular. Monsoons were disrupted. The rain disappeared.

In 1873, a drought began in north China that, three years later, caused the worst famine of China's imperial history. By the famine's end in 1879, it had killed 10 million people in the provinces of Shansi, Honan, Shantung, Chihli (now Hebei) and Shensi.[12]

The Manchu Empire had no solution for the crisis. Its granaries had long since been emptied or else filled with badly stored grain that had spoilt. As the death toll soared, British missionaries and merchants in China felt they could no longer watch this catastrophe unfold and do nothing.

They formed a committee for a China Famine Relief Fund. To raise money, a Chinese pamphlet was translated and published in London, illustrated with woodblock prints by a Chinese artist.[13]

You can still find a copy of the pamphlet in London in the library of the School of Oriental and African Studies. This is a place so full of the energy of focused young people that it frequently erupts in a snatch of melody as a program opens on a laptop, or with a thump as books are unloaded quickly to signal the start of an afternoon's slog. It all melted into silence as I turned the pages.

On the first plate, there are quaint etchings in black and white that look innocuous. Here are little people with uptilted almond eyes who seem to be industriously building a house. In fact they are taking it apart to sell, piece by piece, saving only the thatch which they will eat.

As each plate progresses, the expressions on the faces of these delicate figures turn from relative composure to distress and then to horror – three people clothed like tramps linger to say goodbye to a little boy as a well-dressed man stands placidly waiting to take him away; a husband is distraught when he discovers his wife hanging from a beam while, in the background, his neighbour throws himself headlong into a torrent. On another page, two barely clothed men squat on the ground slicing meat off a corpse with a knife. In a denuded forest, skeletal men wander like the walking dead, a dark ooze around their feet: 'Coffins are not to be got for the corpses nor can graves be prepared for them. Their blood is an indistinct mess on the ground, their bones lie all about.'[14] The caption holds little back.

People from these provinces of north China began to leave. By the end of 1876, more than 10 million people from the five worst-affected areas had migrated to Kiangsu

province, just north of Shanghai. Roads were said to have turned black with refugees.[15]

Those who clung on through these devastating years were finally driven out of their homes in the winter of 1878, when wolves descended from the mountains to enter villages in packs. They devoured babies, children and the weak.[16]

Far to the south, in my great-grandfather's province of Canton, in addition to the domino effect of migration from the north, they were experiencing particular meteorological problems of their own. The same powerful climatic force that dessicated the north brought floods along the coast down to where Law and his family lived, and where they were already struggling.[17] The Taiping Rebellion had destroyed many farms in the south and any land that remained had become exhausted by years of over-intensive farming. Now floods submerged even those.

Whole villages were washed away by the incessant rain. Bodies floated in the floodwater, unclaimed. When it seemed it could not be worse, swarms of locusts and mice appeared out of nowhere to devour anything that remained.

As food became scarce, the stories that swept down from north China began to resonate most fearfully: desperate fathers were selling their sons, and husbands their wives. Men and women stripped the bark off trees to eat till these were bare.

Whole families committed suicide rather than face what was to come – which did come. At first the living ate their dead. Then came rumours that people murdered for meat. My great-grandfather, Law, was fourteen.

'Why did you leave?' A simple question becomes impossible to answer.

The famine affected everyone. I know that my great-grandfather's family was desperate because his father,

Hongxi, had come up with an uncompromising plan. He was going to to leave China with his two sons but without his daughter or his concubine.

Hongxi was acutely aware that his family might perish in the teeth of uncontrollable forces – God save them from ever becoming like the people of Shansi in the north – unless they did something to reclaim the initiative. As ever, money was key. If you had money you could buy food on the black market, or fortify your home against storms, or rebuild it after its destruction in a flood.

You could earn money by working abroad. This had become easier. The country's Manchu rulers had once forbidden emigration, worried that Chinese men on foreign soil were free to plot their downfall. However, in the nineteenth century the Manchus began gradually to ease restrictions. At first they were yielding to pressure from the Americans, the British and the French, whose colonies relied on indentured Chinese labour after slavery was banned. Later, during the famine years, when grain reserves were inadequate and a weak administration was incapable of organizing relief, it was just easier to let the starving hordes go.

In the middle of the nineteenth century, most Chinese emigrants ended up in that fabled land the Cantonese called the Golden Mountain, on the west coast of America. So many Cantonese men had gone there since the start of the California Gold Rush in 1848 that resentment grew against them in the American towns: the Chinese were simply too cheap and worked too hard. Now the US was planning a virtual moratorium on all Chinese immigration, not just on indentured labourers. It would sign its Chinese Exclusion Act into law in 1882, but already the effect of its intention was being felt.

With America to be off-limits, and similar gold rushes

petering out in Australia and New Zealand, the destination for many Cantonese in 1881 had become Southeast Asia, where they could mine tin and antimony, or trade in pepper. Law's father Hongxi had his eye on Singapore, nearly 3,000 kilometres across the South China Sea. It had an unsparing climate that was humid and malaria-ridden but he likely had a contact there.

In the nineteenth century, mutual aid societies were organized in the colony for Chinese immigrants. The Kong Chow Wui Koon is one of these, a league of clans from my great-grandfather's part of Canton – clans being sort of co-operatives to which all men and women of the same sur-name belonged.

It still exists, its main hall dominated by an enormously long and beautiful blackwood table running nearly the length of the room, with matching carved chairs on either side. Colourful lion's 'heads', props from the association's dance troupe, look down benignly at visitors.

On one of my visits to Singapore, I found myself there talk-ing to Michelle, one of its secretaries, about the earliest travellers from China. She said that it was rare to bring both your young sons with you on such an uncertain journey unless you had a connection in the colony that you believed was extremely reli-able. It was likely to have been someone in whom Law's father placed much faith. Though my great-grandfather turned seven-teen when they arrived, his younger brother was still only thirteen. That he was present with his elder brother and his father was a sign either of great hope or great desperation.

Perhaps Law and his brother felt excitement at first when they heard that they were to be part of this exodus of men leaving behind certain poverty for adventure in the unknown. They might have pestered returning clansmen to tell their stories of the southern seas. A monkey as big as a man!

Snakes *bigger* than men! Birds all the colours of the rainbow and one with feathers of gold – catch a few of those, and you'd have your fortune made. Then you could buy a rhinoceros in the market!

To pay for their voyage, Law's father would have sold whatever of value he still owned, making up any shortfall with help from his extended family. Or he may have borrowed the money for the fare from their clan association. It would, of course, have to be repaid and not just with money but through the complex system of obligations that only the Chinese understand.

By the late nineteenth century you could travel to Singapore by steamer from Macau or Hong Kong, services that were run by European companies and were much more expensive than a passage by traditional sailing junk. Law's village in Sun Wui was located near the West River, one of the tributaries of the Pearl, navigable along its entire length. Law, his brother and their father could embark on a junk from any of its landing stages to sail directly into the South China Sea. From there, in the winter with the northeast monsoon[18] behind them, they would be carried south down to Malaya.

Law's mother had died when he was younger, during another period of famine. His father's concubine looked after his brother, his sister and himself. Law would have been close to his sister. It would have been for her sake also that they were going to Singapore, to earn her dowry for the security that only marriage into a respectable family could provide.

While Law, his brother and his father were away, his father's concubine and his sister would be on their own. Of course there was extended family to keep an eye on them, but everyone was struggling. The two women were unhappily aware that until their men returned, their situation was precarious.

*

As the day of their departure draws near, Law becomes noisier as his sister grows quieter.

'What feast will you cook us, Sister? I will need to eat enough to last me till I come back. I want a whole suckling pig to myself, and a goose, and shark's fin in my soup!'

His sister tosses her head and pretends to sneer: 'You'll be lucky if I make you soup from my old shoes!'

Somehow she finds the money for a small chicken and some fish (perhaps she pawned one of the last pieces of their mother's jewellery) to prepare a special dinner for the night before their departure. She works all afternoon in the kitchen, gutting the fish, draining the chicken's crimson blood through the slit she has made in its throat, chopping rhythmically as she minces fresh lard with her cleaver before rendering it into oil in a hot wok.

Like all Chinese women, she cooks to protect. When she washes the earth off the ginger and spring onion so recently lifted from the ground, when she slices into them to free the power of their smell, she is willing them to be alchemical, to turn chicken and fish not into food but armour for her brothers. If she can do that, the impossible might be possible and she would see them again.

At dinner, she fusses over her father and her brothers to disguise her grief. Their stepmother hovers in the background like a sorrowful shade. Young Law's excitement at their imminent departure has begun to evaporate as he sits eating while his sister moves constantly to and from the kitchen, rarely meeting his eyes, almost as if she cannot bear to look upon his face. The next morning, on the quayside, the euphoria has all but vanished.

'Get on the boat, get on the boat!' the stevedores are

shouting, and the huge crowd of men starts to jostle towards the water.

'Don't cry,' Law says helplessly to his sister. She could not be put off coming to watch them board their boat. As the frenzy of embarkation begins, Law sees her as if for the first time. She looks very small and lost. She looks suddenly like their mother. He feels a sharp, familiar stab of pain.

Awkwardly he picks up his bundle of clothing with one hand, while with the other he tries to support her. Distress is tightening like a band around his heart.

'You'll see us again in no time but you won't recognize us! We'll be wearing gowns of silk and smoking from pipes of ebony. We'll dress you like a princess, in more gold and jade than you could ever imagine!' He can feel her body shake with sobs.

Someone is pulling his arm and he is finding it difficult to breathe. He tries to hold on to her but his chest feels so oppressed, he has to gasp for air.

He lets her go, briefly, to look for his father. The crowd immediately pushes them apart and he is carried on a tide of men coursing towards their boat. He fights to turn his head towards her, struggles to raise a free arm over those around him to wave to her. But she does not see. Her face is frozen in anguish as her eyes search the crowd.

'What are you doing, brother?' The man behind gives him a shove. 'Get a move on!' Law twists round momentarily to protest and when he looks back towards his sister, all trace of her is gone, lost in the ocean of men. He blinks back the tears that suddenly sting his eyes. He feels a heartache so bitter, it's in his mouth. He has to spit it out. It's a relief to board the boat and to let seasickness take over.

2

I met Nick in Shanghai in 1983 at a shipping and shipbuilding conference. We were both journalists based in Hong Kong.

Shanghai was only seven years past the end of a brutal Cultural Revolution. Nobody was sure what was acceptable and what was not. The city's only French restaurant was hidden down a side street in a speakeasy, whereas the Peace Hotel had resurrected its pre-Revolution band whose ancient musicians, dressed in Mao suits, played Glenn Miller. They squinted at their scores through state-prescribed spectacles with round frames, like schoolteachers on a musical tea break. Shanghai was where the unexpected could still happen.

We drank sweet cocktails made from fiery *mao-tai* and afterwards strolled alone on the nearby Bund, deserted except for a cat and a full moon. We found out too late that this was because all transport in the city stopped at 9 p.m.

As there was no taxi or bus to take me back to my hotel 4 kilometres away, I had to spend the night in Nick's room at the Peace Hotel. He gave up the bed in his junior suite to cram his 6-foot-6-inch frame on to a sofa designed for two small Chinese people. This made no difference at all the next morning to the Shanghainese bell-hops in the corridor, who sniggered just the same when we appeared, murmuring things to each other too soft for us to hear.

Being English, Nick thought it discourteous to put me in a taxi before a 'proper breakfast' at the restaurant. I emerged from the hotel feeling queasy from so much fried food first thing in the morning, including post-Cultural Revolution Shanghai's own version of European sausages. But the taxi-ride was soothing. 'The Butterfly Lovers' Concerto' played on the radio as I was driven through roads lined with plane trees, flooded in early autumn sunshine.

We decided that we would marry in Hong Kong, a mid-point between England and Singapore.

On both sides there were many unfathomable mysteries to the wedding we were organizing, but I found our wedding invitations the strangest. Traditional Chinese like bright red and gold cards printed with phoenixes and dragons. Red is for happiness, gold for prosperity. The dragon symbolizes man, the phoenix, woman. (Subtle it is not.)

By the 1980s, modern Chinese women everywhere began to prefer soft Western colours and motifs that were a little more discreet: silver bells, for instance, or a pair of doves. However, any fond imaginings that I had along the lines of entwining pastel ribbons were firmly swept away by my fiancé in favour of something stark and white. While it had become common to see Chinese brides dressed in white, white was and still is the colour of deepest mourning. It is what you wear when a parent dies.

These were austere, even ugly, invitations, and rather large. I was assured that they were English and traditional. They were on folded thick, stiff paper that was blank inside with engraved black script on the outside, designed to stand securely on a mantelpiece in England and to be easy to read without appearing to snoop – except few homes in Hong Kong had mantelpieces and we certainly didn't have them in Singapore, where one sweltered in the equatorial humidity and heat. These black-and-white cards were funereal in their simplicity. Were people being invited to a wedding or a wake? In that spring of 1985, South Africa ended its ban on inter-racial marriage for the first time. In London, the Brixton race riots would flare up after the summer. The scope for incomprehension between cultures was still vast.

But there are ways round anything. In Singapore, among the Chinese, it is the groom's parents who pay for the wedding reception; in England, it is of course the bride's. We simply paid for it ourselves, the sort of compromise that would see us through our future together.

After I was given away by my mother's brother Peter at the Anglican cathedral of St John's, we had our reception at the Foreign Correspondents' Club. Family and friends from Singapore, England and Hong Kong meeting for the first time chatted easily together in the language of a commonwealth – my mother in a cheongsam, my uncle Peter's wife Luan in her Malayan sarong and *kebaya*, the men in Nick's family in morning suits, the women wearing hats – though I was still bemused when my brother-in-law Joffin, in his best man's speech, made a tally of Nick's old girlfriends (previously undivulged), an English tradition of which I had not been forewarned.

That spring day in 1985, a family wedding photograph was taken in this British colony. At the time, I did not realize this was fifty years exactly after another spring day, in 1935, when a family picture had also been taken. Ours marked a beginning. The other, of my mother, her cousins and their grandfather on his last journey home, represented an end.

After we married, we moved to Malaysia where we had both found work. We settled eventually into a house in Kuala Lumpur that sat in the middle of a large lawn. The garden was empty except for a small knot of *nibong*, a graceful palm with fine fronds that hang straight down like a girl's fringe. We planted orange-flowered heliconia on the lawn's perimeter. We put in a frangipani tree. We grew ginger, and basil, and four-angled bean.

By now our son Victor was born and my mother was a frequent visitor as Kuala Lumpur was only a fifty-minute flight from Singapore. She loved our habit of a cold gin and tonic in the warm evenings, and she liked complaining about our housekeeper with whom she had a competitive relationship over the baby.

When we relocated to London and the journey from Singapore was much longer, after our younger son Arthur was born, my mother stayed with us for months at a time. We asked her to move in with us but, though she adored her grandsons, she refused. She found our child-centred lives too restricting.

I struggled with a baby and a young child and life in an unfamiliar place. I coped by taking it out on my mother. When she was with us I found her intensely annoying, but when she returned to Singapore I was full of regret for my impatience. I missed her as I missed, viscerally, our garden in Kuala Lumpur – how it smelt after the rain, how every plant flourished all year and flowered whenever it wanted, on a whim.

Our English garden was complex and secretive and followed a private code, much like this new country. Daffodils and tulips nosed up in the early spring like moles sniffing the air, dying politely to give way to a dwarf magnolia's star-shaped flowers and the small mauve blooms of its companions, two sister azaleas.

Others followed in strict order: purple lilac, amethyst wisteria, pink weigela, stripey Nelly Moser, hollyhock allsorts;

on and on, right up to the last roses, flame-coloured crocosmia and late dahlias. There was etiquette and formality. If I put in something that was spring flowering, that was what it did. It would not oblige like its tropical cousins, careless of the seasons. What did 'annual' or 'biennial' mean? They meant nothing in the evergreen, ever-flowering garden that we left behind.

Just as Singapore meant little here. It felt disheartening to be so redundant to the old imperial power that made us – whereas every Singaporean schoolchild knows that it was the Englishman Raffles who 'founded' Singapore, an old-fashioned word that disguises as much as it describes.

My school history books never mentioned that Thomas Stamford Bingley Raffles was the son of a slaver, born on a slaver's ship. Nor that it was by sleight of hand that he produced the thriving British settlement for which my great-grandfather Law would sail.

3

When Law's junk reached Singapore the voyage had taken nearly two weeks, their meals served like slop from buckets in the airless hold where he had been mostly confined with hundreds of men. My mother had said her grandfather was seventeen years old when he arrived, so this would have been 1882.

The pitching and rolling of the junk was intolerable to start with but he would have got used to it, as he would have the growing stench of the men around him. They slept in hammocks or on the planking, crammed together with barely any headroom, their belongings jammed between them in bundles and baskets. Every inch of space was used and shared with a variety of vermin, especially cockroaches which crawled everywhere, even into one's ears.

Nothing would have prepared Law and his younger brother for this, or their father. Everyone they spoke to in Canton would have talked about the journey's end, not the monotony and the misery of the journey itself. Why put off the emigrants before their travels had even begun? The three Law men would have struggled with seasickness and to care for each other, but there would have been no doubt in their minds that this was the right thing to do. They were committed to their course. There was no other option. They would have made a tally of their days left afloat. The thought of arrival would have kept them going.

Most of the other passengers on their ship were coolies or

indentured labourers, signed to cutthroat brokers on irreversible contracts. Their tickets had been bought for them – the fare to be extracted back later – unlike Law's father, who paid for their tickets himself with the help of his family or clan. A man would have to be beyond despair to indenture himself and both his sons.

'Coolie' is an uncomfortable term but truthful to its time. By the middle of the nineteenth century, many Chinese and Indian labourers had replaced their African brothers in Europe's plantations and mines in Cuba, the Caribbean and Southeast Asia. They were supposedly better off than slaves because they were indentured, but to all practical purposes their contracts enslaved them.

By 1865, slavery and the slave trade had been banned by many countries[1] but you could still hire a coolie and treat him little better than a serf. He was often 'recruited' through trickery or worse. Kidnappings from villages near the south China coast had become so bad (whole villages emptied of their able-bodied men) that kidnappers faced the death penalty in China if they were caught. Seven years after Law's voyage, a coolie broker was beheaded near Canton for spiriting away young men to Singapore.[2]

But there were also destitute men willingly lured by the offer of work in foreign lands with the cost of travel deferred. In fact, men on the infamous 'credit ticket system' earned nothing till they settled their passage debts, which could take years. They were treated like slaves, herded on to ships and ferried to lives so grim that they could only find oblivion in the opium that was readily supplied at a price, plunging them further into debt.

In 1874, China was so alarmed by the number of coolies dying in Cuba – two-thirds in twenty-seven years[3] – that it sent an official commission there. Its members met Chinese men who had been maimed by their employers, who had been blinded or had their limbs fractured, their flesh lacerated, their teeth struck out or their ears mutilated. The suicide rate was high. When a coolie found at the end of an eight-year bond that he was 'free' but still too poor to buy a passage home, he might hang himself or cut his own throat. Some coolies threw themselves into the sugar cauldrons.[4]

At least the coolies on Law's boat were not in chains or under locked hatches as they had been on early labourer ships to Latin America. In 1872, 640 coolies had died when they were abandoned by the crew, trapped in the hold of the *Don Juan* when it caught fire on leaving Macau.[5]

The captain of Law's boat has restricted visits up on deck only because there are too many passengers. But as their junk sweeps southwards[6] towards the equator, men are pushing their way up, protesting. With the sun high and bright overhead, it is stiflingly hot in the hold, especially since the junk has slowed right down to pick its way among the many flat islands strewn like green pebbles in the shallow sea around them. More men surge out from below. Law slips quietly behind them. He blinks in the bright sun even as he exults in the fresh air as a light breeze skims over his hair. Then he watches in wonder as they finally approach their destination.

Law could have reasonably expected Singapore to be a proper settlement, but the town that is emerging out of the blue haze of the afternoon is more imposing than he ever imagined. There are buildings in a grand style he has never seen before, some of them as tall as small hills. One of these is white, with a steeply pitched roof rising narrowly to a needlepoint in the sky. Someone says it is an English temple.

They go past fishermen's shelters that are wooden shacks on stilts in the water. Women are bathing under them in full view of every man on ship and shore, their hair tied up, their brown skin glistening in the sun. Although their bodies are loosely wrapped in thin cloth, their shoulders are bare. They seem unconcerned by their immodesty, but Law averts his eyes for their sake.

Looking away towards the town beyond the casuarina trees that line the seafront, he sees carefully demarcated roads on which white men ride horses. The men are completely covered up in peculiar tight trousers (how uncomfortable they must be) and long-sleeved jackets. Their shirts are buttoned up to their necks. Some of their women are in open carriages and hold over themselves little umbrellas made of light cloth. Law cannot help but think that these would be useless in the rain.

Sixty-two years have passed since the January day in 1819 when Sir Stamford Raffles left the island of Penang on a mission to beat the Dutch. This was not *quite* with the blessing of his employer, the East India Company, and completely against the wishes of his host, the Governor of Penang.

Raffles had fallen from previous glory to run an unimportant station in Sumatra named Bencoolen, but he couldn't help being the gifted strategist that he was, driven by patriotism. He did not have explicit permission to lead the convoy of seven ships waiting for the tide to turn outside the harbour in Penang,[7] so he stole from his bed at dawn to row out to them. He planned to take them south, down the length of the lobster-claw shaped Malay Peninsula, to a tiny outcrop perched just beyond its reach like a delectable morsel.

Trade had flourished since the eighteenth century between two great spheres: Europe and India on the one side, China and Japan on the other. Between them lay the Malay Archipelago. The quickest route across was either through the Malacca Strait, which Holland controlled from Malacca; or through the Sunda Strait, which Holland controlled from the vital port of Batavia, now called Jakarta.

These were not free ports. The Dutch were not inclined to share.

Raffles found this infuriating because he had once been lieutenant governor of Batavia, after he helped the British conquer it in 1811. He had inherited a decrepit economy which he revived only to learn, four years later, that it would be handed back to the Dutch because Britain needed Holland as an ally against Napoleon.

Far from now treating the English with some favour in the China trade, the Dutch were progressively cutting them out. Knowing that Penang was too far to the north of the Malacca Strait to be useful to the British, they hurried to occupy even the least significant harbours at its southern end, conceding not even a fingerhold's clutch on the area.

But the Dutch had reckoned without Raffles. He could speak and read Malay. He had a reputation for being impetuous. He had heard of a place close to the trading heart of the Malay Archipelago which had fallen into obscurity, though it had been known to Malay and Chinese traders since at least the fourteenth century. Its unprepossessing coast was one reason, edged with mangrove swamps. Its small population of vexatious pirates was another. Its name was *Singapura*.

Its nominal ruler was a Dutch ally, but he did not live on the island. Crucially, Raffles knew that he was not the previous chieftain's eldest son and heir. He had stolen the throne from his brother.[8]

Once on the island, Raffles had this deposed older brother

located and brought to him; then Raffles persuaded him with smiles of 'infinite charm' and words as 'sweet as a sea of honey'[9] reluctantly to accept his restoration by the British. In return he was to allow the British their trading post.

The Treaty of Friendship and Alliance was signed with fanfare on a beach. Guns were fired; flags were raised. The moment required sufficient ceremony to suggest legality.

Before sailing back to Bencoolen, Raffles drew up a town plan. He gave the island its own garrison and installed a British Resident and Commandant. Then he threw it open as a free port. He calculated that Holland, sitting on most of the East Indies, would rely on diplomatic negotiation with England first, rather than immediate war. In this narrowest window of time, his little colony would have to grow important enough for the British to want to keep and defend it.

In the event, Raffles very nearly provoked an Anglo-Dutch war over Singapore for which the East India Company never quite forgave him. But he was to be proved right. Singapore would secure the Far Eastern trade for the British and, after the opening of the Suez Canal fifty years later in 1869, would eclipse every port in the region owned by the Dutch.

Law's boat draws alongside the quay with a jolt, but they remain on board for at least another hour before an expectant rustle among the crew makes him look in their direction. They have lowered a ramp and two men are now coming on board from the dock. Law is suddenly seized with anxiety. These men are white, pale as ghosts. He has no idea what to expect.

One of the two appears to be the elder though it is impossible to tell from their appearance, as both have hair the colour of straw. But his partner is deferential to him. The older man stands on the gunwale, clears his throat loudly, and starts to speak.

At first, Law cannot understand him. Then a horrified wonder fills him. He glances over quickly at his father, whose mouth has fallen open. It cannot be, and yet it is: the white man is speaking some sort of Cantonese!

The island that Raffles claimed for Britain had about a thousand residents, mainly Malay sea gypsies. By the time of Law's arrival in 1882, the population had grown to more than a hundred thousand.[10] Only five thousand of these were European, though every significant European power from France to Austria–Hungary had a diplomatic presence here, as did America, Brazil, Hawaii and, of course, China. Three-quarters of the population were Chinese, specifically young Chinese men from the south coast of China. The free port that Raffles set up had also become an entrepôt for human lives. The British needed Chinese coolies to cut down jungle and to build and work their mines and plantations, as did the Dutch in the neighbouring East Indies.

Coolies were ill treated on the whole but most abominably at Deli in Sumatra, where Dutch tobacco plantation owners were vicious, like the Spanish in Cuba. They were hampered neither by legislation nor scruple.[11] If you were horse-whipped or thrown into a well as punishment, who would help you?

Law strains to hear the man, whose assistant is handing out leaflets printed in Chinese. Most of Law's fellow passengers cannot read so one of the leaflets is quickly passed to him. Looking through the characters, he learns that the two men are from something called the Chinese Protectorate, set up by the white governor of this island to help Chinese people.

In Singapore, Chinese secret societies routinely snared new arrivals with offers of work. The would-be labourer who followed these gangsters would find himself locked in a filthy cell before being bullied into a contract most favourable to the gang in terms of commission, least favourable to him in terms of his labour.

The British appeared to be offering a merciful alternative. This was to put Chinese immigrants in safe houses until they found work, when the British would read through their terms for them to make sure that these at least appeared fair. The Chinese Protectorate apparently provided this service for free.

Curiosity fills Law. He has never known the imperial government in China to give assistance of any kind to ordinary people without wanting something back. He looks at the men around him. They are all like him – the front of their scalps have been shaved while the rest of their hair has been left long and plaited into a single braid, a queue, sometimes derisorily called a 'pigtail'. They wear this to show their submission to their foreign Manchu emperors but they are all here because their Manchu leaders have been unable, or unwilling, to help them.

The time has come, finally, to disembark. Law climbs out of the boat with his brother and father. All three clutch their possessions as they walk down the gangway. Black dust rises around them from the coaling sheds. The shriek of a steam winch punctuates the noise of engines and the shouting of the stevedores. Law feels as if he has stepped through an invisible curtain of hot vapour to be immediately drenched in his own perspiration. Yet the glare of the day is so blinding that despite the humidity and the heat, some workers have put on brimmed hats made of felt, presumably the only ones they could get hold of.

'Look over there,' his father Hongxi says suddenly, turning around and gesturing with his chin in the direction of a moored ship. It is empty except for a trail of Chinese men who board the ship up one gangplank and come down another.

They seem to be working in pairs. Each man has one end of a short, thick pole on his right shoulder, from which hangs a large basket loaded with black coal. It looks heavy, but the men climb up to the ship steadily, emptying the contents of their baskets somewhere on the steamer before going back down to the quay. Then they return to the coaling shed to fill up and start again. They work ceaselessly, like ants.

Law stares silently at this sight of his countrymen, but there is no time for reflection. Theirs is not the only boat unloading its human cargo. Law sees a group of young Chinese girls teeter tentatively down a ramp. They look lost, but there is no mistaking the woman who bustles forward from the dock to take charge of them – middle-aged, hard-faced, swaying her hips deliberately as she walks – nor the looks of some of the men appraising them. One of the girls reminds him of his sister. He thinks of her with a pang.

'Follow me,' his father is saying, and they plunge into a noisy, jostling crowd like the one they left behind in Canton, in the weeks before that now seem like years.

Around them, Chinese men are calling out but they all sound unfamiliar. The Chinese here are from various provinces in coastal south China. Their different dialects are like different languages. Law and his father push through the throng, straining for intonations that they might recognize. At last they catch the genial Sun Wui vowels of their part of Canton. His father approaches a tanned and stocky man who, to Law's relief, replies in their native Cantonese.

'Oh yes, older brother,' the man says to Hongxi, speaking less roughly to him than he has just done to another. 'I was told about you. You're from our headman's district. As soon as I've organized these little pigs' – he gestures dismissively to some anxious-looking men – 'we'll get you sorted. You can ride with me in that rickshaw.'

Not for nothing was the coolie trade called the 'pig business'. There were always coolies who died en route, while still aboard ship, from ill health: some were opium addicts; others sick through sheer poverty. As brokers were paid for the men they supplied, avaricious agents routinely overfilled their ships with coolies, deaf to the suggestion that overcrowding also killed men. It was more profitable to carry 600 men and have as many as 250 die, leaving 350 live coolies, than to carry 300 and have them all survive. Unlike pigs, dead coolies could not be sold for meat.[12]

Conditions were so intolerable that, though starved and weak, these men sometimes fought back, usually with tragic results. In 1859 there was a mutiny on board the US clipper *Flora Temple*, on its way to Havana. The crew fired on the coolies to confine them below deck, but the ship struck a reef and sank. The crew escaped. All 850 coolies drowned.[13]

There were mines in British Malaya and Sarawak where sick coolies were worked until they died, then simply carted up and dumped by the road. The idea of nursing a coolie back to health was simply idiotic when he was from a tribe as numerous as it was wretched. If one lot of Chinese died, another could be shipped out.[14]

When the agent is ready, he climbs into the rickshaw, something Law has only heard of but never seen. This cart is drawn not by an ox or a mule, but by a man like himself. They are common in Hong Kong, but not yet in Canton. The agent beckons to his father Hongxi, who looks uncertain. He follows, gingerly. When the rickshaw puller picks up the long shafts between which he is standing and sends the cab rocking backwards, Hongxi lets out an unhappy yelp. But the runner is off, clutching the two handles as if his life depends on it. Law and his brother follow quickly on foot, jogging lightly with the other coolies.

Out on the broad road, there are carriages hitched to small ponies and more rickshaws. Great carts rumble past on massive wheels, drawn by bullocks and steered by half-naked men, their heads wrapped in turbans, who stand majestically on platforms between the wheels, legs akimbo and whips in their hands. The oxen they drive are handsome creatures, with gleaming pale cream or dark brown hides, better fed than the countrymen Law has left behind.

The layout of the town was as Raffles had envisaged, with Europeans, Chinese, Indians and Malays settled comfortably each within their own districts.

The Chinese lived south of the Singapore River in terrace after terrace of two-storey shop houses, all covered with a light blue or yellow wash.[15] To the European, these looked satisfyingly oriental with their roofs of curved terracotta tiles laid vertically in a ridge and furrow pattern. But to any Chinese these terraces appeared foreign precisely because they were so alike. Even the streets running between them were disconcertingly wide and straight. In Canton, no two dwellings were the same and the narrow lanes that curved and wound between them did so deliberately, to shake off evil spirits.[16]

*

At last they stop. They leave the bright heat outside to enter the dark, slightly cooler interior of a deep house. The agent gestures to Hongxi and his younger son to wait for the headman and tells Law to take all their bags up some wooden stairs to the dormitory that will be their home for the foreseeable future.

After their boat, this room seems infinitely smaller. There are thirty beds crammed together, and thankfully there is no stench.[17] The beds are empty, their inhabitants at work.

Law feels confused, overwhelmed suddenly by a wave of loneliness. Will it always be just this? This bleak dormitory offers neither devastation nor hope.

As his eyes adjust to the gloom, he sees that he is not alone. There is another man, stick thin, in a corner of the room, lying on the plank that is his makeshift bed, his body turned towards the wall. He hardly moves. Is he alive? Suddenly the silence of the empty dormitory is split by the sound of the old coolie's cough, hacking and continuous.

Law gulps the stale air in short, shallow draughts, but otherwise he is frozen. He holds on tightly to their luggage as he stares in dismay. He might be watching the ghost of his future self.

4

When my mother grew frail with age and found it difficult to travel, we flew to Singapore every year to see her. When she grew even older, house-bound and vague, I went out twice a year.

My tiny mother was born in Singapore in 1917 when it was a British colony. She was taught at schools run by English and French missionaries. She sang songs in English. 'Daisy, Daisy' was a favourite and, later, the words that made me sad: 'Darling, I am growing old, silver threads among the gold'. Though of course her hair was once jet-black.

She spoke to her mother in Cantonese, but to her siblings mostly in English – a sort of English, with Cantonese inflections and a sentence construction translated directly from Chinese. 'You like what?' for 'What would you like?' 'You like or not?' instead of 'Do you like this?'

They each had two names, one suitable for the British island on which they lived, and one Cantonese for the Chinese land from where their grandfather came. None of them could write their Chinese names with characters. Instead, they wrote them out how they sounded, with English letters.

My mother married late, which was unusual for a Chinese woman of her generation. She wanted only one child and wished for a daughter, which was also rare when Chinese men and women yearned for sons.

She loved pretty things and, oddly for someone so gentle,

shiny sharp things – pocket knives, nail scissors, a lady's kimono dagger hidden in a slim black lacquer case on which *Fujiyama* was painted in gold. She was an inveterate spend-thrift but, held back by her modest pension, she was happy window-shopping. My mother's sister Eunice, younger by twenty-four years, was always there for her but Nick also got her a live-in carer, Corazon (his affection sharpened perhaps by relief that his mother-in-law never wanted to move in with us). In her eighties, my mother tottered about in shop-ping centres with trusty Corazon and a walking stick. They looked at jewellery, teapots, bedding, anything.

When I visited, she loved retelling the stories from her childhood that had enchanted me as a girl: how she bor-rowed the children of passing peddlers to make up teams with her cousins for rounders after school; how early on Sunday mornings they coaxed money from their grandfather for treats by rapping incessantly on his partition wall till he slipped coins under it to silence them; how an aunt inadvert-ently killed her beautiful infant son by feeding him crushed pearls for his complexion; and how the only time my mother saw her gentle grandfather angry was when she pushed her little brother down the stairs. My own childhood had been quiet, spent mostly at home alone with the cook. Later, after my father died when I was ten and the cook left, it was quieter still. My universe was my mother.

On those hot, still Singapore afternoons, it hardly mat-tered that my mother's stories were in fragments. Prescience is a gift accorded only to the few. It is distance, conferred by age or geography, that makes important the piecing together of things, to see what they might make.

I reassured her brightly at the end of each visit that it would be no time at all before we saw each other again. Only six months. 'Only'! The unspoken question that hid like an ache each time that we said goodbye was, is this the last?

As she grew more feeble over the years, I phoned her every day that we were apart. It was easier than ringing two or three times a week to hear her go through the motions of working out who I was, the disembodied voice that called her 'darling'.

We flew to Singapore for her ninetieth birthday, to throw a party for her. I had a *samfoo* made for her to wear, in French lace for the tunic top with its mandarin collar, and matching silk for the trousers. I chose a cheerful leaf green for her ensemble to offset the increasing bouts of sadness that she felt, the fear of dying. 'Morbid thoughts', she called them. We were already so far apart, Singapore from London. She could not bear to think of an even greater span between us.

Now, when I visited, she was not interested in much. The stories had petered out. Instead, she sat uncomprehending in front of the television with Corazon, her Filipina carer. I kept her company at lunch and at dinner and filled the hours between at the National Library in Singapore, reading up on history I had omitted to learn as an indolent child. I knew that I wanted to find my great-grandfather, but I did not know how.

Just before Christmas in 2010, when my mother was ninety-three, Corazon rang me in London to say that I should go at once to Singapore. My mother was in hospital for no more pressing a reason than old age, from which there could be no recovery.

If we had to be separated in the later stages of her life, at least we were together at the end. When I asked the young Malay nurse on duty for more morphine, she hinted gently that it was fear, not pain, that was making my mother's heart monitor rattle so alarmingly.

I held my mother's hand and repeated over and over the one psalm that she still remembered, which we had said together every day over the telephone for years in anticipation of this moment. The heart monitor grew quiet. It was the middle of the night. Her constant stream of visitors had left and we were alone. I was grateful for the privilege. She gave my hand one final, tiny squeeze and was gone. I felt incredibly proud of her, that at the end she was able to gather up all the courage that she had, to leave.

There were not many people left to tell about her death. She had outlived her brother and sister, Peter and Florence. There was only Eunice, much younger, and all the dear nieces and nephews in Singapore and abroad who had kept an eye on her these long years. Nearly everyone in the 1935 photograph had now died. The only two left were Hou-Seong, the youngest, and a girl in a frock next to their grandfather, the little cousin of whom my mother had been so fond. Angelina or 'Annie' had left Singapore as a young woman to work as a nurse in Ontario. She had settled there and was now in her eighties.

Annie was kind on the telephone, sad to hear that Violet had died, though there were moments in our conversation when she seemed slightly disorientated, even muddled. I phoned her again after my mother's funeral in January. It was Chinese New Year and I knew that Annie, who had never married, would be on her own. It reminded me of my mother. I was not sure when I rang that she would remember me. By her own admission she was taking Valium regularly as my mother had done, to help her sleep. I had seen how Valium seemed to exacerbate dementia.

Unexpectedly, she claimed instantly to know who I was, automatically responding to my apology for not ringing sooner with, 'Oh but *I* should have phoned you,' though she didn't have my number. She started to ramble. She talked about her cousin Bernard in Vancouver – also my mother's cousin – and his recent kidney transplant. Bernard is twenty-one years older than I am and he'd left Singapore when I was little. I'd never met him, nor had I ever spoken to him before, but Annie was telling me that I should call him – not only that, but that he'd been waiting for me to call! Now I was certain she was confused or had confused me with someone else. We carried on chatting awkwardly, two people unused to each other. I could hear rustling in the background. Then she said: 'Here's his cell-phone number. Phone him.'

'But, Auntie Annie, I don't think he'll know me.'

'Oh?' She sounded surprised. 'But we've spoken about you.'

She was so persistent that, when I rang off, I had promised to get in touch with her cousin Bernard Law, my uncle and the last of Law's grandsons still alive. His father was the younger of Law's two sons.

A strong, vital voice answered when I eventually phoned. Like Annie, he seemed unsurprised that I had called. 'We've spoken before,' he insisted, although I knew that we had not. But he was clear in his mind who I was – the daughter of his cousin Violet, whom he last saw decades ago.

Bernard turned out to be a raconteur, and it was only at the end of a long trans-Atlantic conversation that he casually mentioned a book tracing our branch of the Law family over twenty-six generations. Chinese family trees, even one so relatively modest, are not at all common. They imply not only a degree of scholarship among the men who started it but that later members of the family were educated enough to update it through the centuries. Ours was a thousand years old.

'None of us can read it,' he admitted. 'It's all in old Chinese.'

He said he would get his son John to send me a copy. Bernard's other children were James and Jacqueline, but only John had married. He was middle-aged, with one daughter. None of my great-grandfather's great-grandsons had fathered sons. His male line was dying out.

I got in touch with John in Toronto – until now an undiscovered second cousin – who sent the family archive in a file attached to an email. It was a dense compendium, packed with Chinese characters. Among my cousins in Singapore, I am the only one who can read a very little Chinese as we were all educated in English. But this was overwhelming.

John and I had no further communication till about six months later, when I received another email with the photograph of a baby. I had no idea that John's wife Li had been pregnant but here he was, their newborn. A boy. He was going to carry forward the surname that was even older than our branch of the family – the name 'Law' came into existence during China's Zhou dynasty, in 700 BC.

My cousin John Law has a voice just like his father Bernard's, big and resonant. The first time that I met him, John was in London on holiday from Canada with his petite wife Li and their children, six-year-old Zoey and her one-year-old brother A. J. John was not just any cousin. Together with Li, he had extended our great-grandfather's male line by another generation: the infant in the high-chair, protesting with a piercing shriek at being given purée from a jar when his sister had a savoury dumpling speared on the end of a pink plastic chopstick.

I had arranged for us to have lunch in the cavernous

interior of the New World in London's Chinatown. I chose the restaurant for our rendezvous, imagining that the adults could chat while A. J. crawled about with his sister skipping around him. Spacious Chinese restaurants are very tolerant of children behaving like children. Unfortunately, two-thirds of the restaurant was closed for the summer and it had crammed its entire clientele on to one floor. We were squashed around a table that the dim sum carts could barely squeeze past. The children were confined disconsolately to their places.

I was trying to manage the moment – pouring tea, taking in how John and his family looked and sounded, looking after my cousin Delice who had flown in from Sweden to join us, while at the same time deflecting the baskets of dim sum that the waitresses were tossing on to our table with the abandon of jugglers high on amphetamines – when John called out from across the table: 'Li is from Beijing and knows a bit of old Chinese. She says that our family tree shows we're not even originally from Canton. We're from Henan, fourteen hundred kilometres away!'

What?

It seems that the Canton chapter of our story also began with a journey.

5

China moved out of mythical into recorded history in 1046 BC when the ancient Zhou dynasty began. In theory the Zhou existed for nearly eight hundred years but in reality this included a stretch of three hundred years, beatifically named the Spring and Autumn Period, when its reign was tenuous as its vassal states competed violently with each other for dominance. One of the most troublesome of these was the Chu.

There was a large group of people related by kinship who felt increasingly harried by the Chu. They were forced to move their homes many times, but Chu soldiers always found their villages again, to pillage and to burn. These people decided that they had to flee far to keep safe.

From as long ago as they could remember they had lived north of the great Yangtse, the Long River. They resolved to cross it. To its south lay the deep unknown: what waited there? They had only their legends as a guide.

The journey required great courage. It was desperation that pushed them on. They would have lost many people in their 800-kilometre trek across rivers and mountains, but eventually they found a place that they liked near a river called Miluo, north of present-day Changsha. They decided to stop here and to rename themselves Luo or Law, after the place. It reflected their great hope that this would be where they would settle for generations to come. It was 689 BC.

But change is the constant that drives history.

The great river could not keep back their enemy. Eventually, the town that they had built near the Miluo fell to the Chu and the Laws had again to uproot themselves, even though this was where they had felt most at home. We know this because they kept the name of the place after they scattered, following rivers that were branches of the Yangtse. Some headed back north, guided by the Han tributary; others travelled south along the Xiang into Hunan. They continued to call themselves Luo or Law.

Over subsequent centuries, my distant ancestors continued to swing north or south of the Yangtze depending on the fortunes of their princes. They produced high achievers, a handful of men who worked as ministers or imperial advisers in the Han, Western Jin and Eastern Jin dynasties.

Eventually, following the see-sawing of capital cities across China as dynasties came and went, some of our Laws ended up in a capital back north of the Yangtze River. This was near modern-day Kaifeng in Henan.

It was the tenth century. The Tang dynasty had just ended, in AD 907, but the Song dynasty was yet to begin. The vacuum was filled once more by competing hegemonies – the Five Dynasties and Ten Kingdoms. None of these 'dynasties' lasted more than sixteen years.

A boy named Law Yanxiang was born right in the middle of this period, and with him, the origin of my branch of the family, the Canton Laws.

Yanxiang grew up to be clever, talented in poetry and fluent in the classics. This meant that he was a scholar. He must also have been physically robust because he was made an officer of the imperial army in the last of the Five Dynasties, the so-called Later Zhou which flared, as briefly as a firefly, for just nine years.

Rather impressively, Yanxiang was more adept at surviving than his imperial masters. He was given another military post when the Song dynasty took over in AD 960 with Kaifeng as its capital. He was twenty-four years old and married.

Life was presumably stable and calm for four years before he received a cruel instruction: Yanxiang was to move 1,235 kilometres south, to the northernmost expanse of the region not yet known as Canton Province. He was to head for a place called Nanxiong near a pass through the Nan Mountains. This mountain range runs from east to west just north of Canton for more than 1,000 kilometres. It guards the Canton region like its own Great Wall. Nanxiong was remote and primitive.

It is true that the Emperor's officials were often sent great distances to serve him. It is possible that Yanxiang was picked to defend the town and the pass from the brigands who preyed upon them. It is also possible that as he was strong, young and virile, he was to be a pioneer. Thirty years later, Canton would be administered as an entity for the first time.

Even so, it feels like exile.

Yanxiang's departure from Kaifeng would have been difficult. Though he was only twenty-eight, he knew that if he ever saw his family again, they would all be much older. The journey would have been dangerous and arduous, through miles and miles of uninhabited, undulating land. When at last he reached the Mei Pass[1] to arrive at Nanxiong, he would have found the people strange and their dialect unintelligible.

Despite this, he embraced the future. It was probably in Nanxiong that he married the second wife mentioned in the genealogy. Their descendants became the Canton Laws. After this, the clan account does not reveal much more. We do not know if Yanxiang ever saw his first wife and family in Henan again.

Yanxiang did right by his clan. The Song dynasty was glorious but did not last forever. Soon enough, tribes of barbarian Jurchens invaded its capital at Kaifeng. The Song court was obliged to relocate south of the Yangtze, at Hangchow, where eventually it was crushed by the Mongols under Kublai Khan. Many of our Law ancestors would have died in the interregnum. But the branch of the Law clan that Yanxiang started in distant Nanxiong was safe, able to slip beyond the reach of the ravaging Mongols far to the south, nearly to the sea, close to another river system – the Pearl.

I know the story of Yanxiang only because I finally found a translator. There are ten thousand characters in the clan book. They sit like motifs on the page. They are impenetrable.

The language is archaic, the characters are old, and the dates in the book are calculated according to emperors' reigns in imperial China. They need adjustment to the Gregorian calendar to make contemporary sense.

My translator would have to know not only classical Chinese but history and, of course, be able to render it all into English so that I could read it. Despite a grant from the National Heritage Board in Singapore to help me in my search, such a person had proved elusive. Young, bilingual Chinese learn modern, simplified characters and aren't familiar with the old dating system. Older Chinese, schooled in traditional characters and the imperial dating system, are not comfortably bilingual.

I was about to abandon my search when a friend in Hong Kong emailed to say her former colleague might be able to help. Christa thought that Chun-Wai, a PhD student in history at the University of Hong Kong, had the sort of 'old-fashioned mind' which she reckoned to be a requirement of the job. Crucially, he was able not only to deal with classical Chinese and the old dating system but, after a previous spell at the University of Cambridge, could turn it all into recognizable English. I wrote to him and he said 'yes' and offered to do it all to his own deadline: one month. I felt as if I'd won the lottery.

But when the translation arrived, my heart sank. Antiquated Chinese becomes antiquated English. There was too much of one sort of information – many of the men have three names each which seem interchangeable (birth name, style name, art name) – and too little of another: the women are mentioned only in passing, typical of Chinese genealogies. Wives and concubines are referred to by their maiden names, and daughters are named through the men they marry.

But at least I could read the genealogy at last. I was surprised by how reassuring it felt to scan a list of names – except, of course, it is more than that. It is a litany of the people whose genes I share. We are each the sum of the families who came before us. We can never shake them off, therefore we are never alone. Our tribe is embedded inside us through the genes of our ancestors. We are part of an infinite arc, a continuous sequence of souls. I was beginning to understand the power of Chinese ancestor worship, how it comforts like religion.

I am delighted to confirm that my great-grandfather was indeed born in 1865 (that was a very lucky guess), in January. He would have arrived in Singapore with the winter monsoon as he was turning seventeen, just as my mother had said. He speaks directly from the past in the introduction to our clan record: 'I have learned that trees must have roots and water must come from a spring. Lineages are important to human beings. The proper way to be a human being and filial son is to trace the origin of the lineage, to memorialize the ancestors.'

When I read the genealogy, I feel a connection not only to my great-grandfather, but a sense of how he connected to *his* ancestors. They are, of course, also mine. 'Genealogy is to a clan as history is to a country. A country without its history is unthinkable even for one day.'

He pleads with his brother and their cousin in a joint preface: do not lose your past; do not lose your way.

6

Yanxiang's descendants in Canton could have easily lost their way but they had their genealogy to guide them. It was how they oriented themselves far from the centre of power (the shifting capitals of China always to their north).

Life wasn't easy for them in the delta and many became farmers labouring in the fields. They could have succumbed to permanent self-doubt. But their clan record reminded them that there were ministers and prime ministers in their collective history, men asked to serve emperors because they had distinguished themselves in the imperial examinations.

They were the exemplars to emulate. They inspired every Canton Law to keep trying, to fight to learn his characters. It meant that even when life became very, very hard, they could dream of not being labourers.

In the nineteenth century, it was finally the turn of my close ancestors in the Canton Delta to elevate themselves through the Emperor of China's marathon examination system.

China's civil service had been meritocratic since the seventh century, unlike Britain's, which ran on feudal lines until the eighteenth century. China's would eventually inspire change in the British system.[1]

This meritocracy relied on triennial examinations that were astonishing in their difficulty, though this did nothing to put off applicants. In China, primogeniture was not practised, and titles could not be passed from father to son.[2]

Every generation had to earn for itself the prestige and riches that were assured with success at the imperial examinations.[3]

In theory, anyone could have a go at entering the Emperor's civil service. Woodblock-printed books had been widely available from the tenth century. But in practice, it was still only the well-off who could afford to educate even one of their sons. You had to buy the books and you had to hire a tutor. Most of all, families struggling to survive in precarious times had to write off the economic contribution of one of their sons. He could study for years, through adulthood, in vain.

First, a boy would be tutored from age eight to complete his general classical education by age fifteen. In those seven years he was expected to memorize 400,000 characters,[4] or roughly 200 characters a day. These were from the *Analects* of Confucius, the conversations of Mencius, the *Spring and Autumn Annals*, the *Book of Changes*, the *Book of Documents*, the *Book of Poetry* and the *Book of Rites*.[5] What he was not expected to learn was mathematics (only for merchants) or science and technology (for farmers).

If he were capable of carrying on, there were preliminary assessments at the county level which, if passed, qualified him for tests at the district or prefectural stage where about half the candidates failed. Then he was ready to sit at the provincial level which was the real starting line for the actual civil service race.[6] Finally, there was the metropolitan examination at the capital of the prevailing dynasty.

The tests took place in locked halls or other secure arenas. Near where my great-grandfather grew up in Canton, the prefectural examinations were held in a field dotted with narrow cabinets resembling commodious Chinese coffins standing upright. Each entombed a scholar with just enough room for a table and a kettle in which to boil water for his tea.[7] He was there from seven in the morning till it grew too dark to write. He was allowed out only once, to go to the lavatory.

The reason for this severity was that cheating was rife. One local Canton family supported itself for years off the earnings of its talented son at the examinations. He sat in his box in the field passing answer-notes to servants whose masters had paid for them. He contrived every year to fail, so that he could turn up again the next.[8]

You needed greater cunning at the provincial level when books no bigger than matchboxes, filled with microscopic writing, might be secreted in the hem of a gown or the sole of a shoe.

After an interminable period of study, only a much-reduced number of candidates arrived in the capital for the metropolitan examination where the very best graduates earned themselves a royal assessment at the palace before the Emperor.[9] By now, many students were middle-aged, having prepared for this moment for decades.

In the middle of the eighteenth century, a Law was born in the Canton Delta who passed sufficient civil service tests to be made a junior officer of the Qing dynasty. His son Zezi would also do well in the imperial examinations and be awarded the title of *wenlin lang*, an officer of the seventh grade. Zezi clearly prospered because he was able to educate his ten sons born to his wife and two concubines. One of these sons was Law's father, Hongxi.

I don't suppose that life in Zezi's household was conducive to ease: imagine ten brothers and half-brothers constantly being measured against each other. Each boy's happiness for the other is tempered by envy or regret, cooled by his own need for his father's recognition.

Unluckily for Hongxi, he had a half-brother, Hongzuo, born just months before him in the same year. They were among the oldest of Zezi's sons. Their mothers would have minutely compared their achievements, and it would not have been lost on Hongxi that his brother was better. Hongzuo was admitted to the county school at the age of twenty-two, whereas Hongxi only managed the preliminary tests for the civil service examinations. This was a lot to live down.

It is possible that Hongxi's father Zezi was sympathetic to his situation and bought him a position. Hongxi would later become an officer of the ninth grade, more an honorary title than actual office. This title would be no help to him whatsoever when jobs became scarce.

To make things worse, Hongxi's younger brothers excelled even more as scholars. Several qualified for the prefectural school and were singled out for commendation. The standout success was Hongxi's younger brother or half-brother by two years, Hongxia. He passed the demanding provincial-level examinations, second highest of the civil service tests, and won the eminent title of *juren*, broadly equal to a master's degree.[10] He would be appointed county magistrate.

Hongxi was painfully aware of his scholarly shortcomings and what his brothers and their wives thought of him. Then his wife bore him their first son in 1865. This propitious event was followed tragically, months later, by the unexpected death of Hongxi's 'twin' brother. Hongzuo was only twenty-eight, his promise unfulfilled. Hongxi may have transferred his failed hope in himself and the lost hopes of his brother on to his baby boy.

The pressure was always on this child, my great-grandfather, never on Hongxi's younger son who was clearly not academic. I believe that Law was sent to school or tutored to complete his early classical education because, as I would find out later, Hongxi trusted his elder son's capacity for academic study. But Law did not have the luxury of continuing his education in China as his uncles had done. Circumstances had changed immeasurably since his grandfather Zezi's time.

In the nineteenth century, local bureaucracy flourished as Peking's central government disintegrated, which benefited Zezi, a city official. He had a life of prestige and success and he was fortunate to die six years before the terrible famine in north China reverberated through the regions of the south. The same Manchu mismanagement that allowed him to prosper had failed to plan for this contingency. A famine would become a crisis.

Zezi's family descended from plenty to want. Some of them became so desperate they had to leave their home for the primitive Nanyang. For one of his grandsons, the dream of joining the Chinese civil service would always have to be just that.

Zezi did not live to see his family's decline but if he had, he would know that he had done everything that he could to protect them, by educating his sons. It would have comforted him that they, in turn, had schooled the next generation.

Now, in Singapore, only one thing stood like a shield between my great-grandfather and the fate of a coolie: the fact of his education.

7

Hongxi pauses before they reach the headman's room and turns to face his sons: 'Boys, look sharp and be eager. We need to make a good impression. Everything depends on this.'

They are finally face to face with the clansman for whom they have an introduction from China, a man whose businesses deal with everything from importing rice or coolies to running the gangs who move goods and build houses.

The man is seated at a table on which are books of accounts, a cup of tea and an abacus. He is short and has, Law thinks, the pleasing plumpness of one who has plenty to eat. But he also has a canny face and small, sharp eyes that miss nothing.

Now they rest on Law and his younger brother. The clansman turns back to their father: 'I have work for one such as you, of course, but these two . . .' He tails off meaningfully.

Hongxi speaks quickly, smiling all the time. Law knows from experience that this means his father is nervous.

'My elder son can read and write too. He's a bright boy. He will pick up anything,' their father says, and carries on without pause so there can be no interruption: 'As for my younger son, you can see for yourself he is almost as big as his elder brother. He is strong. He can fetch and carry . . . I will make sure he is useful to you.' Both Law and his brother nod vigorously.

The clansman makes to look dubiously at the two lads. He sighs expansively and begins to fan himself with the letter of introduction in his chubby fingers. 'Well, let's see what they can do. I can't pay them of course, not when I have no idea if they can put in a decent day's work. But they can have some of the rice off our table, to keep them going.'

Hongxi promises that his sons will work hard. He makes them kowtow to their clansman, to show how they are humbled by his generosity.

At first the three of them may have stayed in a dormitory for new arrivals, shared mainly with men who were destined to be coolies. Then they would have moved to a rented room in one of the narrow but substantial houses that still exist today in Singapore's Chinatown.

One of these has been turned into a museum. It replicates interiors from the 1950s, not the 1880s, but it still gives me an idea of how Law, his father and his brother may have lived – I just have to make it several notches worse.

For instance, there is only one lavatory at the end of a corridor of cubicles, and it adjoins the kitchen. The night-soil man and his buckets have just one access, through this corridor and the main stairs. The whole arrangement looks unsavoury now in this recreation of the 1950s. It doesn't bear imagining how it would have been in 1882.

I peer into each of the cubicles. They are typically 7 feet square – and separated by wooden partitions that reach three-quarters of the way up 8-foot-high walls. There are no doors, only makeshift curtains made from lengths of cheap cotton. In one room, there are two wooden platforms, one above the other, against the wall. Each platform is a scant 5 feet in length and just over 2 feet wide. These would be two beds. There is a narrow table against the opposite wall. If my great-grandfather, his brother and their father lived in such a room, this would have been their third bed, though it is even shorter than the other two.

'I'm the smallest,' Hongxi says. 'I'll go on the table.'

Law glances at his younger brother. He is growing so quickly that in the few weeks they have been in Singapore, he has nearly overtaken both Law and their father in height. Their clansman has been making full use of this strong young lad, not yet fourteen, never interested in books, much more interested in doing things. He is sent wherever an extra pair of hands is needed, literally – taking letters from one place to another, unloading goods, cleaning. He has recently been apprenticed on a building site.

Law imagines with pain the sort of future that stretches ahead of his brother. Will he be carrying bricks like a coolie even when he is old?[1] Will he still smile every night, after a day's labour, as he does now?

In Canton they had lived in a large house with extended family, but there was plenty of space outdoors where you felt free. Here they share one small space in the middle of an unfamiliar city. Some evenings Law longs for the moment that they lie in their darkened room and he can finally let his worries unknot and dissolve into silent, pricking tears.

But eventually the routine of everyday life, even in this strange place, takes over.

My great-grandfather would have had no words to describe the array of people in Singapore, most of whom he would never have met before.

The Reverend Bethune Cook said that only Constantinople or Cairo could compare: 'Here come Arabs and Negroes, there natives of India – Tamils, Parsees, Marattas, Bengalis, Sikhs,

Assamese, and Afghans; there Siamese and Annamese, there Cingalese and here Burmese; Jews from Baghdad and from Europe, Armenians and Turks, Bugis from the Celebes, Dyaks from Borneo, and Battas from the mountains of Sumatra.'[2]

Yet it was the Chinese men he met that Law would have found the most extraordinary, from provinces in China he barely knew existed, who seemed like him and yet were not. They spoke dialects as different from each other's as Spanish is to Romanian. It was an upside-down world where one of his countrymen might understand a Malay man better than he might Law.

Of all these Chinese, the most peculiar were those who were born in Malaya and who, inconceivably, had never set foot in China. They were the exotic offspring of Chinese traders who had travelled to Malacca in the fifteenth century and married local Malay women. Later, these families imported Chinese wives for their sons, but they still all spoke a mixture of Malay and the Chinese dialect of their great-grandfathers, usually Fukienese. These men were known as 'Baba' and their women, 'Nonya'.

Baba men dressed like other Chinese men. Nonya women wore Malay sarongs with blouses called *kebayas*, and cooked curries with ginger and coconut. The men could not read or write Chinese characters but they could read and write in English. Sometimes, they even put on the costume of an Englishman.

'We're going to have some fun today, young brother,' their clansman chuckles. 'You're finally going to meet a Baba! He's coming to visit with one of my customers to talk about our silk from China.'

The clansman's client is a middle-aged man in the usual

Chinese attire of dark tunic over loose trousers. His young companion is dressed very differently. Law is shocked to see that he is all in white, as if at the funeral of his father or mother. But he is clearly not bereaved because he wears gold – forbidden when mourning – and looks very cheerful and pleased with himself.

His suit of white cotton drill is carefully pressed and buttoned all the way to his neck, where two gold studs fasten the high collar. His trousers are not baggy like Law's but tapered, as if to draw attention to the shiny leather shoes on his feet.[3] The leather looks stiff to Law, unlike the soft cloth of his own shoes. He wonders if they might hurt.

Glancing at Law, the well-dressed visitor pulls out a gold chain from one breast pocket to check the time ostentatiously on his fob watch. Then, when Law's clansman tells Law to take notes, and he works away with a brush on his calligraphy, the visitor scribbles into his notebook with a dip pen.

When the clients are served tea, the young man is handed a tin of condensed milk from which he ladles out the sticky white mass with a spoon into his cup.[4] Law cannot help gasping out loud. His clansman glances over to him and grins. Later, he teases Law.

'You think it odd that he defiles his tea with that stinking cow's milk? He will even eat unsliced meat with a dagger and a spike, like a barbarian!' The clansman scowls, then spits: 'Phah! *He's* no Chinese, but he does have the ear of the British, those red-furred devils.'

In this cultural and auditory melee, Law was beginning to understand the dialects of the other provinces of China. From their jumble, he was able to separate Fukienese from Chiuchow or Hakka, to recognize that the same Chinese characters for 'eating rice' were pronounced 'sik fan' in Cantonese but 'jiak bung' in Fukienese, and 'sik pon' in Hakka. He was also picking up Malay and the odd Arab phrase. He was even managing a bit of what the Klings, or Tamils, spoke. Law was discovering that he was a linguist, which would have surprised him. He had grown up hearing nothing but Cantonese. Most Cantonese people had no ear for anything except their mother tongue.

'Your son is clever, no doubt,' their clansman told Hongxi. 'I haven't met many men from our Canton villages who pick up what the Klings say. But what would really be useful is if he could learn the devil-men's tongue. They're the bloody masters, get me? This whole damned place is run by them. Those goddam Babas are ahead of us in learning English. It helps them wipe the fattest arses. Now, if your boy could understand the white devils, and talk to them on behalf of us Cantonese, *that* would be something.'

Hongxi was delighted. Here was the chance they had been hoping for, something they could work towards. He had always believed that his elder son was special, even as a baby, destined to be a scholar with a bright career. If Law succeeded in learning English, there would apparently be work for him in the colonial administration.

They found that there were English classes that taught pupils in their native tongue, whether it was Malay, Tamil or a Chinese dialect like Cantonese. It probably astounded both father and son that the lessons were virtually free.

The colony's hundred thousand Chinese were run by only a handful of British administrators. They desperately needed Chinese employees whom they could understand, but new immigrants from China were nearly all uneducated and struggled to learn English.

By the time Law arrived in the colony, the British had set up primary and secondary schools to teach English, though expectations were low. One requirement for a scholarship to the government service was, simply, 'colloquial familiarity' with *Aesop's Fables*.[5]

Law had already been trained to study by his tutors in China so it would not have fazed him to discover that learning English would take seven or eight years. It was a long commitment in the life of a young adult, especially in the days when life expectancies were short. But it was the sort of commitment that their little family was ready to make because the situation was entirely familiar to them: as in China, a middle-class household made sacrifices to educate one of its sons in the hope that he would bring them success and honour – except that in Singapore, it would be through the British, not the Chinese, civil service.

There was a school in Chinatown on Cross Street, south of the Singapore River.[6] But my mother told me that her grandfather had gone to the Raffles Institution on Bras Basah Road, north of the river.[7] To get there, Law had to walk northeast beyond his patch of Cantonese Chinatown, past the familiar landmarks of a Hindu temple and a Coromandel mosque. He then had to go through Fukien and Chiuchow territory to get to New Bridge Road and on to a bridge built many years before, no longer new, to cross the Singapore River.

'Have you never been to the market?' Law's younger brother was astounded. Already, he has seen more than Law. 'It's not very far from your school, just a little eastward before you cross the river.'

Law slows his pace to take in the wonderful things for sale

in the market, a welcome diversion from the tightening in his chest whenever he remembers that this will be his first day at a Singapore school. (He has no idea what to expect.)

There are great branches of coral, dazzling white, or violet or red.[8] There is jackfruit from the jungle nearly as long as his arm, its thick green skin split open to reveal golden yellow flesh. Whole carcasses of pig and goat hang from hooks, their heads hacked off. Flies swarm around them in the heat. The smell makes Law feel a little queasy.

He moves on quickly to marvel at the mousedeer and ant-eaters in cages, and a huge lizard with a poisonous-looking tongue that flicks out at the passers-by who dare to stop and stare. Finally, he halts in amazement, not to look at the dead python near his feet, its belly still bulging with the form of its hapless four-legged meal, but beyond it at the magnificent tiger lying on the ground. Its fur glints, truly like gold, in the sun. Law dares not go any nearer in case it is still alive. He has heard that tigers in Singapore kill and eat one Chinese coolie a day.[9]

He turns north again, and hurries on till he sees the river ahead. Then he pauses to gaze across the water. He is on the south bank where two-storey shop houses crowd together, cheek by jowl. Something about their crammed appearance marks them out as being Chinese. How different things look on the north bank, where the European godowns or warehouses are in an orderly arrangement. They are punctuated by government buildings whose neo-classical form Law does not comprehend, though he senses their desired effect: that they have important purpose.

Law finds the timber bridge that he must cross before walking another kilometre to his school. Most of his fellow students are from Fukien province. Law tries chatting to them in their own dialect when, suddenly, the door swings open and the teacher walks in.

Law recognizes him at once. He is the white man who spoke to them on their boat when they arrived. His name goes round the classroom in a wave of awed whispers: Pi-Ki-Ling.

The *kilin or ch'i-lin* of Chinese myth is a fabled hybrid with a dragon's head, a unicorn's horn, the hooves of a horse and scales on its body like a fish. William Alexander Pickering is similarly composite, an Englishman who speaks more types of Chinese than most Chinese. He looks very curious with his sandy-coloured whiskers and beard and hair. He seems ancient to Law, though he is only forty-one years old.

Law struggles to understand this man's English and is relieved when he begins to speak in what sounds passably like Fukienese. Then Pi-Ki-Ling asks, in tortured but unmistakeable Cantonese, 'And one of you is a man from Canton?'

Law feels like a moth dropping closer and closer to a flame, unable to escape. He is required to stand up and to converse with this odd-looking and monstrous-sounding man, sometimes in the man's strange Cantonese, sometimes in Law's own peculiar English, until they begin to comprehend each other.

Law shakes his head in disbelief as he walks home that evening. He thinks of the tiger in the market, the anteater in its cage, all the extraordinary things that he has seen. Nothing is stranger than this: who would have thought in the morning that by the end of the day, he would be standing no further than an arm's length from a devil-man, and talking to him?

8

Before my mother died, before she grew forgetful, in the happy days just after my arrival in Singapore to visit and before she began counting down the days to my departure, there was time for her to reminisce. She told me that her grandfather was an interpreter. She thought that he worked in a magistrate's court. He looked after women, she said, saving them from prostitution against their will. She told me that his name was Law Foong-Siew. She could not write the Chinese character for 'Law', only tell me that it meant a kind of net. She spelt out his name for me in English.

At the time I had no idea that I wanted to do anything with the information. My life was crowded with the minutiae of raising a young family in London while caring for her from a distance.

I stayed on after her funeral to tie up her affairs. As I knew I would not be back in Singapore soon, I thought that I should try to trace the grandfather she so clearly adored, though it was unlikely that I would find him. She had given me scarcely anything to go on, not much more than a name.

By the last decade of the nineteenth century, there were still very few Europeans in Singapore. Two-thirds of the people living on the island were Chinese, with the Malays and Indians making up about another third.[1] Europeans accounted for a scant 3 per cent.[2] Most Chinese would never have spoken to an Englishman. Some might never even have seen one, and yet my mother had claimed that her grandfather actually worked for the British. In 1881, only eighty-three Chinese on the entire island were on the government's payroll.[3] Was it really possible that my great-grandfather was one of them? Even if his name was actually on an official register, how would I recognize it?

When British officers took down the personal names of their Chinese subjects, they simply wrote down in letters how these sounded to them, however they liked, using a whimsical system of transliteration. So, while my mother did know that her grandfather's surname was written with the Chinese character for 'net' or 'gauze', when spoken out in Cantonese and written in English, it could be Lo, Law, Loh, Luo or even Lor.

I could be looking for any number of permutations of 'Law Foong-Siew', which was simply how she had written his name. It could, for instance, be written instead as Lo Fong-Siu or Lor Fung-Seow or something I had not yet imagined. I was full of doubt that I would find him, but it would be worth knowing that I had at least tried. Mentally I filed it away under 'hopeless', and turned to the next item to research before leaving Singapore.

My mother had been a pupil at the Methodist Girls' School. It was one of the best on the island but a long way from her home in Cantonment Road. I'd wondered how, as a little girl, she'd made the journey each day. It was only when I asked her that she said her aunt Fanny was already a pupil there and had taken her. If this was true, it would mean that three generations of my family's women had gone to the school before it was even a hundred years old – Fanny, my mother and then me.

We had lived, fortuitously, near the Methodist Girls' School but it had become so popular that when my mother tried to enrol me, they were already full. Undeterred, even though she wasn't at all pushy, my mother had gone in person to the school, found one of her former teachers who still recognized her, and begged for a place. I was beginning to realize that this was down to the aunt who had made such an impression on her: that it was important to educate a girl well. I wanted to find out more about the woman who'd had such an impact on my upbringing.

My school used to sit on a small hill grandly named Mount Sophia, probably after Lady Raffles.[4] It had since moved to new buildings, in a new location, at the end of a long drive. In Singapore, the humidity is high by 10 a.m. and I arrived hot and perspiring on a sunny, cloudless morning for my appointment to look through the school's archives.

The part-time archivist was already waiting in the quiet of the library, looking dauntingly fresh and poised. When she was my teacher, we had all idolized her; later she became a respected headmistress of the school. Now retired, her black hair had grown splendidly white. Every strand was in place.

She didn't remember me. She wasn't impressed by people who claimed that they were writing books. She was used to keeping bothersome girls in line and she was stern: it was unlikely that there were records from the 1920s when my great-aunt would have gone to the school. Over the years, compilations had been borrowed for research and not returned. It was clearly a source of irritation.

Ready to get on with her day, she picked up a register book and ran an elegant finger quickly down various pages to demonstrate the futility of my quest when, to her own surprise, she said, 'Oh, there she is, Fanny Law.' My great-aunt's name was spelled out in faded black ink and, next to it, under the column 'name of parent/guardian', was a name I did not recognize. It was not the one that my mother had given me, Law Foong-Siew, but a quite different one: Law Quan-Yee.

I was vaguely aware that Chinese gentlemen sometimes had various names to reflect the different stages of their lives, their different passions or associations.[5] It was the vogue for men of letters. But I didn't think that it applied to my great-grandfather. I thought that he came from a family of farmers. I was not yet in touch with my uncle Bernard in Canada. I did not know that a family genealogy existed. At this point it would be years before I'd manage to get it translated.

Therefore I had no idea that Law males were educated or that they picked fashionable nicknames for themselves known as 'art names'. There was no way of knowing that Law's birth name was Quan-Yee whereas my mother had remembered his art name, Foong-Siew. Instead, I worried that if my mother had got something so basic wrong, how could I rely on anything else that she had told me, including where she thought that he had worked?

Later, at lunch, when I moaned to friends about the impossibility of finding my great-grandfather, one of them told me that he had rather a good connection at the National Library. He phoned her at once to ask for her help. Despite this kindness, my expectations were low as I set off after lunch to see what I could find.

The characterful and extensive 1950s red-brick block once occupied by Singapore's National Library has gone, demolished to build a tunnel to ease traffic in the city. The library is now within a modern high-rise building on Victoria Street that no one really notices. There is every reason to be dismissive of something that merely adds to the urban sprawl, but it is wonderful to be inside. The airy atrium of young trees makes it feel peaceful although you are just feet away from busy roads. Fast, quiet lifts glide up and down to take you between floors with views of the city.

My friend's contact assigned me the help of a researcher, Mazelan, who took me to their microfilm section and suggested that I look through old copies of the *Singapore and Straits Directory*. Its civil service lists date back to the late nineteenth century.

I squinted dutifully through everything from the late 1880s when I thought my great-grandfather could have worked for the British. Law Foong-Siew was nowhere. He was not among the Chinese Interpreters of the Supreme Court and he was not in the Police Court where young thieves, merely children, were flogged for stealing cloth slippers. He was not in the Attorney General's office, nor in the Sheriff's department.

But there was plenty in the *Directory* to interest and distract: at the General Post Office, there was uncollected post waiting for men and women with evocative names straight out of Maugham or Conrad (H. Orienter, Joaquim Jovellar, V. der le Baron); or perhaps from an early Cluedo game (Reverend Codrington, Captain Crane). Who were these people? Where were they when their post lay dumb and patient in a room while those who sent them waited impatiently, or even desperately, to hear back?

They couldn't all have been victims of the wild dogs that roamed the island in the 1880s, whose infected bites were so fatal that they were culled regularly on fixed dates by licensed gunmen. It was up to you to check the calendar for the colony's official 'dog-killing days' and to keep your canine house-fellow chained if he were not to be mistakenly shot. That was if he had not already been killed by one of the island's venomous snakes, the most common of which was the *Naja tripudians*, dangerous because of being nondescript, brown and plain with only a whitish stripe on its throat. The *Directory* pointed out that as it was not as distinguishable (nor distinguished) as its Indian cousin *Naja naja* with spectacles printed on the back of its hood, this species of cobra was probably more deadly.

My afternoon was beginning to slip away. I had to wrench myself from Mr Fraser and Mr Neave trumpeting the virtues of their patent machine. It could print gentlemen's and ladies' visiting cards in 'a variety of fancy types in a few minutes'. You could tell that they were proud of their new business from the size of their advertisement where, as an after-thought, they also mentioned their sideline in aerated water. I grew up with 'F and N' orangeade, cherryade and ice-cream soda. It was fizzy drinks that would make Mr F's and Mr N's fortunes.

Back to more dull lists, this time the Chinese Protector-ate's. William Pickering still ran it as Singapore's first and only Chinese Protector since 1877.

Pickering had been sent to sea at sixteen, a pale boy with a round face.[6] He found himself sailing deep into the East – beyond Burma, Siam and Malaya – where he was most smitten with the people of China whom he found 'ever liv-ing backwards, as it were, on the wisdom and mandates of their ancestors'.[7]

At twenty-two, Pickering joined the Chinese Imperial Maritime Customs Service near Foochow. Out of sheer boredom, he taught himself all the dialects of the south China coast to become the rare chimera that Harry Ord, first colonial Governor of the Straits Settlements, had for so long (and so hopelessly) sought.

Ord had struggled to control Singapore's Chinese since he

arrived in 1867. Three-quarters[8] of these belonged to secret societies that were organized according to different dialect groups.[9] As they could not understand each other they had numerous quarrels, some of which exploded violently into riots. One ended in three hundred houses burning down.[10] But as neither Ord nor his British staff spoke any Chinese, none of them could intervene. Ord had heard of Pickering's extraordinary linguistic ability while both were home on leave in London. He offered Pickering a job at once.

As soon as Pickering assumed his duties in Singapore, he picked out the leaders of every gang and told them – in a dialect that each could understand – that if they could not control their men, they would be deported back to China to their former lives of drudgery. The rioting stopped at once.

By the time my great-grandfather moved to the colony, Pickering had become monumentally successful. He was revered by the secret societies that once opposed him. They invited him to private initiation ceremonies to which no other outsider was allowed.

But the colony's administrators gave him little recognition and no help. Pickering had to carry on boarding the growing number of ships to Singapore himself, to register the tens of thousands of Chinese immigrants who were flooding in each year. He was also asked to translate for the police, to fight illegal prostitution and gambling, and to be the Registrar of Societies. All the triads turned to him to settle their quarrels, which only added to his workload.

By 1887, Pickering had been Protector for ten years and was beginning to feel a little worn and tired. One day, while he attended to the usual stream of Chinese supplicants at his office, he looked up to see a burly man walk in and take aim at him with an iron axe-head. Luckily it was the blunt end that hit him, or it would have split his skull.[11] The Chinese man who threw it later said that he only meant to scare Pickering off his master's illegal gambling business, not to kill him.

But the blow had been hard and though Pickering survived, even able to run after his assailant and to arrest him while bleeding heavily from his wound, the years of overwork took their toll. He had a nervous breakdown. He left Singapore with his wife Ellen on convalescent leave, officially retiring in 1890 at the age of only fifty.

The running of the Protectorate was left to the gentler, milder Francis Powell. But Powell could not manage the range of dialects that Pickering had commanded. The need was greater than ever for Chinese interpreters who could provide a translation in English. Besides the Eurasian Second Clerk J. S. Fernandez, Powell had eight Chinese staff to help him. These were the Chief Clerk Quek Yan-Hye and his third, fourth and fifth clerks, two additional interpreters, and two Chinese detectives. None had the surname Lo or Law.

The next year, 1891, Powell's Chief Clerk was still Quek, but the Eurasian Fernandez had left. In his place there was a new Second Clerk and Interpreter, a young Chinese man, twenty-six years old. His name was Lo Kuan-Yi.

The light of my microfilm projector was dim. I rubbed my eyes and checked the name, again and again, against the name in my notebook. I could scarcely believe it, but there was no mistake. The name in my notebook was spelt differently in English, Law Quan-Yee instead of Lo Kuan-Yi. But it was undoubtedly for the same Chinese name.

My great-grandfather had materialized out of my mother's stories.

9

Tragically, Law's father died in 1890, just short of seeing his son achieve their dream. Hongxi was only fifty-three. The next year, 1891, Law joined the Chinese Protectorate of the British Straits Settlements, the nearest thing that father and son could imagine to the imperial Chinese civil service.

I know how it is to be ludicrously protective of your children even when they have grown up. It feels very sad that Hongxi might have died still worrying about his boys. But he would have known at least that Law had been picked the year before, in 1889, to be one of just three Chinese student interpreters in the colonial service. It was almost certain that a promotion would follow. His elder son was going to be all right.

It was in London that I found another entry on my great-grandfather. The School of Oriental and Asian Studies has issues of the *Singapore and Straits Directory* that are missing from the National Library in Singapore. They are stored in a little-visited basement that is somewhat spooky (my steps echoed as I walked through its empty corridors), but my exploration proved totally worthwhile.

This time my great-grandfather was registered as 'Loh Quan-Yi' rather than 'Lo Kuan-Yi', but I have become something of an expert on the various English spellings of his name.

To have found him unexpectedly in a list of student interpreters for 1889 was wonderful: another fingertip's clear space in a badly smudged window, a gap through which to peer into the past.

My great-grandfather then disappeared from the colonial register the following year, 1890, but reappeared in 1891. It seems likely to me that, in 1890, he had returned to China to bury his father. It was imperative, as the eldest son, that he be at his father's funeral.

The note in the family genealogy on his father's death is brief. It does not say how or where he died, in Singapore or in China. If he had died in Singapore, Law would have had to take his father's body back to Canton.[1] This was what filial sons did. They fulfilled a parent's wish to return to the motherland. Law would have had to borrow funds for the expense unless his uncles in China clubbed together to help him. In addition to the shock of sudden bereavement and the tumult of unexpressed feelings, he would have worried about money.

In Canton, Law would have seen his sister and stepmother again, probably for the first time in nine years. His sister was by now married to a Mr Du, still living in the Pearl River Delta. Hopefully, she had borne him the sons that would give her status in his family, and protection from a mother-in-law's bullying.

On the other hand, Law's stepmother Mo had poorer prospects than ever, now that her husband was dead. In the genealogy, she is designated as a concubine rather than a second wife. She may not have had children of her own, certainly not sons. She died the year after her husband Hongxi, perhaps of hopelessness. She was forty-six years old.

My great-grandfather was twenty-five years old at his father's funeral and, I am going to assume, unmarried. (Chinese genealogies have no marriage dates.) It would have been nearly impossible for a student with no income to have had a wife. But now that he was about to work for the British in Singapore, he had become more eligible – though his bride might still have to be from a family fallen on hard times. No one who could afford a decent dowry would want their daughter moving to the Nanyang. It was another of my mother's favourite stories, how her grandmother had discovered her fate.

Miss Li of the Pearl River Delta looks around her and frowns slightly. The street outside the temple is crowded with stands that are indistinguishable one from another. They all have paper posters dyed red or saffron, covered in bold, black calligraphy proclaiming the expertise and triumphs of their owners.

She turns helplessly to her mother, who is here as her chaperone.

'There's Tang *sifu*, the Master,' Mrs Li says, pointing to a man talking intently to the woman seated next to him. A small crowd is gathered round them. 'Everyone knows him. He tells your future like an adventure. Look at the people listening to him – they almost dare not breathe! He knows what will happen just by looking at the shape of your nose and the size of your ears, and where the moles grow on your face. Also, if your eyes are close together or far apart.'

Miss Li suppresses the desire to measure the space between her eyes with her thumb and forefinger just as her mother adds, flatly: 'But we can't afford him.'

Miss Li allows herself a look of mild disappointment which her mother ignores as she nudges her along, past the stall selling incense shaped into spirals or sticks as thick as bulrushes, some of them the height of a boy; and quickly past the fortune-teller singing loudly in a rasping voice to attract the attention of passers-by. Mrs Li is disapproving. 'Drunk, if you ask me. I wouldn't go to him if he charged nothing.'

Finally, they stop in front of an old man with a wispy white beard. Old is good. Old means he's been in business for a long time and still has customers. He's not totally hopeless then. And he's not expensive.

The man puts down the book rolled up in his hand that he has been reading top to bottom, right to left. Mother and daughter sit down on the wooden bench opposite him. Mrs Li haggles a little on the price; then she gives him her daughter's time and date and place of birth. He hands over to Miss Li a wooden canister full of flat bamboo sticks, to shake gently until just the one spills out.

He picks it up and looks thoughtfully at the tiny characters etched on it like spiders' writing. Then he reaches for his *Almanac of Three Lives*, the ancient book that offers a glimpse into your life before this one, when you were beggar or prince or just infuriatingly ordinary; your life now and in the near future; and the life to come (non-committal, very brief), after we die as we must to be reborn.

The old fortune-teller finds the place that he is looking for and shows it to the women. On the page there is a picture from a woodblock. A lady in a long, belted dress typical of earlier dynasties is alone on an open road, an umbrella in one hand and a bundle of clothing in the other. Miss Li stares, uncomprehending, before she is aware of her mother's dismay. Then it's clear in a flash. She is destined after she marries to live far from home, so far that she may never see her mother again.

This prediction will come true, and a year that began in

utter misery for my great-grandfather will end for him (if not for others) feeling slightly miraculous.

There is a provision in Chinese custom that allows a filial son to marry within the first hundred days after the funeral of a parent. After this window he would have to wait three years, the traditional mourning period. Law's family may have invoked this contingency. He was the right age for marriage. He was in the right place. Marrying now would save the expense of another trip back.

It seems reasonable to assume that Law did marry in 1890 even if there are no wedding dates in a family genealogy because, the very next year, his first child was born.

Law would have found it bewildering to be plunged straight into his own wedding after the funeral of his father, especially as all the preparations were made by other people – his uncles would have whisked him through the arrangements. It might have felt uncomfortable, even disloyal. There would not have been eager anticipation.

At a Chinese wedding, the bride's face is hidden by an opaque veil till the end of the nuptials. The groom sees her face for the first time only in their bedchamber.

Law's hands tremble as he raises them towards his bride. He pauses, confused. His heart still aches for the man who gave up everything for him, who was buried only weeks before. Law was clothed in mourning white and weeping; now he is dressed in red and expected to smile.

But the bright colours and cheerful faces of this day work their charm to distract him, and the noise of cymbals and firecrackers have muffled the memory of monks chanting. Slowly, he lifts the red veil over his bride's headdress. He finds himself staring into a pair of calm eyes. His heart starts to beat freely.

Law married a woman who was three years younger, whom we know initially only by her surname Li. It would be her good fortune that the husband she was to follow, to a place so far from everything familiar, would turn out to be kind.

If it was not love at first sight, they certainly grew to love one another. They left China to live in a room in Singapore that they may at first have had to share with his younger brother, Quan-Kuan. The young interpreter and his wife managed somehow. Their son, Cheng-Wah, was conceived over Chinese New Year in February 1891, the Year of the Rabbit, and born in November. His arrival was regarded as deeply auspicious. He was followed three years later by a baby sister, my grandmother Mong-Han or 'Virtue'.

10

In 1894, the year that my grandmother was born, China and Japan went to war for the first time. She would feel its devastating effect only long after she grew up, though it was subsumed by other conflicts. It would begin further wars and was itself started by a war. In a way it had begun with tea.

Tea was brought to Europe from China in the seventeenth century and made fashionable in England by a Portuguese princess, Catherine of Braganza. The English developed an unquenchable thirst for this infusion but buying more tea was difficult: China wanted payment only in silver (the Manchu Emperor, fighting rebellion around his empire, needed silver for his armies). Britain's silver was running out.

The British sent their first diplomatic mission to China in 1793, looking for two-way trade. This was before even Law's great-grandfather Zezi was born. Its chief envoy was Lord Macartney, to whom the Emperor of China handed a letter for King George III so blunt that it was bruising: '. . . we possess all things . . . and have no use for your country's manufactures . . .'[1]

This wasn't entirely true. There was one thing that ordinary Chinese did want and which, after their failed trade mission, the British were happy to supply illegally.

The Chinese had known opium since the tenth century.[2] Boiled in water, it was a common cure for sunstroke. It took another five hundred years for its aphrodisiac properties to be revealed to the Chinese court. There it remained, in the aristocratic domain, until the late seventeenth century when Chinese pirates took over an island formerly occupied by the Dutch. On this island, now known as Taiwan, ordinary people smoked pipes of tobacco with opium.

This habit jumped like a flea to the nearby provinces of Fukien and Canton on the Chinese mainland.[3] It began to spread uncontrollably from the end of the eighteenth century as opium supplies increased, boosted by the British after Macartney's fruitless expedition.[4] The East India Company grew its opium in Bengal and Bihar and sorted and packed it with industrial fastidiousness at Ghazipur. The quality was superb.

By now Law's grandfather Zezi had been born. No one knew it, but these were the declining years of China's power. Though Zezi grew up in relative prosperity and would himself prosper, Western imperialism was about to rear up, setting off a sequence of conflicts that would end in a war calamitous for my family.

At first the East India Company sold just enough contraband to pay for its tea, about 270 tons a year.[5] But the stream of smuggled drugs became a flood when the Company lost its monopoly among the English on the China trade. Britain's Charter Act of 1833 allowed all merchants into the market, and they were rapacious. Between 1820 and 1840, opium imports into China grew by more than 800 per cent, from 270 to 2,500 tons a year.[6] Chinese addicts were in their millions.[7]

China's Manchu rulers understood opium's potential to devastate the working masses. They tried in vain to rein back the illicit imports. Tensions would build and break in 1839 in the first of two Opium Wars between Britain and China, fought at sea off Canton. China would lose not only from inferior firepower but because most of its soldiers were addicts. Seven out of ten soldiers in its southern army, recruited from Fukien and Canton, were invalided out of service from opium abuse.[8]

All this took place before my great-grandfather Law was born but he would have learned of it as he grew up. Older Chinese men burned inside with the injustice of it. His grandfather had lived through both Opium Wars and Law's own father, Hongxi, was twenty-three years old when the Second Opium War ended and legalization of the opium trade was forced upon China. Its consequences would stretch far. Not only would opium-smoking be treated as a recreational pastime without the stigma of a deeply dangerous drug, but this model of coercive imperialism would inspire followers. Law himself, and his family, would experience both aspects of this dark legacy.

Japan had once looked up to China, and it was troubling to see it impotent against the West. Then, in the summer of 1853, Japan itself became the target. The Americans, recognizing the persuasive eloquence of superior firepower, anchored four black-hulled warships in Edo Bay to show off some serious artillery. They left their demands and returned for an answer eight months later with double the number of ships and a hundred guns. The Japanese opened their ports.

Two years later, when the British felt that they no longer wanted any restrictions in China on their opium 'trade' and preferred it legalized, they launched the Second Opium War on wholly spurious grounds and won it with the help of the French. Together, they then fell upon the Emperor's Summer Palace in Peking, looting it of its treasures. Next, they set fire to its thousand acres to leave it burning for three days till it was a desert of grey ash and rubble. Its once magnificent buildings and gardens are gone. Its ancient gingko trees can never be regrown.

By 1861, China and Japan had signed away privileges in the so-called Unequal Treaties not just to Britain and America, but to France, Russia, Holland and Prussia.

In the treaty ports of China and Japan, foreigners controlled the customs duties and kept troops to protect themselves from local laws. In an affray with the natives of the town, foreigners could walk free whereas the local authority was obliged to arrest and punish its own people.[9]

China was too busy crumbling under the weight of Manchu decrepitude to confront these injustices. But across the water in Japan, there were men preparing to effect great change.

By the time my great-grandfather was born in 1865, dissatisfaction had grown in Japan over the weakness of the Tokugawa shogun. In 1868, when my great-grandfather was three years old, young samurai[10] pushed aside the shogunate to bring back a collaborative emperor in what is called the Meiji Restoration.[11]

These low and middle-ranking samurai were ready to challenge the unequal treaties. Remarkably, they understood that it was possible only on Western terms. Their country would have to be recast in the mould of the West.

Once, Japan had venerated China – but it was no longer the example to follow. Two countries long joined by their reverence for Confucius came to a crossroads, and went their separate ways. In China, Confucian ideas and the classics would continue to underpin the Chinese examination system, even after proving inadequate in a modernizing world.

*

Hongxi watches his first-born son on his mother's lap. His little hands are playing with the strand of her hair that he has pulled free. She chides him gently as she tucks it back in place, laughing softly as he giggles and struggles to pull it free again.

Hongxi's eyes rest with pleasure on his son's full forehead, then on his straight nose and broad, square chin. All these features presage success. He dreams of his son's future, of the career that he might have, better than Hongxi's own. His son will receive a thorough education in the Chinese classics. Already, he can recite from that ancient primer for children, the *Three Character Classic*: 'The three mighty powers of nature are Heaven, Earth and Men. The three great celestial lights are the Sun, the Moon and the Stars.'[12]

Over the East China Sea in Japan, they no longer believed in such learning. A Confucian education had failed to protect their country from the mercantile marauders of the West. Instead, the young leaders of the Meiji Restoration went to Europe and America for the knowledge to transform Japan. They returned to strip away feudal privileges, dismantle the samurai class, create a national army, introduce national education. They put in place a constitution with an elected parliament like the West's.

What has taken one paragraph to describe required more than twenty years of committed and sometimes violent reform. No other country in the world except Russia has managed so much change in as short a time.

Japan had modernized to become predator, not prey. In 1884, when my great-grandfather had grown into a young man newly arrived in Singapore and learning English, Japan compelled Korea to sign a treaty on trade. Korea, like Japan once, was closed to all foreign countries except China. The treaty divided Korea into pro-China and pro-Japan factions that clashed repeatedly until – with the confusion of a Korean peasant rebellion thrown into the mix – the armed forces of China and Japan went into Korea ten years later in 1894 to support their respective allies. My great-grandfather was in Singapore with his young family and he was not troubled by this collision if he thought about it at all. It was far away, it was fought over reasons that seemed obscure, and he expected China to win. It never crossed his mind that the hallowed Chinese Empire could fail.

But Japan now had a professional army and navy that were backed by the railways, shipyards and munitions factories built over the previous two decades. Its army followed French and Prussian models. Its fleet was based on the British Royal Navy. All its advisers were European.[13]

China's army and navy, on the other hand, had troops that were addicted to opium and officers who were corrupt as a matter of course. They packed their shells with cement instead of explosives.[14]

China lost the first Sino-Japanese War in just nine months. This started the chain of events that, ultimately, would be terrible for my family.

The British Library is very different from the one at SOAS. There are no shelves among which to flit haphazardly like a happy bee, choosing books at whim to leaf through. Instead, you pick out publications from a vast catalogue to have them delivered to one of the library's reading rooms. Depending on the book or document, this can take seventy minutes or two days. But I am not complaining. It is astounding to have access to this world-famous and venerable collection, a privilege that it confers on even its country's most ordinary residents.

My preferred reading room is Asian and African Studies on the third floor. My stack was one short. It took the librarian some time to locate the missing item.

I thought that I had ordered a book about Japanese prints from the 1894–5 war. In fact, they were the prints themselves.[15] There were more than 170 triptychs, each about 70 centimetres by 35 centimetres, in a box too enormous for one of the regular shelves. I staggered to the nearest table to put it down and open it up.

Warriors and cavalry, banners and cannon fire leaped out, their purples, vermilions and greens vivid from the European aniline dyes embraced by the artists of a modernizing Japan. History was literally at my fingertips as I lifted out folio after folio. The flag with the red rising sun flew everywhere.

These Meiji woodblock prints depict the Chinese as craven Orientals who grimace cartoon-like in their death throes,[16] whereas the artist Nobukazu's Japanese officers are in European uniform, have nearly Caucasian features (and European beards), and look heroic.[17] Their captives are lined

up, kneeling, to be beheaded. Severed heads, stained with carmine, collect in the foreground.

Were these the starting steps towards a narrative to justify how the Japanese might treat their neighbours, and how later they could plunder their resources? Japan had not expected to win its war with China so quickly. Victory was sweetened by the spoils: there was a huge indemnity paid by China; there was territory. There was a valuable steel battleship.[18] Once savoured, imperialism Western-style would not be easily given up.

Japan had revered China for hundreds of years until the Opium Wars. Now any lingering respect was turning to disdain.[19] Meiji thinkers urged their country to 'leave the ranks of Asian nations and cast our lot with the civilized nations of the West'![20] They wanted not just to embrace the institutions of the West, but no longer to be considered Asian. It was a dangerous point of view.

But history forms in secret spaces, unknowable till it has emerged. Your future may be its captive.

My great-grandfather was fixed to his present. He had his hands full in the Chinese Protectorate working as its Second Clerk and Interpreter, and whatever he read about China's defeat was played down by the patriotic Chinese press in Singapore. He had more immediate preoccupations in the Nanyang. In 1895, the year that China lost its war with Japan, he had a third child, a girl. He named her Mong-Lan or 'Orchid'. His young family was expanding.

Whereas I have been given hindsight and I know that a fledgling bird of prey grows broad wings and strong talons. There will be death. There will be war. Japan will embark on a trajectory from where there will be no retraction until its catastrophic end.

Fourteen years after he arrived in Singapore, my great-grandfather was still poor. Despite a supreme effort to better himself by learning English, he couldn't afford a house for his wife and three children. The interpreter and his family lived in rooms.

Monthly rents for houses in 1896 were fifteen Straits dollars.[1] His salary was about twenty dollars. He should have been paid more but he wasn't, even though he was one of only about a hundred Chinese[2] out of the 190,000[3] in Singapore who could speak, read and write in English and Chinese.

I had no idea of the formality of the process by which this Chinese man became an official interpreter for the British — the years studying English, the internship, the official appointment and then the assumption of specific duties. Law was more than just a translator. He wasn't simply gadding about chatting in two languages. He was one of the administrators. In the Protectorate, 'clerks' weren't minions.

In a colony where most of the people were Chinese, the Chinese Protectorate was the most important of its government offices. The agency's clerks were privy to information that affected their people directly. Only the Department of Police was held in as high regard. It was considerable to have been the Protectorate's Second Clerk and Law worked in a department of nineteen officers, five of those directly below him.

But it was not enough.

When Law's father, Hongxi, left China for the Nanyang with his two young sons, the plan was not just to survive but to thrive. However, Singapore's colonial bureaucracy turned out to be nothing like China's civil service – there, the prestige of office opened many doors; here, there was no opportunity for personal enhancement. Nor was there a clear route to wider career advancement, at least not for a Chinese man like Law.

And Law's timing had not been good. Because he had to leave Singapore in 1890 for the funeral of his father, he had joined the Chinese Protectorate in 1891. When the position of chief clerk became vacant in 1892, he was deemed too inexperienced to be promoted.

Instead, my mother had said, he was 'in charge of protecting women'. Her turn of phrase at the time had struck me as quaint, before I learned that such a thing as a Chinese Protectorate existed or that William Pickering, its first Protector, had set up a shelter for women called 'Office to Protect Virtue'.

In those early days, there were roughly six Chinese men to one Chinese woman and practices were rife among the men which Pickering found 'unEnglish, unChristian, and abnormal'.[4] He felt that it was his duty practically to encourage prostitution, which was legal in Singapore. But he wanted to save from the sex trade those women who had travelled to the colony in good faith to find honest work.

Under Pickering's guidelines, my great-grandfather had to make surprise visits to the grimy premises in Chinatown that served as brothels, to write his reports in English as an interpreter. Inside these places, dispirited women in crumpled *samfoos* waited. They got up with expressionless faces when customers walked in, to disappear with them into cubicles screened only by thin, stained curtains.

His work was partly to register and interview new arrivals, preferably out of the earshot of their 'madam', so that he could ask if they were there against their will. Pickering's safe house was for those wanting to escape the brothels but the girls did not always dare leave, too terrified of the gangsters who ran the business.

Law hands out a note to the new girl with the pale face. She has not managed to rub off the tear stain dried down the side of one cheek. When she stretches out her hand to take the ticket from him, he sees a purple bruise on her arm. Someone has been beating her. There is nothing he can do if she will not leave with him now. The current Protector is William Evans. Law explains gently: 'Trust me, the white chief has a good heart. I know you cannot read, but this note has his guarantee that he will protect you if you decide to go.'

He can see that she does not believe him. It is usually too late to save the girls once they are in a brothel. The best time is at the dock but the secret societies are very good at stealing girls past the Protectorate's officers.

He has finished for the day. He gets up. A little girl runs into the hall. 'Who is that?' Law asks. He suddenly misses his two young daughters.

'Oh, she's Precious Lily's,' the brothel owner says, gesturing carelessly to a booth where one of her more seasoned women is silently submitting to a customer. Law catches the hard glint in the brothel owner's eyes. As soon as she is able, the child will follow in the footsteps of her mother.

*

Law was growing disheartened by his work. His salary was no compensation for the misery that he felt. In 1896, when his wife was expecting their fourth child, Law had himself transferred from the Chinese Protectorate to Gaols, under the Inspector of Prisons. He was thirty-one years old. He was now the Chief Chinese Clerk but in charge of just one interpreter. It seems a desperate move. Two years later, he is down in the register as 'on leave'. The year after, 1899, he disappears from the colonial service altogether.

He has gone into business with his brother.

He would have agonized over the change – in China, business- and tradespeople were the lowest social category. Above these were the artisans and, above them, the landowners and farmers. Near the very top were the scholar-officials, of whom Law felt very much a part. But he realized that his progress under the British was limited. His English was simply not fluent enough, not like a Straits-Chinese man's who had been taught the language from childhood.

Besides feeling that he was betraying his ancestors, leaving the colonial service was a huge risk to take. Law wouldn't have wanted to make life any harder for his family but he had no savings to fall back on. He might have borrowed money. He would have needed his wife to be on side. She would, understandably, have had her doubts.

'Is it wise?' The former Miss Li has long been known as Law *tai*, Mrs Law the interpreter's wife, mother of four healthy children, two of whom (how clever!) are boys. 'Perhaps your new job just needs more time?'

Law shakes his head. He has two sons now. Cheng-Wah is eight years old and Cheng-Liang, whose birth brought so much joy, is three. The pressure on Law to succeed is great.

He knows his father had hoped that he would flourish in the colonial service and he tries not to think about this. When he does, his disappointment in himself still feels raw. But he is desperate. He needs to be able to help his boys make something of their lives.

'It's been three years. Promotion isn't likely or it would have happened by now. And what would it be? A little extra money? It won't be enough. I want to give you more.'

Law's younger brother, Quan-Kuan, who was hopeless with books, had something infinitely more useful in the cut and thrust of an evolving town: an instinct for business. Far from being dragged down by the building industry for which he worked, he had risen with it. Construction was booming. There were now 150,000 Chinese in Singapore, and the border of their Chinese quarter was extending all the time to fit in more arrivals. This was good for the Cantonese who came to Singapore as carpenters and artisans and who dominated the building trade.

But Law understands his wife's anxiety. 'It is a risk, of course it is. But I still have my contacts in the Chinese Protectorate. Working with my brother could earn us more than would ever be possible in the government service. Then I could move us into a house. You wouldn't have to share the kitchen or the lavatory with so many families.'

Wrestling with his anxieties at the turn of the new century, my great-grandfather had at least the distraction of an unusual visitor who was nearly his age and from the same province in China.

A certain Dr Sun Yat-Sen blew into Singapore like a

typhoon in 1900, on an impetuous mission to save a friend. There was no getting away from this bizarre case. The Chinese newspapers were full of it. For a while, it made the Chinese of Singapore feel that they were in the mainstream of China's current affairs, rather than eddying in its backwaters.

This Dr Sun had been given a private English education in Hawaii by his older brother, an ex-coolie who became so fabulously wealthy that he was called the other 'King of Maui'. Sun trained in western medicine but turned his back on the profession to be a revolutionary firebrand. Five years before, he had tried to overthrow the Manchu regime in China. His attempted coup was badly organized, and therefore easily foiled. He had since become a fugitive with something of an international reputation.

He had sought freedom in London but was kidnapped by the Chinese Legation and confined at their quarters in Portland Place to be deported and executed. Word got out to an English friend, who raised the alarm. When the London newspapers publicized his plight, Sun was released. He fled to Japan.

Kyushu,[5] closest to the Chinese mainland, had become a haven for rebels like Sun. Although Japan had embraced Europe, there were still those Japanese who worried about Western imperialists and their intentions. They believed Japan was safer if it was joined with China against the West. But first the Chinese had to be helped to throw off the moribund reign of the Manchus.

Sun had made good friends among these Japanese, one of the most loyal of whom was Miyazaki Toten, a larger-than-life character with a full pirate's beard and a fondness for the geisha house.[6] Oddly, he would have a lasting effect on my family – Miyazaki was the reason for an unscheduled visit by

Dr Sun to Singapore which, in turn, would be pivotal in the life of Law's elder son Cheng-Wah.

Miyazaki was from a family that had dedicated itself to the Chinese republican cause. Now, he was mysteriously in Singapore with a large sum of money on him. He was looking for a man called Kang You-Wei.

No Chinese in Singapore would have heard of Miyazaki Toten; not all may yet have heard of Sun Yat-Sen. But everyone knew Kang You-Wei. He was China's most famous reformer, still in all the history books. In 1898, he had his young Manchu Emperor Guangxu issue a raft of sweeping reforms that included, fatally, one to eliminate corruption. This drew the ire of Guangxu's aunt, the redoubtable Empress Dowager Cixi. She placed the Emperor under house arrest and ordered Kang's death by 'slow slicing'.

In 1900, when my great-grandfather was struggling in his first year away from the umbrella of the colonial service, Kang arrived in Singapore still dodging attempts on his life. He was, understandably, a little jumpy.

Sun Yat-Sen had been trying for some time to speak directly to Kang, to persuade him that they should join forces. But Kang had rejected his advances. Kang was Chinese but a constitutional monarchist, loyal to the Manchu Emperor. He wanted no taint from revolutionaries who were looking to depose, forcibly, the Manchu regime.

Imagine Kang's distress when Miyazaki, not exactly invisible with his wild eyes and bristly black beard, turned up suddenly in Singapore at the home of the friend with whom Kang was quietly staying. He knew Miyazaki and to whom he was linked. It was going to look as if Kang had planned an assignation in Singapore with anti-monarchist revolutionaries and their money. What kind of death would the Empress

Dowager recommend for him then? Kang threw himself on the mercy of the British administrators, denounced Miyazaki as a Manchu assassin, and had him arrested.

Dr Sun was in Saigon trying to raise money for his revolution when he heard the news. He went straight over to Singapore at considerable risk to himself. The Manchus had just set up their legation in Singapore and the British were eager to accommodate them. Sun was arrested almost as soon as he arrived.

'Look at this,' Law shows his wife the sheet of Chinese newspaper. He is avidly interested in Chinese politics so he's certainly heard of Sun Yat-Sen.

She glances up from her mending without much interest as he adds, 'I've no idea why that Japanese *ronin* is so important, but Dr Sun's just got himself thrown into prison because of him!'

'Just think,' his wife says archly, 'if you were still working for Gaols you could have met them both.' Law wonders, not for the first time, if he did right to leave. His salary from the British had been minuscule, but it was at least dependable.

Luckily, Sun had influential Chinese friends in the colony, who arranged a meeting for him with the Acting Governor, James Alexander Swettenham.[7] It is possible that Swettenham was swayed by Sun's confident English, debonair dress and dignified presence. Apart from anything else, Sun could explain directly in English that the money Miyazaki carried on him was meant for overthrowing the Manchus, and that therefore he could not be working *for* the Manchus. Both Sun and Miyazaki were released.

Sun would eventually return to Singapore to set up a branch of his underground resistance movement, the Tong-menghui, which organized readings and talks on revolution in China.[8] By then Law's eldest son Cheng-Wah was a teen-ager, a top student at a deeply nationalist school. There is every chance that he might have attended some of these meetings, maybe even seen Sun Yat-Sen during one of his many visits to the colony. Certainly, Cheng-Wah was aware of Dr Sun. When in 1910 Cheng-Wah went to college in Nanking and in that very city the following year Sun Yat-Sen was made provisional president of the new Republic of China, it must have felt thrilling. Cheng-Wah would join Dr Sun's political party, the Kuomintang, to become an active member in Singapore. It would determine his fate.

But back in 1900, after their release, Miyazaki was banned from ever setting foot in Singapore again whereas Dr Sun was banned for five years. As soon as his ban was lifted in 1905, he was back. He was in the colony to ask its wealthy and patriotic Chinese to fund his cause against the Manchus. He could not have timed it better. The unimaginable had happened. The Japanese had dared declare war on Russia the year before. They had just won.

At the end of the first Sino-Japanese war in 1895, Japan was given territory by China that had included Dalian. But Russia argued that Dalian – with its year-round ice-free port and strategic location – was far too important to belong to any foreign power. Together with France and Germany, Rus-sia pressurized Japan to return Dalian to China, only to then occupy that whole peninsula for itself on a lease from China.

From Dalian, Russia encroached on Korea, threatening Japan's security: there is only the Tsushima Strait between Japan and the Korean peninsula. Japan had tried to reach a settlement with Russia over this, but talks collapsed in 1903 in the face of Russian intransigence.

By this time, Japan was in a bilateral pact with Britain, the most powerful imperial nation in the world. Britain also worried about Russian intentions in the East. It had asked Japan – now with a modern navy of its own – to be its partner in an exclusive naval and military agreement. Their Anglo-Japanese Alliance was signed in 1902 to 'unrestrained joy'[9] in Japan. It was the first time in history that an Eastern and a Western country were collaborating as equals. It also carried the implicit understanding that in a war between Russia and Japan, Britain would remain neutral. This gave Japan the confidence to confront Russia.

Now in May 1905, after nearly sixteen months of fighting, Admiral Togo has ambushed and decimated Rozhestvensky's Baltic Fleet in the Strait of Tsushima, obliterating Russia's international naval dominance in the process. Russia would have to surrender its leased Chinese territory to Japan.

This is electrifying news. It is the first time in the modern age that an Eastern country has beaten a major power of the West. If Japan can defeat the Russian Empire, perhaps Dr Sun can overturn the Manchus. Singapore's Chinese millionaires may appreciate the comparison between Sun's proposed revolt in China and Japan's success. They may be generous. They are feeling wealthier than ever from the prospect of a rubber boom – unlike my great-grandfather. It is five years now since he left the Chinese Protectorate, but he still carries his indigence with him like a tortoise and its shell. He may have to move his family from two rooms into one.

12

The merchants of Singapore might be thriving, but my great-grandfather and his brother Quan-Kuan were not. They were learning that though the margins in their construction business were generous – you could charge ten thousand dollars to build a small warehouse yet you only had to pay your coolies seven dollars a day – the serious money was to be made elsewhere. They were too late for tin mining, but the new business of rubber plantations was just taking off.[1]

Clearing land to plant rubber was a hugely expensive enterprise that was beyond the brothers' resources, but they could hang on to the coat-tails of this rising industry by providing a very particular service to its workers.

Opium was the medicine of the roughly treated coolie and gambling was his comfort. The coolie removed the jungle by hand to dig in each new rubber sapling. He believed that opium healed him after a day of backbreaking labour while gambling subdued his loneliness. They helped him to forget that his destiny was to provide cheap labour to the British. He was reluctant to work at all if even these needs were not met, although, ultimately, they made his lot more wretched by swallowing up his pitiful, hard-earned cash. The British, who needed coolies for their colonies, were uneasy at first about peddling opium and gambling. But in the end it was simpler to take the view that the Chinese would seek depravity, whether lawfully or not[2] – in which case their vices might as well be legalized and provide revenue for the state.

In 1900, half of government revenue in Singapore was from opium.[3]

The colonial administration collected such income indirectly, through 'revenue farmers'. It charged these men a rent in return for the freedom to gather and keep opium duties or to organize public gambling. Would-be farmers had to apply for these rights, an expensive procedure often undertaken by syndicates. Successful applicants then sub-let their rights to smaller operators.

The process was cheaper in British North Borneo, a wild place managed by a chartered company under the protection of the British Crown. In 1905, this company removed the export duty on rubber to encourage its expansion.[4] Coolies were vital to this enterprise, therefore their requirements had to be met. The opportunity to run a gambling farm presented itself to Law if he were willing to relocate to Jesselton on the northwest coast of Borneo. Borneo was more than 1,000 kilometres from Singapore and few businessmen wanted to move there, but opium and gambling were cash operations. You couldn't run them from afar.

'Will you be all right while I'm away?' Law looks imploringly at his wife. He wants her to ask him to stay though he knows this choice does not exist. She shrugs. Then she nods to reassure him: 'Of course we'll manage. You have to do what you must. I'll pray for your protection and wait for your return.'

There is no other way. Already she buys mainly fish for their supper, the cheapest food in the market. There isn't always money even for that. Sometimes, she is reduced to asking for fish that would be thrown away, left out for stray cats on the street. She catches the fragments of conversation around her as she puts the scraps in her basket, her cheeks burning. 'The interpreter's wife . . .'; 'Oh, not any more'; 'I didn't recognize her! She's grown so *thin!*'

Law will have to leave the wife and children he adores to live alone in an isolated frontier town. He will miss his daughters' happy chatter, the serious expressions on their faces when he arbitrates a quarrel with their high-spirited brothers. (Even Cheng-Wah joins Liang in provoking Orchid, tickled by her quick temper; Virtue always sides with her younger sister.) He will miss how his wife floats through it all, keeping relative order with no more than a hand on a shoulder or a shake of the head.

But here is the chance to pivot them out of want into surplus.

Law was as driven as any Chinese to wear self-sacrifice lightly if it meant a better life for his family.

Did he also stop to consider that he would have to exploit, ruthlessly, men worse off than himself? He knew that the gambling business entangled in debt miserable men who might never free themselves from bondage. Law had studied the classics. He understood that humanity was as important as duty.

But the world that my great-grandfather knew was harsh. He found that he could not travel with his full set of Confucian values. He would have to jettison a few. He chose duty to family over humanity to others. For better or worse, he plunged in.

In 1907, Law's wife had another baby, a girl. It was eight years since he left the colonial service, and eleven years after their last child. Their family already had two sons and two daughters, like matching pairs. They would have to squeeze a little closer in their two rooms, each eat a little less. If they had to have another child, a son would at least have brought hope of a fortunate change in circumstances. Not another daughter.

Girls were considered such a blight in China that burglars warned each other off any household with five daughters or more.[5] Obviously, the family would have nothing worth stealing. It would have been impoverished by creatures that needed to be clothed and fed but contributed nothing. There were Chinese men who, if they only had daughters, would say that they were childless.

But an unexpected pregnancy after the interval of a decade cannot help but feel hopeful, the smell of moisture in the air after rainless days, especially when it ends in the birth of a healthy baby, even a girl.

Life was still precarious for my great-grandfather. He was forty-two. By the reckoning of those times he was already approaching old age. He had struggled to be something that his ancestors could be proud of, a scholar and a civil servant, but in this curious place called Singapore – so different from China – it had counted for nothing. He had tried to rise up in its bureaucracy, but it was like climbing a hill of slipping sand.

Yet, since leaving the British colonial service to dip his hands in the muck of commerce, he was still struggling. It would have saddened his father Hongxi that he had made this sacrifice for nothing. Law must have felt a failure.

His new baby allowed him to step back briefly from his worldly preoccupations to exercise a little of the learning and originality that set him apart from the other immigrants, even the coolies who had become tycoons. He did still have his education. No one could take that away.

All Chinese men understood the importance and magnificence of boys: they grasped your lineage in their hands and passed it on through millennia. Because sons were so important to the Chinese, the clan often chose a shared name for an entire generation. The generational name for Law's sons was 'Cheng', which means 'clarity'. His elder son was Cheng-Wah, and his younger son and fourth child was called Cheng-Liang.[6]

Girls, on the other hand, meant little to the clan. Chinese men in early Singapore were mainly merchants or coolies, preoccupied with making money. Their daughters were typically named 'Jade Girl' or 'Golden Pearl', simple names after some imaginary piece of treasure revealing greed rather than taste.

Law was different. He had come from a region of China where girls had intrinsic worth. He chose his daughters' names with as much care as for his sons.

His eldest daughter was 'Mong-Han'. 'Mong' means to dream of or to aspire to; 'Han' means virtue, all its attributes from serenity to forbearance. The girl who would become my grandmother was to cultivate in herself the qualities that really mattered to Confucian Chinese – loyalty, self-restraint, courage. It was an instruction manual in a name.

His middle daughter and third child was called 'Mong-Lan': Lan is an orchid, specifically the orchid that Confucius loved. The cymbidium symbolizes virtue. Its leaves are arching and graceful, its flowers demure and modest. In the poetry and paintings of ancient China, it represents the scholar and the gentlewoman.

'I've been thinking', Law says, 'of a name for our new daughter.' He is in Singapore to visit his family.

'Oh, yes?' His wife is tidying their small room. The children have finally fallen asleep next door, but it won't be long now before the baby wakes for milk.

'I want her name to have something to do with virtue, like her sisters'.'

His wife glances over at the baby. She thought she heard her stir.

'You know how Confucius liked wild orchids, how they could grow even on the steep sides of a gorge where it was rocky and inhospitable?'

Before cymbidiums were tamed by the scholar-gardeners of China, they were found only in the forest. They comforted Confucius when he was old, ignored by the princes and dukes of a China not yet unified. They had listened to him once when he taught that those born with power and wealth are responsible for those born without. But he had become irrelevant, an unwelcome itinerant with a dwindling band of followers.[7]

Hiking through the hills in his sixties, looking for refuge, he could always be cheered up by the sight of a cymbidium: '. . . when two people understand each other in their inmost hearts, their words are sweet and strong, like the fragrance of orchids.'[8]

The flowers of a cymbidium have a scent that is subtle yet powerful. It can drift 10 feet or more. You inhale it before you see it. It gave Confucius hope that his words might travel far.

'He admired their resilience and he loved their perfume. I would like to call our baby Mong-Fan.'

His wife looks at him. It's been good to have him home. She arches an eyebrow; then she smiles. 'That's lovely,' she agrees. 'It will suit her very well.'

*

Law may have regarded Confucius as a kindred spirit when he named his youngest daughter Dream of Fragrance. Just as the orchid's enduring scent had inspired Confucius, so she would help him to soldier on.

She was known by a diminutive, Fan-Fan, and she turned out to be a lucky charm. A year after her birth, the world went mad for Henry Ford's Model-T, the automobile for the masses. Cars needed tyres which needed rubber. Rubber prices began to climb in what would be a five-year surge.[9]

More land was turned into plantations, more coolies brought to Borneo to work the land and squander their wages in gambling dens, profiting the men who ran them. The great risk that Law took in leaving the impecunious certainty of the Chinese Protectorate was finally paying off.

Around this time, Law moved his family into their own house in Singapore, a phenomenal achievement. Like any entrepreneur, the gambling concession wasn't his only project. There was also investment in timber, and in gold and silver mines.

Number 31 Cantonment Road still exists, one of a row of terraced houses marooned near a knot of modern expressways. Public Works has thoughtfully planted a bed of rain trees and spider lilies to screen off the traffic and the noise.

The houses have wooden shuttered windows on the first floor that open to Juliet balconies.[10] Their narrow frontages disguise deep interiors. Number 31 is now converted into offices, but in Law's day it had a reception room on the ground floor with an interior courtyard, a kitchen beyond that, and a room at the back for a maid. It still has its staircase made from Malayan mahogany.

My great-grandfather would have seen himself living here for a long time, though he might have dreamed of one day moving to something even bigger, when his sons married and their wives had babies. Installed in this fine house with his loving family, he must have been wrapped in a veritable fleece of contentment. But tragedy slipped in to lie beside him, an unwelcome bedfellow.

In 1909, when their baby Fan-Fan was nearly two years old, his wife died. In Singapore, where the mortality rate was higher than in either Hong Kong or India, the trusting girl who left her Canton village to follow him had turned into a statistic, one of the nameless many to die from childbirth or cholera, dysentery or malaria.

How much Law loved her is reflected in the great change that he made to his family's genealogy: he named her. Ten years after her death, when their eldest son Cheng-Wah was commissioned to update the clan lineage, Law had Tsui-Chan's personal name put in with the place where she was buried. This was completely against tradition. No other woman in the previous one thousand years had been given the same privilege, to be identified in this book beyond her surname at birth.

The two parts of my great-grandmother's name combine to suggest beauty, especially the beauty of clear, green jade. Tsui-Chan was forty-one years old.

My grandmother Virtue, fifteen, took the place of her mother in running the household, consoling her younger brother and sisters, being a confidante to her older brother. But perhaps the vacuum that Tsui-Chan left threatened to engulf Law. As devastated as he was by his wife's death, he got himself a concubine – a girl older than Virtue by a year.

I can only imagine the feelings that this triggered in my grandmother and the pain that it caused, that a girl little older than herself should move into their home to share her father's bed and to assume the space that her mother once occupied.

Virtue, Orchid and their little sister Fan-Fan stare wordlessly at the girl whom their father is presenting to them. The girl drops her eyes as their father says, 'You can call her Little Aunt and she will help you around the house.' But they don't want help. They want their mother. Or to be left alone.

In 1910, the year after his wife died, Law sent his two sons to college in China. He had always hoped to educate them there, but perhaps the timing was expedited by the acquisition of a young mistress. It would undoubtedly be awkward to have his nineteen-year-old son around his seventeen-year-old concubine.

Cheng-Wah left Singapore for Nanking with his younger brother Liang, fourteen years old. They were joining the prestigious Chi-nan or Jinan Academy. It had been inaugurated four years earlier under the auspices of the Manchu government, specifically to provide a higher education for overseas Chinese.

The brothers were not in Nanking for very long before something epochal and unexpected took place in China. In October 1911, a series of mutinies sprang up spontaneously in central and southern China. They would unseat the Manchu Empire.

Revolutionary groups had mushroomed around China as dissatisfaction with the Qing dynasty spread. But they were badly organized. In the city of Wuchang, the leader of one accidentally exploded the bomb that he was building and had to be hospitalized. Police investigating the incident at his home found a list of his fellow revolutionaries, including scores of names from the province's own government-sponsored New Army.

Facing arrest and certain execution, these men had nothing to lose from immediately launching a revolt. Panic can be the grease that makes the wheels of revolution turn: they routed the local viceroy, installed a military government and, flushed with success, invited other provinces to do the same. In less than a month, three-quarters of China's provinces declared themselves free of Manchu rule.[11] Almost inadvertently, an impossible dream was coming true. China was on the brink of becoming Asia's first republic.

Dr Sun Yat-Sen had been fundraising in America, removed from these events. He rushed back to China. Though he had not organized these rebellions, his was the recognizable face of the revolution. He was sworn in as provisional president of the Republic of China on New Year's Day of 1912.

There was only one obstacle. The Manchu child emperor Puyi was still on the throne and Sun did not have the military means to force his departure. Sun had to hand over his presidency to an influential Chinese member of the Manchu government, Yuan Shi-Kai. Yuan had the loyalty of the military and the power to persuade the Manchus to leave. In February 1912, the last Emperor of the Qing dynasty abdicated.

The college where Law had sent his sons immediately suffered from a lack of political patronage. Jinan Academy had been a pet project of Qing royalty. Now that China had become nominally republican, nobody wanted any longer to be associated with its unpatriotic Manchu past.

Both brothers were back in Singapore by 1913, where they were employed by their former school as a trainee teacher and a teaching assistant. Even so, the family genealogy loyally claims, they 'raised the prestige of the clan'.

13

My grandmother Virtue grew into a conscientious young woman with a carapace of reserve.

She died when I was nine years old but I have no memory of talking to her or of her hugging me. I know that she held me at least once. There is a photograph of me lying in her arms as a baby. She is looking not at the camera but down at my face, examining me. She isn't smiling.

Her protective shell must have hidden something soft inside because I remember trailing behind my mother and grandmother to the cinema to watch a procession of sad films. She loved sad films. There was one we saw repeatedly that was probably her favourite. It was a celebrated romance that had been told and retold for over a thousand years.[1]

Fourth-century China was a fractured and impermanent place where the Huns had gained control of the north and driven its Chinese aristocrats south to present day Nanjing. Here, they set up a vibrant court and continued their sybaritic ways with little regard for the future. Their Eastern Jin dynasty was condemned to be short-lived, a mere 103 years in the span of time, but it is remembered for its black glazed pots, its poetry and a story. It was only the story my grandmother ever cared about. Only the story mattered.

Butterfly Lovers

There was once a wealthy merchant with many fine sons and one beautiful daughter. His sons went to school to prepare for the imperial examination; his daughter was tutored at home to read and write. She was intelligent and learned quickly. Then she wanted more. All the expensive, intriguing gifts her father bought her counted for nothing – the songbird in its gilded cage, even the combs for her hair made from kingfishers' feathers of a blue brighter than the sky could ever be.

She asked to go to a class like her brothers to study the classics, to learn to quote freely from that repository of ancient poetry, the *Book of Songs*:

> *'Fair, fair,' cry the ospreys*
> *On the island in the river.*
> *Lovely is this noble lady,*
> *Fit bride for our lord.*[2]

'But that's impossible!' her father exploded in anger. 'How can you sit in a room full of strangers? You know that only whores and servants go among men!'

But times of flux are also times of freedom. In exile, Eastern Jin women were no longer resigned to being confined to their homes. They had begun to visit each other, accompanied by their maids.

Persuasive as well as clever, the girl convinced her father that if she and her maid were to disguise themselves as men, they would break no conventions as women. They could take off for Hangchow, the city of poets, where she would enrol at a school for a period of study, after which she would come home.

In lakeside Hangchow, one young man stood out in her class. He was not rich, you could tell from his clothes, but he was handsome and modest and treated with kindness this secretive and somewhat effeminate new classmate.

The two became close friends who studied together and laughed at the same trifles. They talked about everything, sometimes about nothing. They had no secrets between them but for one.

'If only you had a sister, dear friend,' the scholar sighed, 'I would feel I know her as well as yourself.'

To which the girl, now deeply in love, replied, 'But I do and you shall meet her soon.'

Winter came and went and came and went again. When the first peonies appeared on their third spring together, a summons from the girl's father arrived: she was to return at once.

The two friends found it hard to part, but the scholar promised that he would visit his schoolmate, whose town was not so far from his own. Once he had sat the imperial examination, he too would have to go homewards, whether in triumph or defeat.

In fact, he passed with many honours and was conferred the post of county magistrate in Ningbo, close to where they both lived. On his journey back, he stopped joyously in the town of his dear friend to give him the news.

To his bewilderment and wonder he was met not by the young companion of his schooldays, but by a captivating girl at once exotic yet familiar. She floated towards him smiling, her silk gown the colour of cherries, her long hair dressed in gold pins from which dangled little gold leaves.[3] She smelt of orchids and musk.[4]

The two friends were free at last to fall in love. But they were not free to marry. The young woman – once the scholar's soul mate, now his sweetheart – had been promised since birth to the son of a powerful family near Ningbo. It was because she had come of age that she had been called home.

When the girl's father discovered their secret romance, he was furious. He ordered the young man out of their house. The scholar returned, distraught, to his home and then to the new post where he had dreamed, briefly, of arriving with his bride. He died soon after, of a broken heart.

The girl submitted numbly to the preparations for her wedding. The day arrived when she bade her family good-bye to travel to the groom's town. After the marriage ceremony she would belong to his family forever.

The wedding party travelled towards Ningbo with the bride borne in a sedan chair. Coincidentally, they had first to pass the place where the scholar had been buried. As they drew close to her lover's grave, the sky grew dark and a wind began to blow so strongly that their group could go no further.

When the bride heard that they had stopped near her lover's tomb she begged to visit it just this one time. Her servants relented.

At the scholar's grave she wept such bitter tears that perhaps the earth itself felt moved. It rumbled and then began to shake, violently. The tomb split open, the bride leaped in as her servants watched in horror. At once the grave closed over their young mistress.

In an instant the air cleared and the sky brightened and two white butterflies emerged from the tomb to flit and circle around each other, in endless courtship.

True lovers can never be parted. True love has no end.

*

Late on a Singapore afternoon, as the heat was going out of the day and it no longer hurt the eyes to look directly at the sky, a young Chinese man walked with his two colleagues back to their home for a cup of tea.

They were all teachers at the Yeung Ching School in Chinatown which the young man had just joined. He taught English, learned at one of the colony's free government schools. He was lucky to have had an education. Unlike his new friends, brothers who had studied abroad at an academy in China, he was poor.

In a house on nearby Cantonment Road, a young woman laid the table for supper and went lightly up the stairs to look out of a bedroom window for her brothers. To her surprise she saw three young men strolling up the street, not the two she was expecting. They were laughing together when the man in the middle, a stranger, looked up.

Later, he would say it was love at first sight.

He glanced up at a terraced house to see a young woman lean out over a Juliet balcony, her hair tied back to reveal a long oval face, delicate features and serious eyes. She looked at him without smiling.

'Who is that?' he asked in wonder.

'Our sister,' the brothers replied, almost in unison.

At least this is how my mother said her parents met.

14

The First World War broke out in Europe with no more of a nuisance to Singapore than the internment of its German civilians. These included, regrettably, Herr Hackmeier of the Tingel Tangel Club. His cabaret on Bras Basah Road had a ladies' orchestra staffed by a contingent of Polish women. For fifty cents, one of them would dance with a lonely young Englishman.[1]

War in Europe cannot displace the rhythm of courtship and the time is undoubtedly right for Law's older daughters to marry. Matchmakers buzz around Virtue, twenty and Orchid, nineteen, like flies that smell fat on a dish.

But then the swirl of the wider world catches even this little British colony in its wake. The Sultan of Turkey declares a jihad against Britain, France and Russia,[2] counting on Germany to shore up his collapsing Ottoman Empire. In 1915, Muslim sepoys from India, who defend Singapore for the British, mutiny on the rumour that they will be sent to Turkey to murder fellow Muslims. They roam the streets of Singapore killing Europeans on sight.

Everything stops for a while, though this is Chinese New Year in the middle of February, a good time for matchmaking. Law keeps his family indoors. The barracks where the Muslim troops are based is only a march away. He doesn't want his children caught in an affray. He has heard rumour that the soldiers have killed, whether by accident or design, Chinese and Malay civilians.

Life returns to normal when the British seize the sepoys with the help of the Japanese, Britain's allies, stationed nearby on their warships. Law must return, reluctantly, to the necessity of getting his daughters married.

Law understands why his daughters must marry but it doesn't cause him any less pain. He has grown to depend on them. Virtue is utterly reliable and Orchid's ebullience always makes him smile, even if she is sometimes acerbic with his mistress. It is true that he still has Fan-Fan, only eight years old. But with much older sisters and brothers, she is growing up quickly.

Yet what could Law do? It was the duty of every Chinese father to try to pair his daughters off with worthy boys from good families. Many such families would be pleased to make a connection with Law. He was now doing rather well, even if not as well as his younger brother Quan-Kuan with his row of fine houses on Ann Siang Hill and a wife who went to mah-jong parties with a basket stuffed full of banknotes. But it had not been forgotten that Law was once Second Clerk and Interpreter at the Chinese Protectorate. His standing in the Cantonese community was still high and he had brought up nice-looking and capable daughters.

With the help of matchmakers, Law would have looked for commendable young men whose astrological charts were in harmony with his daughters' own. Then they could at least have a fair stab at happiness.

However, he was to be confounded by Virtue his eldest daughter, who took charge of the process for herself. She had set eyes on a young man and decided, with modern and unnerving resolve, that she had found her own match. It was probably inevitable that one of Law's daughters would fall in love with their brothers' colleague, once he started to visit regularly. How many single men did young women meet? Only, Gilbert Chang was penniless.

He was from a distinct group of Chinese that other Chinese called 'guest people' or Hakka. They were the descendants of refugees from north and central China escaping invasion and war in earlier centuries. Many eventually settled in south China, on infertile land that no one else wanted. Hakka people would have a profound impact on the history of China – Sun Yat-Sen, the father of the Republic and Deng Xiaoping, the founder of modern China, were both Hakka. But in the Canton province of the eighteenth and nineteenth centuries, they were merely the rural poor.

Chang's father had died when he was little. His mother had somehow raised the money to take them to Singapore, where she had a sister who had married. She worked for her sister as a maid in exchange for a room and the freedom to send her son to school, where he learned enough English to want to call himself 'Gilbert' and to find work in a Chinese school teaching English, not paid very much.

'Listen to me, young lady.' Law waves a fan wearily about his face. It is thirty years since his arrival in Singapore, but he has never got used to the lack of seasons. On the equator, every day is the same: unyielding blue skies, oppressive heat.

'After you marry, you will live with your husband and his mother in two small rooms. Can you bear that? No – don't interrupt, let me finish.

'They are penniless, Mong-Han, and they are not Cantonese like us. They are Hakka people, so pitiful that in China they have no province to call their own. You would never have met this young man if we lived in Canton. It is only possible in Singapore, such a small, jumbled-up place. What will happen when you have children?'

'But he is educated, Pa Pa, he has an *English* education like you. He will have prospects. He will make his way. We are young and I will help him. We won't be poor forever.' Virtue's face, sometimes nearly austere, is radiant.

In the end, Law simply gives in. He hasn't the heart to object. He has become indulgent with his daughters (he can hear them giggling now in the next room). Orchid looks like their mother; Virtue has her temperament. Fan-Fan is turning out to be a combination of the two.

Virtue followed her heart by picking an impoverished husband, but Orchid was destined for riches.

As soon as word got out that Virtue was to be married, a matchmaker went round to Law's house with a proposal for his middle daughter, Mong-Lan. She had blossomed like the beautiful flower after which she was named.

The cymbidium is celebrated as a metaphor for refinement. Gentlemen gardeners of the Song dynasty had pots made specially for this orchid that is so genteel, even its roots are well behaved. They will grow straight down if they can, through a compost of burned earth, bone ash, and dried goose and goat manure.[3]

But the prettiest of Law's three daughters was also the most fierce. Law had reckoned without the tropical *jinn* that swirl around the equator and infuse Singapore's flora with indelicate fragrances and immodest blooms. His second daughter grew up less like a cymbidium, more like the native *Grammatophyllum speciosum,* a Tiger orchid larger than life and not so much striped as spattered with angry brown marks.

Mong-Lan was impetuous and hot-tempered. Her speech

could sometimes be so rash that it verged (regrettably) on the coarse.

'Mok-Lan,' her brothers would snigger, changing her name slightly to be the same as a peasant girl's from fourth-century China, the fabled woman warrior who had disguised herself as a man to take her ailing father's place in the army. She was famous for her courage, not for her femininity. Orchid's brothers hoot with laughter when she fights with her legs as well as her hands.

Yet this very lack of daintiness was the reason why the ultra-wealthy Lye family thought she would be the perfect bride for their precious eldest son. They had particular requirements which made her ideal.

The Lye family was Cantonese like the Laws. They had become rich making glass chimneys for the kerosene lamps that every house in Singapore required but which broke all too easily during shipment from China. The Lyes bought property with their money in exclusive European enclaves of the colony, in Scotts Road and Grange Road. They owned jewellery shops. They would own a Studebaker.[4]

But in a generation, the Lyes had turned from hardworking entrepreneurs to progenitors of feckless spendthrifts. Their eldest son was a wastrel. But as he was still only seventeen years old it was possible that Orchid, three years older and of a robust temperament, could keep him in check.

Law was flattered of course that the Lyes, so much richer, should want his daughter. It was a fulfilment of her name: the orchid also symbolizes prosperity. But he worried that, wealth apart, the Lye heir seemed a poor match. It was Orchid herself who persuaded her father to accept the offer of marriage. She saw how Virtue struggled with her downward shift in circumstances since marrying. Virtue had chosen a husband out of love, but was romantic love enough? Orchid was not sure that poverty would suit her. Besides, she had seen a picture of the boy. He was not bad-looking at all.

It is the groom's family that hosts a Chinese wedding. As Virtue's fiancé was poor, her wedding was modest, which was exactly what she expected. Appearances had never been important to her. What lay in your heart was what mattered.

Orchid's, on the other hand, was very grand – which wasn't what interested Orchid either, though she was reluctantly impressed by the dazzling gold jewellery presented to her by the Lyes ahead of the wedding, the ornate sedan chair that came to collect her on the day and, when she returned to her father's home for a formal visit with her husband two days after they married, the magnificence of the whole roast pig that they sent with her.

Later, when the celebrations were over, after her gown of gold embroidered red brocade was packed away, Orchid dealt firmly with her husband's late nights at the music-hall. She impressed him with her knowledge of choice words.

'You did what?' Virtue is incredulous.

'I emptied the chamber pot over his head. I had to. The night before, I'd locked him out of the house, but that didn't make a difference.'

'And now?' Virtue asks, still shocked.

'He's not been out again at night.' There is a triumphant gleam in Orchid's eye.

Soon Orchid was pregnant, sooner than Virtue who had married before her. In 1917, she gave birth to a son, instantly ensuring the continuity of the Lye family line. This was magnificent news in itself but, to everyone's wonder, the Lye family that was already prosperous began to prosper more. This was taken absolutely to be a sign that Orchid's marriage to the Lye heir was not merely suitable, it was blessed by the gods.

The Lyes carpeted her bedroom with silk rugs and showered her with gifts of gold and jade and money, which she sewed secretly into her mattress, saving them for her family.

Three months later, Virtue gave birth to a girl, my mother. But the sisters' love for each other was steadfast. One neither pitied nor envied the other.

My grandfather, Chang, was still struggling as a teacher two years later when Virtue gave birth to their second child, a son. They named him Hong-Kay, 'Thriving' and 'Vast', as in one who brings new and bright horizons. As if in instant fulfilment of this promise, Chang was offered an opportunity that was a way out of their difficulties.

The timber industry had become important in Sandakan, the capital of British North Borneo.[5] Chinese coolies were needed in great number to cut down its forests. There was a proliferation of opium and gambling licences to woo them.[6]

Law had invested in one of these gambling concessions and needed someone to run it for him there. It had to be someone he could trust. His son-in-law Chang was perfect. Not only was he part of the family but he was of Hakka descent like many of the traders and coolies in Sandakan. He was fluent in their dialect.

'Why won't you come with me? Can't you change your mind?' Chang cannot hide his disappointment. He wants Virtue and the children with him in Sandakan. It is on the northeast coast of Borneo and 1,600 kilometres from Singapore.

Virtue frowns. She smooths down the front of her cotton *samfoo*. She has heard that Borneo is full of savages who walk around nearly naked and kill with poisoned darts from blow-pipes. Their victims die within minutes, and then are eaten. The savages keep their homes like charnel houses where the smoked and shrivelled heads of those that they have cannibalized hang from the rafters – skin turned nut brown, hair still intact. It is not where a man takes his wife and babies. She shudders.

'Are you all right?' Chang stretches out his hand to touch her gently. Virtue does not reply.

Chang travels alone to Borneo, still hoping that Virtue will change her mind.

Sandakan is not so uncivilized. There is little illness and plenty of fresh spring water.[7] The English Governor's wife has made a garden out of the jungle in front of her house, and planted it with cinnabar, cinnamon, and gutta-percha trees.[8] When the white sap of the gutta-percha is boiled, it softens to make any shape you want. When it cools, it becomes as hard as wood.

There are creatures here found nowhere else – a black clouded leopard and a monkey with a nose like a tuber. There is a beautiful snake with a bright blue body and a neck of vivid flame. Pygmy elephants hide in forests sprung from seeds that float to the ground on pairs of wings.

You can buy precious Chinese things – sharks' fins and birds' nests – for little money. Sharks are fished in a sea that on clear, still nights turns milky with phosphorescence.[9] The swifts make edible nests in giant limestone caves not far away. They fly in great drifts like dense dark clouds. And begonias, which Virtue loves, grow wild on the limestone soil.

But Virtue cannot be enticed.

*

The First World War has brought abundance to America. Europe needs its flour and grain and its commercial vehicles,[10] which need rubber tyres. The rubber is sent mainly from Singapore, whose rubber merchants flourish. Its newly rich men, Chinese mostly, buy Swiss watches and build mansions. The colony's Japanese dentists fill their cavities with pure gold.

Orchid has had a baby every year since she married. She is bored with child-bearing but she is pregnant again for a fourth time.

This time she will tell no one, not even Virtue, though her personal maid will have to know. She washes Orchid's underclothing. Also, Orchid needs her help to buy the herbs that Chinese use to be rid of a baby – black cohosh or angelica, brewed into a soup. This is not an exact science. Much will depend on the state of Orchid's health and the stage of her pregnancy.

When Orchid was born twenty-five years before and her dear father first looked upon her lovely face, perhaps – crucially – he chose in his heart not the cymbidium *ensifolium* which blooms from summer to autumn, but the *sinense* which flowers only in the spring.

Orchid will have been warned to expect abdominal pains and bleeding, but she won't have expected the pain to last so long or the bleeding not to stop. Her eldest son Pak-Leong is placed by her side, only three-years old, but required by tradition to keep watch as his mother's life ebbs away.

Orchid died from an unsuccessful abortion in the flowering of her womanhood as America's prosperity slumped in 1920 with the end of the First World War: Europe no longer needed as many of its vehicles and cars. Fewer automobiles meant fewer tyres with rubber sourced from Singapore. Singapore's wealth sank in synchrony with America's.

The death of Orchid and the slump in America might just have been chance but the Lye family could only acknowledge their own experience: a tragedy had occurred in their family and life ever afterwards was changed. Orchid, their talisman, had gone.

Virtue fought to keep close to Orchid's young children. She knew where her sister had hidden the gold and money that the Lye family had given her. She cut open the mattress with a pair of scissors and handed it all back. And when her brother-in-law remarried – he was only twenty-two when Orchid died – Virtue asked his wife to fill the place of her dead sister within the Law family. This was the custom of the Chinese, habituated to death on a grand scale. They retrieve their dead how they can.

The new Mrs Lye, a calm, kind woman, agreed to restore a dead stranger to a family of strangers. To the Law family, she became their 'Third Aunt' as Orchid had been, reflecting Orchid's birth order in her father's family.

But the Lyes could not replace the luck that Orchid had brought them. Their fabulous fortune melted away. Gambling debts mounted as Lye businesses foundered, too weak eventually to fend off the Great Depression when it arrived nine years later. Everything would go – the properties, the Scotts Road home, the Studebaker.

Chang and Virtue now had three children, including an infant girl, but Chang's visits to see them in Singapore were necessarily infrequent. He might have earned more than he did as a teacher, but he was still not earning very much. The post First World War depression lingered on in Singapore to make sure of that.[11] The gambling business in Sandakan was languishing. His father-in-law's attention was on matters turned urgent. Law had other businesses also dependent on the wealth generated by the rubber industry, and they were doing badly.

Chang was adrift in Borneo where life had become so hard that coolies, finding they were no longer to be paid, sometimes wandered into the forest and never came out. In the grey early mornings, you could hear them call, *wou wou*, dead men's jeers rising out of the jungle like gibbons' cries. They made even strong men's hearts fail.

When my gentle grandfather Chang first gave himself the name 'Gilbert', it must have summed up all his hopes for his future in a British colony. Now those hopes had vanished, to be replaced by black nights when he felt that he was drowning. He needed someone to cling to, someone whose eyes were not empty like those of the men around him.

Gradually, a rumour carried across the sea – Chang is not on his own – and my grandmother sailed for Borneo and all its savages. She left her two young daughters with Chang's mother in Singapore, but she brought her son Hong-Kay with her. It was important that her husband see their son.

A pair of hornbills appears unmistakably in the sky like a portent, enormous and black with curved white beaks. They fly without noise between the treetops. Chang watches them despondently. His heart is heavy.

Virtue had arrived that morning on the steamer, holding tightly to the hand of their three-year-old son. Her face was tense. She spoke little on their short journey to the Chinese Hotel where he rented rooms. Once there she would not leave her bed, saying that she was tired and needed to rest the entire afternoon. She had insisted that he go back to work. Now it is early evening. The sun is low in the sky but still bright, and he has gone back to the hotel to take them for a stroll to the bay before dinner.

Their son takes his hand excitedly as they walk from their lodgings to the sea. The little boy looks carefully when Chang points out where a small monkey hides in the branches of an ironwood tree. On the beach, Hong-Kay runs to the sea's edge, watched closely by Virtue. He laughs as he retreats before each advancing wave. Afterwards, they go to a restaurant in a large shack covered by a roof of palm fronds.

Chang calls the waiter over and orders what he hopes Virtue will like: a big silver fish caught only hours earlier and steamed with strips of ginger; venison from the jungle fried with spring onion; live prawns boiled briefly and served with a dip of sliced chillies in soy sauce. There is a stir-fry of tapioca leaves which Chang thinks may intrigue her, followed by sweet potato baked in a banana leaf.

But when the dishes arrive, Virtue says she is not hungry.

After dinner, a girl approaches their table, smiling. She has a broad face and slightly coarse, flat features, but pretty eyes and a lively air. She greets Virtue respectfully. She pours special after-dinner tea into small china teacups. She picks up Virtue's son and carries him on her hip, though she hands him back immediately when Virtue calls for him.

Virtue finishes her tea quickly. She wants to go back to their room. Her heart is beating so fast she can feel it throbbing in her throat.

'Oh! So soon?' the girl asks, disappointed. But Virtue has already got up. Taking her son's hand, she walks swiftly out of the restaurant. Chang follows silently.

*

My grandfather had broken no Chinese rules by taking a mistress. He lived at a time and in a culture where women were regarded as chattels. Successful men were expected to acquire mistresses as status symbols, or if their wives had not produced sons. But my grandmother had borne Chang a son, and she had brought the child with her to remind him.

Chang promised Virtue that she would always be his only wife, but he would not give up his concubine. He had taught the girl to be respectful to my grandmother, to bring her hot water in the mornings with which to wash, to wait quietly with a towel, to kneel when serving Virtue her tea.

All the same, my grandmother sailed back to Singapore knowing that she could not bear to be with Chang any more, nor to live with his mother. Once, she believed in everlasting love. Now that simple trust was gone and the idea that she could be in their rooms when he visited, still dependent on him for money, was intolerable. But there were few alternatives for a woman in her situation. She could not be reabsorbed into her father's household.

There was a taboo that persisted from previous centuries to prevent the return of women already offloaded successfully through marriage. China's rural economy simply could not cope with unexpected extra mouths to feed. The shame of taking back a married daughter was reinforced by a superstition: if such a daughter were allowed back permanently into the family home, she would jinx it.[12]

Therefore, when my grandmother returned to Singapore, she was resolute. She took with her to a nearby beach her five-year-old daughter, her three-year-old son, and her eighteen-month-old infant tied on her back by a criss-cross band of cloth. She held each older child by the hand. She walked them slowly into the sea.

'Nobody wants us,' my mother remembered her saying. 'This is what we must do.' It was only my mother's frightened cries, and her brother's, and how they tried to hold their mother back by pulling at her clothes, that made her stop.

There was nowhere else for her to go but to Cantonment Road, where her father lived with her brothers and their wives according to Chinese custom. Law, Cheng-Wah and Liang gathered with their youngest sister, Fan-Fan, fifteen years old, to listen to what Virtue had to say.

A decade had passed since the fall of China's last dynasty, but Confucian attitudes still held the Chinese back. Many believed that China could only progress if it unshackled first from this 2,000-year-old association and the superstitions that clung to it.

Three years before, in 1919, students at Peking University had led a revolutionary movement proposing the radical new idea that everyone, even women and peasants, should have a voice. Now Virtue was using that voice, *her* voice, to say she would not share her husband with another woman. Monogamous love was a modern and a fundamentally European idea. To traditional Chinese, it was not valid. Even her brothers, who were abreast with current thinking, were taken aback.

It was apparently their youngest sister Fan-Fan who gave breath to the thought slowly forming in the minds of her family's men. Fan-Fan had become friends with their Straits Chinese neighbours, whose attitudes to women were very different – more modern, less traditional Chinese. *They* wouldn't cast off one of their own. Fan-Fan's family couldn't possibly abandon Virtue, especially not since their father's work for the Chinese Protectorate had shown them the depths to which women and children could fall if there was no one to help them. They lived in a British colony where the people who ran it renounced superstition. Might they not do the same?

But were Law and his sons ready to ignore an ancient Chinese prohibition, to cast in their lot with new beliefs? Which man would willingly condemn the rest of his family to help just one daughter or sister? Self-preservation is a potent force.

All three men looked deep within themselves to see if they would remain immersed in tradition or dare swim to the surface to breathe new air. Singapore in a trade depression meant life had again turned precarious for an immigrant and his dependent, extended family. Challenging the fates at this

Right to left: Virtue, Florence, Violet, Peter (circa 1923), all in Western clothes, looking to their future in a British colony.

time might be unwise. But the men showed incredible courage. They struck upwards. They took back my grandmother with her three young children.

Later, Virtue learned that Chang's concubine had given birth to a baby, a boy. Chang had picked a name for him that was close to her son's, to show that they were brothers. Her son – their son – was called Hong-Kay. Chang's new baby was called Chun-Kay.

Only Fan-Fan, who now called herself 'Fanny', could console her. She said the children's Chinese names should be left behind like the old ways. She helped choose new English names for these vulnerable children that might ease them into the bright new order for which she and Virtue hoped that they were destined. From now on, Virtue's children were to be known as Violet, Peter, and Florence – my mother, my uncle and my aunt.

15

Fan-Fan was only two when her mother died in 1909, much too young to apprehend the great loss in her life. She was three when her brothers left for college in China the next year, shrinking her family further. Therefore, the sisters who became her surrogate mother and her playmate were her whole world – Virtue, sixteen, and the exuberant Orchid, fifteen. How they lived their lives, how their lives turned out, shaped Fan-Fan's own.

Fan-Fan was nine when her adored sisters married and moved away. Her father could have sent her to one of the schools that had sprung up, run by European missionaries, except that in 1916 this was exceptional for Asian girls. Only a few hundred on the entire island went to school.[1] They were mainly from the Malayan Chinese families that had been in Southeast Asia for several generations. They were not considered by Law to be 'real' Chinese.

Instead, Law enlisted his sons to tutor their youngest sister at home in classical Cantonese, particularly the elder of the two, Cheng-Wah. He was twenty-five, back from college in China, now a teacher.

Cheng-Wah delights in taking Fan-Fan under his wing for a proper Confucian education steeped in the ideas of propriety and duty. He fills her head with stories of heroic men and women of the past, patriots who had sacrificed their lives willingly.

'And what is the name of the general whose mother

tattooed his back with the instruction to fight for his emperor?' he asks in Cantonese.

Fan-Fan frowns with the effort to remember: 'Yue Fei!'

'Very good! Good girl!' The young man beams approvingly at his little sister. 'Tomorrow I will tell you the story of the other brave generals of the Song dynasty – how when they all died in battle, their wives took over their armies to defeat the enemy.'

Fan-Fan's eyes grow very round.

Fan-Fan was ten in 1917 when she became an aunt, first to Orchid's son and then to Virtue's daughter. By now she had got to know a neighbour, a little girl exactly her age but with a background quite different from her own.

Tinn-Nyong was the youngest of four sisters and lived with her family in 53 Cantonment Road.[2] The Leongs were not at all like the Laws. Mr Leong had been born in Singapore, where he had inherited a chain of goldsmith's stores from his father. Though his origins were Cantonese like Law's, he had married a Straits-born Chinese woman, a Nonya.

The Straits-born – the Babas and the Nonyas – were those Chinese who had grown up in one of the British settlements strung along the Straits of Malacca – Penang, Malacca or Singapore. They were in their second or even third generations in Malaya and their culture was a unique blend of Malay and Chinese. Their language at home was Malay mixed with the Chinese dialect of their forebears, and English. Baba men were usually educated in English.

Mr Leong had absorbed the values of these anglicized Malayan Chinese. In the Leongs' home, British, Chinese and Malay objects would have mingled unselfconsciously. Sheffield-made cutlery might be laid alongside porcelain plates from Ching-te-chen,³ on a batik tablecloth. Mr Leong did not seem bothered that he had no sons. He had not got himself a mistress to try for a boy.

The little girls soon became good friends even though one spoke only Cantonese, while the other spoke it with a mixture of Malay and English.

Nyong holds a tiny teacup to the red lips of her golden-haired doll. 'Drink tea,' she instructs in English, adding '*Minum teh*' in Malay to make sure that she is understood. Fan-Fan does the same as she pretends to pour from a miniature teapot. She picks up her clay doll from China and swings it gently so its little black plaits sway from side to side: '*Yum cha.*'

It was here at Tinn-Nyong's house that Fan-Fan would have met Straits-born men properly for the first time. These men may have looked Chinese, but they were totally unlike her father. Baba men often wore western clothes whereas her father was always in Chinese dress. They could not read Chinese whereas her father read and wrote it beautifully. They spoke to Fan-Fan in a mixture of English, Malay and Chinese.

There were other things that were different about these Straits Chinese.

They were against concubinage, whereas Law's concubine had lived with them since Fan-Fan was little. They disapproved of opium, which her father smoked. They did not yearn, like her father, to return to China. They were loyal not to an emperor or a president of China, but to King George V and King Edward VII before him. Some of their men had cut off their queues as long ago as 1898 in rejection of the

Manchus in China. Their loyalty was to the British Crown. They were known as the King's Chinese.

Fan-Fan picked up enough English to rename herself 'Fanny', which was what her Straits-born Chinese friends called her. She was thirteen when her middle sister Orchid died and fifteen when Virtue left her husband and moved back to the family home. These would be huge turning points in any life but for Fanny, whose sisters had virtually brought her up, they were devastating. She changed from a carefree child into a serious girl beginning to ask big questions of herself.

Fanny was soaking up new thoughts on women's education through her friendship with Nyong. Straits-Chinese men who had been to university in Edinburgh and Cambridge had set up a school for girls in Singapore in 1899.

A girl who had gone to this school had later been accepted by the medical college in Singapore. Lee Choo-Neo graduated in 1919 when Fanny was twelve, and registered the next year as the colony's first woman doctor.[4] It was true that she was widely considered odd and those greatest of all castigations, 'unfeminine' and 'unmarriageable'. But she had broken the mould. It was no longer unthinkable that a Straits-Chinese girl could be as well educated as her brother.

Fanny was processing through these ideas as she turned sixteen, though they overlay rather than replaced those already sown in her mind by her brother, of Confucian duty and sacrifice. She was growing increasingly protective of her eldest sister Virtue, for whom life continued to be miserable.

Fanny can hear stifled sobs as she walks past Virtue's room, sounds that lie somewhere between a quiet groan and a gulp. She knows that Virtue's children are playing outdoors and that she is alone. Fanny hesitates; then she pushes open her sister's door to find her prostrate on the bed. Virtue sits up immediately on hearing Fanny enter, but her face is turned away. Fanny takes her hand. They sit without speaking.

Virtue's situation was impossible. She had brought opprobrium upon her father and brothers for taking her back into their family home. They were scorned for being foolish and disliked for setting a dangerous precedent.

She was also aware that although her brothers accepted her, their wives could not feel the same. She struggled to make as small a dent as possible in the household budget, taking in sewing to earn a very little money, mending her children's clothes to be reused – but they were growing older and larger and eating more. Her sisters-in-law's tolerance could soon turn to resentment. If she was not already the source of conflict in her family, she had the potential to be so. In the future, after her father died, her brothers might no longer be able to support her.

But she had no way out.

Virtue was *persona non grata* in a Chinese world where gentlewomen arranged concubines for their husbands as acts of wifely devotion.[5] Virtue might have felt that her husband had abandoned her, but by the standards of the day it was *she* who had left him. She would not share him because she foolishly believed in true and monogamous love. This could not be understood. There was no niche in the pragmatic Chinese mind for a woman like her.

Virtue could bear all this but not the fear of what might happen to her children. If, against all expectation, she managed to bring them up herself (who knew how and where, once her father died and his protection was removed?), who would marry her daughters when she could not provide dowries for them? A young woman on her own with no money had very few options.

Fanny knew all this and longed to help her sister. But how? The day was not far off when she herself must marry. Which suitor would agree to take on a sister-in-law and her three children?

She turned the problem over and over in her mind until a solution began to form. Part of it grew from her friendship with Nyong and the progressive ideas of her people, the Straits Chinese.

Part of it sprang from the old country, China, specifically from the area where her father was born, the Canton Delta. Its canny women had won for themselves the right not to marry, to be free of coercive husbands and controlling mothers-in-law. Fanny might find a path somewhere between the two.

16

For hundreds of years the Chinese maimed their children. They described their act of mutilation with two characters – 'bind' and 'fall'.[1]

To make a girl suitable for marrying, the bones in her feet were broken repeatedly when she was four or five years old so that her toes could be pushed under her arches and her heels forced forward to meet them. These stumps were then bandaged tightly with cloth. For the rest of her life she would have to bind her feet (they could never return to normal) and hobble so as not to fall. Chinese society in its darkness and fallacy decided this was beauty.

But her crushed feet might be only the start of years of abuse, since there was no question but that a young woman in imperial China had to marry, even to a brute whose mother might beat her. Stories of ill treatment by mothers-in-law were widespread. Suicides by young brides were common.[2] But Chinese women had believed for literally thousands of years that they had no choice.

This was down to a wooden plaque.

When you died, your soul lived on in a tablet of wood carved with your name. This was both your resting place and your link with the material world – you received food, drink and other comforts placed before it as offerings.[3] A son's 'spirit tablet' was kept in the family home. A daughter's was not. Hers was only allowed in her husband's house. A woman had to marry to acquire caretakers for her soul.

If she was unlucky enough to die before marrying, she became the very thing that struck terror into everyone: the doomed wraith condemned to drift forever, without rest, in the cold mist of purgatory. The Chinese, with their periodic bouts of cataclysmic famine, understood and dreaded starvation more than anything else. They named these shadows after what frightened them most. They called them 'hungry ghosts'.

Therefore a woman must marry, even if a wife's life was misery, enslaved to a husband and his family. But in my great-grandfather's part of Canton, things began to change.

Girls there were treated differently from other regions of China. Female infanticide was lower and foot-binding was less common. On this fertile plain, rice could be grown and harvested twice a year. Women had to pitch in to help in the fields or elsewhere on the farm.[4] This gave them worth.

Because they were useful to their families, it became the practice – unique to this delta – for daughters to carry on living with their parents after marrying, usually for a period of three years. Young wives saw their new husbands rarely, on 'conjugal visits', moving into their husbands' homes only on becoming pregnant. Given the infrequency of the girls' visits (and some judicious birth control), this was rarely sooner than three years. In one case, it took six![5]

Then, in the middle of the nineteenth century, an unprecedented opportunity arrived in the Canton Delta, seized by its women, which allowed them not to live with their husbands at all.

In the 1850s, the silk industry collapsed in Europe after disease in France killed its silkworms and fanned out to infect other countries on the continent. At about the same time the Taiping Rebellion in China stopped silk production in the

Lower Yangtze north of Canton. The Canton Delta stepped up to both disruptions and its silk industry took off.[6]

Workshops proliferated which needed girls to tease the delicate threads off the cocoons without tearing them (their hands not yet roughened by work under a demanding mother-in-law). The wages were very good.

Now a well-off bride could free herself of marital obligations by paying her husband to acquire a second wife. It was part of the contract that she be allowed to keep her status as first wife even though she lived separately from her husband, his parents and his concubine. The understanding was that, after she died, her spirit tablet would be allowed on his family altar table to be venerated by the children that he had with this other woman.[7]

Or a girl could marry a ghost.

Ghost or spirit weddings were a practical feature of Chinese life from ancient times – if you had only one son and he died before he could marry and father children, where were the descendants to make offerings to your spirit when you too died? Disaster could be averted if you 'married' your dead son's ghost to a girl from a poor and willing family and then adopted boys to acquire descendants on his and your behalf. In extremis, if no such girl were available, you married him to a dead spinster, another ghost, before adopting your grandsons.

The cunning women of the Canton Delta turned this round to suit themselves. A girl paid the (usually poor) family of a dead stranger, a single man or boy, for the privilege of marrying his spirit.[8] She therefore acquired a husband without the messiness of actual marriage or second wives. She could adopt children later, the 'descendants' who would one day look after her spirit tablet.

Alas, there were not enough unfortunate men died young to satisfy the ladies of the Delta. But a better solution would soon be possible.

'Pa Pa, may I speak with you?' Fanny asks in Cantonese.

It is mid-afternoon when she enters her father's room. The shutters are closed to keep out the sun. Law is resting, smoking his pipe. Sometimes opium allows him a glimpse of his wife, or of Orchid.

He opens his eyes to look at Fanny. He considers what he sees.

She has the generous lips of someone who gives full expression to her feelings, while her firm chin suggests decisiveness, even stubbornness: as long as that were kept in check, it would be easy to arrange her marriage into a good family. Fanny is growing the curves of a woman who can bear sons.

By the early twentieth century, the world's appetite for raw silk from the Canton Delta had grown enormous. More than a million women worked in the centralized factories that had taken over from the small silk producers that once dotted the countryside.[9] These factories were located near towns far from the girls' homes. Wages had to be even higher to attract them and dormitories built to accommodate them.

The result was a generation of unmarried women used to living away from home, being paid far more than their farming brothers could ever hope to earn. These single women were no longer merely financially independent. They were the breadwinners of their families.[10] Now there was little inclination to keep up even the appearance of marriage. These girls could cancel matrimony if they wanted.

*

Fanny asks her father: 'Please can you arrange a wedding dinner for me? For just twenty or thirty people?'

Law's daydreams evaporate in an instant. He focuses more sharply on his daughter. She doesn't *look* pregnant.

Fanny's dark eyes, often thoughtful, are solemn.

'I want to take an oath not to marry.'

In imperial China, unmarried daughters were considered immature even if they were middle-aged, incapable of independence or thinking for themselves. They were not allowed to go out unchaperoned to mingle in mixed crowds. An outward sign of this subordinate status was their hair, which had to look girlish with a fringe, or be worn long in plaits.

The career women of the Canton Delta wanted to be able to remain single but to be treated as adults. Most of all, they wanted no longer to be consigned to purgatory's scrapheap after they died, simply for being unmarried. They wanted their spirit tablets to be acknowledged.

In return, they would take a basic building block of Confucian society – filial piety – and construct upon it a new concept using as the mortar their spinsterhood status: they would be society's filial daughters, almost as good as sons.[11]

They would support their families with their considerable earnings. They would respect the taboo against adult daughters living in the family house by moving out. To be above suspicion, so there could be no slur on their reputations, they would make public pledges of celibacy. (At the turn of the century, unmarried women in China were still either prostitutes or nuns.)

These women became known as 'sworn spinsters',[12] the working-class feminists of south China.

By the time Fanny was sixteen in 1923, sworn spinster-hood had grown so popular in Canton that it had to be kept in check by an informal rule: only one unmarried daughter per household.[13] But the movement was still only associated with peasant or factory girls, not with the daughters of well-off families. Only unfortunate women had to find paid work. A girl from Fanny's background was expected to marry well enough never to have to earn a living. But her sisters' marriages had filled her with disillusion.

Law shuts his eyes and takes a deep breath. Sometimes, opium also plays unpleasant tricks. He opens his eyes. Fanny is still there.

'I've been thinking about this for a long time,' she continues, 'please listen to what I have to say.'

Fanny decided that she wanted not to marry, and that she wanted to make this intention binding. The Canton spinsters provided her with a framework that was already familiar to her father and her brothers. She would take a vow of celibacy like theirs. But, unlike those Canton girls, she would go on to get a proper education and in the medium of English, though she had never been to school or studied English. It was possible to find respectable work as a single woman in this British colony if she could speak and write the language. Then she could support not only herself, but her sister and her sister's children.

To make this audacious plan work she would require not just unimaginable commitment, but the support of her father.

Law hated the idea. How could a young girl from a good family decide that she would never marry? How could she possibly know? A public spinsterhood ritual not only made Fanny's choice irrevocable, storing up time for regret, but also announced to the world that he had *two* unattached adult daughters in his house (though one of them had been married before). No one could pretend that this was anything but folly. His ancestors would not be pleased.

It seems all the more extraordinary that, despite his reservations, Law should give in to Fanny. Perhaps he had a lingering fear of the suicides that took place in the Canton Delta among girls forced to marry against their will.[14] Perhaps it was Fanny's iron resolve, even so young. Or perhaps it was the value of the unique solution that Fanny offered her father and her brothers to the problem of Virtue. If Fanny's plan worked, she would remove Virtue (and herself) from their responsibility. It was a way out of a dilemma.

They reached a compromise. Fanny could have her English education, but the ceremony to become a sworn spinster would have to wait until she finished secondary school.

Fanny was nearly seventeen when she joined the lowest class of her school in 1924, self-conscious and hot in white stockings and a uniform of pleated navy skirt and white sailor blouse.[1] She was not the oldest in her Primary One class. There was a girl a year older. The youngest was already fourteen.

The Methodist Girls' School in Singapore was founded in 1887 when south Indian merchants expressed the wish for their daughters to be taught like their sons. A young Australian missionary, Sophia Blackmore, was sent from India to instruct her first class:[2] nine beautiful little Tamil girls who sat for lessons dressed in colourful Varanasi silk, gold studs in their noses and bangles on their wrists. Their skin and hair gleamed with scented unguents.

By the time Fanny started, Miss Blackmore's class had grown to more than five hundred students. In a colony now positively teeming with good girls' schools, it was one of the best. It was taking girls up through the Senior Cambridge qualification.

Fanny quickly understood the value of starting an education young. Two years later, she brought with her to school her young niece Violet, my mother. She was planning a new future not just for herself, but for the next generation of women in her family.

'Wake up! It's time for school!' Violet is curled up into a ball. Virtue bundles her off in the dark to the bathroom, shushing her as she begins to cry. It is 5 a.m. Most of the household is still asleep.

'Silly girl, you should be happy, not sad,' Virtue scolds, as she helps Violet into navy cotton bloomers and a white camisole attached to a pleated navy skirt. The box pleats of the skirt are so starched, their edges so precise, they might be made of card. She pulls a stiff white cotton blouse with a sailor collar over Violet's head, and pins on the school badge.

Violet winces as her mother hurriedly runs a comb through her hair and pulls it taut to braid into two plaits. School opens at 7.30 a.m. By noon it will be uncomfortably hot, and her camisole and stiff cotton blouse will soften with moisture and stick.

At first a horse and carriage clattered by each morning to sweep up Violet and Fanny to take them over the Singapore River to their classes. It belonged to a friend and classmate of Fanny's, the daughter of wealthy Straits-born Chinese. Violet loved leaning out of the window to feel the cool air on her cheeks as they clopped across town.

All too soon, the rich girl's family decided that she had learned enough to be literate without the danger of being literary, and that it was time to be schooled in the more important, marriageable arts of cooking, beading, embroidery and the manipulation of men.

Young aunt and little niece continued their journeys to school together by tram or trolleybus, a hot and dusty journey. But Fanny was not to be put off. When she finished her homework at the end of each long day, she made sure that Violet did hers. She believed in the transforming power of education.

As Fanny progressed at school through the late 1920s, the

enlightened European and Eurasian women who taught her and who introduced her to Christianity must have encouraged her to be more ambitious. Might she consider university? This would have been impossible in the decade before. There was still no university anywhere in Malaya, only a medical college in Singapore that handed out diplomas.

But everything changed when the University of Hong Kong started to admit women in 1921 – changed, at least, for those who could afford to travel and lodge there for something as frivolous, or even dangerous, as a higher education. In Britain at the turn of the century, they had believed that women became neurotic if they used their brains too much, particularly when menstruating. English doctors even had a medical term, *anorexia scholastica*, to describe the condition.[3]

But Law must have embraced the idea that his daughter should advance her studies where he could not. My mother remembered that Fanny was given 'the best bedroom' in the house, at the back where it was quiet, so that she could study.

It was my mother who told me that Fanny had wanted to go to university in Hong Kong and that she had achieved her dream – that Fanny's father had been her chaperone but that as he was sixty-six years old and in need of care himself, my grandmother Virtue had accompanied her father and her sister on this enterprise. Virtue had to leave behind her children. Violet, my mother, was fourteen, Peter was twelve, and Florence was ten. I don't suppose they had much say in the decision. Adults were less sentimental about their children in those days. Virtue agreed to stay for six months in Hong Kong before going back to Singapore to be with her children; she would return to Hong Kong after another six months if her father still needed her.

I had no reason at first to doubt my mother. But the more

I learned, the more I realized that it was rare for girls from Singapore to go to university. From the whole of Malaya, only two women studied at the University of Hong Kong in 1928,[4] after which the enrolment of Malayan women just seemed to evaporate.

But my mother had been perfectly clear that Fanny had gone to Hong Kong. While her brother and sister were to remain in the house on Cantonment Road still occupied by their uncles and wives, she herself had been sent to stay with her wealthy great-uncle, Law's brother, as a treat. Quan-Kuan lived with his family in an elegant house on prestigious Ang Siang Hill. My mother was a young teenager, eager to stretch her wings.

But though she remembered the time with her great-uncle distinctly and with much affection, perhaps my mother had confused Fanny's going to university with something more mundane, like the equivalent of a sixth-form college? Or even a ladies' finishing school?

After all, the University of Hong Kong had strict preconditions for entrance. It required applicants from Malaya to have at least five Senior Cambridge credits.[5] I wasn't sure if Fanny even took the examination. Her school needed ten years on average to prepare a girl for the qualification. Fanny had done only eight.

When girls left the Methodist Girls' School, notes were made in the register next to their names to say if they had 'Passed Senior Cambridge', or were leaving simply 'To stay at home' in preparation for marriage. Next to Fanny's, there was only a question mark.

I emailed the University of Hong Kong to find out if they had a record of Fanny. The university was apologetic. Many documents were lost or destroyed in the Second World War when the Japanese occupied the colony. It was going to be difficult to locate my great-aunt.

In desperation, I contacted Dr Chan Lau Kit-Ching, one of the editors of a book on the history of the university.[6] I got in touch without an introduction, a stranger from the internet, but she replied with great courtesy to explain that she had retired. Perhaps I could try her co-editor, Dr Peter Cunich?

I shot off another email without much hope, only to hear back straight away from Dr Cunich. He had just published another history of the university,[7] and had a record of every student who was there before 1945 – so long as his or her file survived.

He had Fanny's.

18

I was sent an extraordinary photograph by my Uncle Bernard in Canada, taken apparently in early 1931 in Hong Kong, of a small group of people.

At first I could not make out who they were: there is a powerful-looking Chinese man, rather grand; there is a gauche-looking girl, unconcerned with how she looks. There is an arresting woman with her hair scraped back to reveal a high forehead. There is a smartly dressed lady next to a little girl.

Then I realized, with a start, that they are Fanny, my great-grandfather Law, my grandmother and, seeing her for the first time, Law's concubine. She is holding the hand of Law's granddaughter Annie.

According to Dr Cunich's records, Fanny had applied in 1931 for a place in the Arts Faculty of the University of Hong Kong where the curriculum had been modified to be more of a teacher-training programme.[1] Of course! Teaching would be the perfect profession for Fanny. It is possible that Fanny was required in Hong Kong for an interview as she lacked the necessary credits for admission. If that was the case, I am gazing at a portrait from that time.

Fanny is wearing a prettily trimmed cheongsam but it is creased and there has been no inclination to smooth it down. She has more important things on her mind: the possibility of a place at university perhaps. She has the distracted air of someone who has been swotting and would certainly rather be somewhere else.

Her father, on the other hand, looks in complete possession of himself. Law is totally different here in this photograph from the one taken a few years later in 1935 – the one that my mother had given me before she died and which had started off the story of my great-grandfather. That 1935 image was then the only one I had of Law and was my single reference point. In it, Law looked like a withered leaf, something that a gust of wind might blow away. Therefore, I had imagined that he had always looked like that – slight and feeble, even as a younger man.

But in this photograph, taken just four years earlier, his physical strength is palpable. He is filled out, solid, anchored. He is dressed in a fine silk jacket and wears the kind of black silk cap that gentlemen wear. His air of authority is unmistakable, and what his concubine wears tells me why. She has emerged at last from the periphery to be examined.

Zhang isn't pretty. Her mouth is a little too wide, her nose slightly too broad. She looks much older than Virtue, not just by a year. But she is dressed very expensively, in a white or cream cheongsam made of stiff material, some sort of lined linen or fine wool. It has the three-quarter length sleeves and contrasting *passementerie* of the latest European fashion. The ornamental edging is opulent. Her leather shoes are two-tone. She carries a matching clutch handbag. She has the style, if not the bearing, of a *tai tai*, a woman of consequence. It is through her that I see that my great-grandfather did make it in the end. He had become wealthy.

Zhang is holding the hand of Annie, my aunt in Canada whom I had phoned after my mother died. Her father was Law's eldest son, Cheng-Wah. In the picture, she is about four years old. Zhang was very fond of Annie, and it was presumably for Zhang's amusement that Law has allowed this little girl to come along.

I can see that Law has provided generously for his family. Even Virtue looks so well-fed, sleek and beautiful – in dark silk and I think wearing earrings – that it took me a while to recognize her. The grandmother that I remember was thin, more like how she looked in the 1935 photograph when, having struggled through an economic depression in Singapore, she had clearly lost weight. Her cheongsam was baggy in the places that she no longer filled, its high collar loose around her neck.

Fanny was enrolled to start at the University of Hong Kong in January 1932 for its new academic year. Her university records show no matriculation qualification,[2] but as the university had so few women from Malaya, it was probably willing to be flexible.

Neither Fanny nor her father seemed fazed by the project

on which they had embarked. In fact, it was an extraordinary undertaking. Its expense and organization cannot be underestimated.

In Hong Kong, only the very well-off went to university. Later in 1932, at a meeting to discuss the building of women's hostels, when the vice chancellor worried that these would be too expensive for middle-class families, he would be told not to fret. Only the richest Chinese could afford to send their daughters to university.[3]

The cost of taking Fanny to Hong Kong was much more than the sum of her tuition fees and maintenance. In those days, Chinese women couldn't just go off abroad on their own, especially not to be among young men as Fanny would be at university. Law would have to be her chaperone until he could find a suitable guardian. He had to pay for lodgings for them all – Fanny was booked to board at St Stephen's Hall near the campus, run by the Anglican Church, while Law rented rooms elsewhere for Virtue and himself. And as they were arriving in the winter, they all required warm clothes.

My great-grandfather had prospered when the price of rubber shot up with a booming American car industry, but that all ended with the Great Depression in October 1929. Its contagion spread swiftly. Between the end of 1929 and the end of 1930, rubber prices halved.[4] Plantations in Malaya laid off tens of thousands of workers. Property prices crashed in Singapore as the brakes were slammed on every other business that gave it riches – mining, building, timber.

Miraculously, Law seemed to have avoided the full impact of the initial blow. Despite a year of disintegrating stock market and rubber prices, he still felt able to take his family off on a jaunt to Hong Kong for Fanny's university interview, bringing along even little Annie on a whim.

Even so, it was quite a commitment to give his youngest child, only a girl, the university education that she craved. Did he always find it impossible to say no to Fanny? Was she so difficult to put off? In fact, Fanny's precipitate departure from her school, after eight rather than ten years, provides a clue.

The currencies of Hong Kong and China were on the silver standard, unlike America's, Britain's or Japan's, which were on gold. The price of silver had already been falling as Europe produced more silver to pay off First World War debt. In 1930, it plummeted further as stock markets tumbled and investors rushed to buy gold. The Hong Kong dollar depreciated by 50 per cent against other currencies, which triggered an export-led boom.[5] Hong Kong's economy was thriving. It had taken off just as Singapore's was grinding to a halt.

Law needed to be in Hong Kong. He desperately required help with his finances. If someone could shore up his businesses in Malaya over this difficult period (in exchange for future profits), he needn't write them off.

If one of his children could have a higher education at the same time, even better. Law had not managed to thrive in the British colonial service. It had been too late for him, raised in China, to bridge the cultural divide. It could be different for Fanny. She was raised in Singapore and an English university education was undoubtedly a brilliant opportunity. It would mean that his family could finally fulfil the scholarly tradition of his ancestors, albeit through a girl.

However, if Fanny wanted to study at university it had to be now. Law was in a hurry. He couldn't wait. The situation in Malaya and Singapore was getting very bad.

There was one more thing to do before leaving for Hong Kong and a modern education, and that was to reach back to imperial China for a public troth of celibacy. Fanny wanted there to be no question of her falling in love. If she did well at university she could have financial independence and need never be trapped in marriages like her sisters'. And she would be able to look after Virtue.

Law tried a last time to put her off her spinsterhood ceremony: 'Why make a vow now that you can never break? Wait till you are older to make the choice. One day you may meet a man for whom you want to change your mind.'

And Fanny had answered, 'I want never to be able to change my mind.'

Fanny carries herself like a bride this morning. This is her wedding day, though she is about to commit not to a husband and babies, but to lifelong chastity.

She bathes in water that has been infused with citrus leaves, to wash away invisible spirits that are unlucky or unclean. She puts on the new silk clothes laid out on her bed, carefully chosen not to be red – the colour that real brides wear – but sober grey or blue.[6] Her female friends and relatives visit her bedroom with presents as they would before a real wedding,[7] but the mistress of ceremonies who attends to her has been chosen not for being the mother of sons, but for being unmarried and celibate.[8]

Fanny's attendant shushes everyone. She is about to begin the most important ritual of the day, which is to arrange Fanny's hair. There is no bridal headdress of gold and pearls for Fanny, but her fringe is swept back like a bride's and pinned. Only girls have fringes. The pins that are used are plain rather than decorative like those on the heads of properly married women.[9] If Fanny's hair had been long enough, it would have been coiled into a bun.

Unmarried Chinese women were not allowed to put up their hair. Instead, their hair was worn loose or in plaits like a girl's, even when they were no longer young. Until they married, women had none of the privileges of adults, not even to go out on their own to the shops. When sworn spinsters in the nineteenth century wore their hair *sor hei*, combed up, it was not a casual expression of defiance. It was subversive, a badge of rebellion weighted with controversy like a suffragette showing her ankles.

There is no need to powder Fanny's face, to make her up like a true bride.[10] When she is ready, she goes down to the family altar. This is a tall, blackwood table where effigies of the household gods sit next to wooden tablets engraved with the names of her father's ancestors. A real bride would not worship here.[11] She wouldn't be allowed to. She prayed only to her husband's ancestors. The privilege that Fanny's men confer on her is exceptional. It overturns the natural order of things, the habit of two thousand years.

Then Fanny turns to where her father is seated and kneels to offer him a cup of tea. The mistress of ceremonies nods to Law, inviting him to repeat after her in Cantonese to Fanny: 'Your hair is combed up like a married woman's. You are no longer a girl. Do not bring shame on us. Do not bring dishonour to our family.'[12]

Everyone understands what this really means: Fanny cannot change her mind about marrying and she must never have a lover. All the people in the room have the Confucian certainty that a woman is better off dead than tainted.

Fanny replies in a clear voice, 'I will never bring dishonour to our family,' and her vow of celibacy is sealed. Law finds that he has been holding his breath. He breathes out. His youngest child has just entered an irrevocable contract with his family's deities. If she breaks it, she will be punished by unmerciful gods.

The spinsterhood ceremony is usually followed by a small banquet. In Law's house, there are three tables of ten to mark Fanny's coming of age. Like all Chinese dinners it would have been noisy, full of loud conversation and the clanking of porcelain spoons against porcelain bowls. In the melee, one sister-in-law might have whispered to the other: 'The old man's mad! One blighted daughter wasn't enough, he's now got two! What will happen to this family now?'

But Fanny wouldn't have heard. With only the people she loved most by her side at her table, she would have been as radiant as a willing bride.

19

The former interpreter and his daughters set off for Hong Kong at the end of 1931, the second time that year. Fanny was twenty-four years old and a sworn spinster. She was starting university in the New Year, the only woman directly from Malaya or Singapore. The other Singapore girl was already in Hong Kong, a pupil at a convent school.

Undulating green mountains rise out of a blue sea as their boat steams towards busy Victoria Harbour. Junks of all sizes bob alongside, their red sails open like giant paper fans. Fanny had noticed many things about Hong Kong before, but not that it was also beautiful.

They transfer from ship to shore in a bumboat and are deposited on Hong Kong island to be fought over by rickshaw men. Law has somehow to pick several rickshaws for his family and their luggage, while placating the rest. Then they career into the traffic towards Wan Chai, where Law has rented rooms. Fanny will move into student accommodation in the New Year.

When they step out of their lodgings on Lockhart Road, they are swept up by a throng. Everyone walks quickly. Hong Kong has double the number of people of Singapore on less habitable land.[1] They are nearly all Cantonese. There are few Fukiens, or Chiuchows, or Hainanese. You hardly see any Arabs or Indians.

The men wear fedoras to keep their heads warm. The

women of the bourgeoisie wrap up in long wool coats over their ankle-length cheongsams. One occasionally flashes past with a maid hurrying behind carrying the shopping, her long plait of dark hair swinging with the effort and the haste.

Fanny turns to her sister: 'Look,' she says, pointing to a man staggering along to market with the carcass of a hog on his back, almost as long as he is tall – its head behind his head, its front hoofs tied round his neck, its back hoofs hanging just above his ankles.

Law reminds Virtue and Fanny to hang on to their purses – who hasn't heard of the colony's pickpockets? – but pauses to admire the whole roast ducks that dangle, glistening, in a restaurant window, as plump and princely as cardinals. Beggars crouch outside the polished brass doorway, hands cupped. Well-dressed men step past without stopping to feast inside, followed by their *tai tai* wives draped in diamonds and furs. The colony is known for the ostentation of its rich and their indifference to the poor.

It is easy to go across the island from Lockhart Road for a quick inspection of Fanny's university ahead of her transfer. A tram links Wan Chai to Pok Fu Lam where the university is halfway up a hill. They disembark, switch to sedan chairs, and are each carried uphill, swaying, by pairs of men. They are dropped off in front of tall wrought-iron gates which they have to go through to climb a hundred steps to the university. It is a little tiring for an old man but when they arrive at the top, they are impressed by what they see. The main building looks like a small castle with turrets. Double-storey colonnades support a central clock tower capped by a small dome.

On the way back to their lodgings they may have stopped at St John's Cathedral, to see where it was. Fanny was already a

Christian, an Anglican, and it would have been where she could go for Sunday service. It is oddly pleasing to think of Fanny where Nick and I would marry more than fifty years later.

Before Fanny's academic year began, there would have been time to visit some people to whom they had been given an introduction. The Chens had a son who was also at the university.

The Chinese middle classes are no different from those elsewhere, and their hosts would have resented the adjustment that they were required to make to their routine for people they had never met, simply to please a mutual relative or friend with whom they were probably no longer in regular contact. The living room would have had to be tidied and dusted, the windows cleaned, the table runner washed. There would have been some discussion over which local cakes to buy for tea. I imagine they would not have been at all sure that they wanted to meet this man and his peculiar daughter, but they would have had to welcome them with the ceremony that custom dictated.

A smiling maid greets Law and his family as she places cups of tea on the crochet table runner (laundered to snow-white perfection) and lays out dishes of unshelled peanuts, cut fruit and biscuits made from mung-bean flour.

Their hostess turns to Law: 'I hear your daughter is very clever.' She bares just enough of her teeth in a smile to emphasize her insincerity. 'Not many girls go to university,' she adds, meaningfully. Both Law and Fanny hurry to soothe her with suitably emollient and modest replies.

But as Law is a learned man who has led an adventurous life, the reservations of their new friends gradually dissolve to be replaced by genuine interest, when they hear the front door open and the maid's greeting, 'Young master!' and light steps through the hall, and an attractive voice call out, 'Father! Mother! How exciting! I know you've invited your friends from abroad to visit – but you didn't mention they were coming today. You're trying to keep them to yourself!'

Like most educated men in Hong Kong, their hosts' son would have perfect manners and beautiful Cantonese, full of the refinement missing in the Singapore version of the dialect. His thick, black hair would have been cut short and glossed, European-style. When the Manchu dynasty ended twenty years before, the long queues or braids that Chinese men wore – their sign of submission to Manchu rule – disappeared overnight in Hong Kong.

Young Chen greets Fanny's father and older sister first, as is correct, then addresses Fanny, briefly resting his eyes on her before he turns the full beam of his charm and attention back on to her father. It gives him time to take in what he sees. Fanny is not at all what his disapproving parents had led him to expect – some sort of odd bluestocking, rather plain.

Anna McCormick at Hong Kong University Archives had kindly scanned me a page from Fanny's file with a photograph attached. Fanny's hair is cut to a very short bob, ending around her ears. It is parted on the right, with a silver slide to keep her hair off her face. If the intention is to appear severe, she has not succeeded. It only draws attention to the oval symmetry of her face.

She looks very different from the gawky girl in the photograph taken nearly a year earlier, at the start of 1931. There appears to be a touch of lipstick, very light, on her lips. Perhaps her spinsterhood oath provides a protective mantle and

she is safe to be herself? She is wearing a white blouse with a round neck and loose, long sleeves with what looks like a silk-screen print of foliage and flowers on the bodice. The overall effect is enchanting.

Chen would not have found it disagreeable to be enlisted by his parents and Fanny's father to be her guide during her first days at university, though they would have been on different courses. Chinese men went to Western-style universities for the practical degrees in science and engineering that could usher China into the twentieth century.

Because there were so few women on a campus of hundreds of men, Fanny was always easy to spot. There were not many places where the ladies could hide. There was such scant provision for them that between classes, they sometimes simply waited in the corridors.[2] The students' union building did have a tearoom – but first, you had to run the gauntlet of staring, inquisitive men.

Chen smiles as Fanny describes the first, terrifying days of her course. She is comfortable confiding in him. He listens as if he understands her perfectly. She finds herself looking out for him, pleased when she sees him waiting outside her lecture room. There are only six women to seventeen men in her class[3] and the English lecturers delight in singling out the girls, inviting the 'ladies first' to answer questions.[4]

'But how can the professor ask for my opinion on what he's teaching?' Fanny shakes her head, bewildered. 'He is my senior in every way. I would never dare show him disrespect by telling him that he was wrong, or even right!'

Chen grins. 'Of course. We Chinese are taught never to question authority. That's part of the reason why China's struggled to modernize. But we're in a Western university and this is the way of the West. It's how they have progressed. I myself believe that we should embrace Western practice, though of course many of my fellow students do not.'[5]

When the Manchus were removed in 1911, at first many Chinese intellectuals embraced the European Enlightenment just as the Japanese had done before with such tremendous success. But they felt betrayed when, at the Paris Peace Conference following the end of the First World War, the West gave China's Shantung province – birthplace of Confucius – to Japan. This sparked off a huge student protest in 1919 called the May Fourth Movement. It swept through Peking and Shanghai. After that, though young Chinese intellectuals accepted the necessity of some political and cultural reform along Western lines, they became far more circumspect about the West.

At the University of Hong Kong, the men's choice of dress neatly divides those who want everything Western (from science to politics) and those who want practical access to Western technology without sacrificing the Confucian ethics that had underpinned Chinese civilization.

The former were in Western suits; the latter dressed in the fashion of the Chinese literati, in long Chinese gowns slit up the sides and worn over trousers. Those in Chinese dress hoped not to be accused of being less Chinese for studying at an English university.

'So you think I'm too *gweilo*!'

Fanny laughs at Chen's Cantonese slang for a European or an American: 'devil-man'. The young man has invited her to a teahouse near their campus. He takes off his jacket and loosens his tie.

'You can dress how you please!' she replies in Cantonese, smiling.

'But you think it wrong to follow the West?' he asks as he pours tea into porcelain cups. He loves teasing her. He likes seeing her cheeks colour slightly. It's very pretty. His eyes are twinkling but she finds herself saying with vehemence all the same:

'Not at all. I come from a British colony too. I just don't see why, to be modern, we must give up all Chinese ways. Surely we can have the best of the West with the best of the East?'

Chen looks suddenly serious. 'Fah-nee' – he pronounces her name Chinese-style – 'you cannot take one thing from the West but not the other. Over there, they believe that to progress you must be allowed to think and speak as you please. Here we accept authority without question. We dare not use reason if it goes against tradition. How can we be modern and scientific when old ideas cling to us? They are the chains that hold our country back.'[6]

It has been two decades since the Manchus were deposed yet China has not progressed. Sun Yat-Sen had tried to introduce democracy when China first became a republic, but it proved impossible to change in an instant the mind-set of millennia. For thousands of years, ordinary Chinese had simply obeyed their emperors. They were more comfortable with that.

In 1912, after just over two months as provisional president of the Republic of China, Dr Sun gave up his post to Yuan Shi-Kai in the hope that Yuan, with his military influence, could push through reform. But Yuan quickly turned on Sun to take down the scaffolding of democracy. In December 1915, Yuan gave up any pretence of wanting an elected parliament. He declared himself Emperor of the Empire of China.

But Yuan died unexpectedly six months later, in 1916, and China reverted to the chaos last seen after the Tang dynasty fell in AD 907 – not one country but a string of competing fiefdoms run by warlords, from the north right down to the far south.

China split into two. In the north, there was a militarist government based in Peking and recognized by America, Britain, France and Japan.

In the south, Dr Sun's parliamentarian group[7] set up its own government, backed by southern warlords who grew poppies for revenue. Whole swathes of the countryside were a blaze of red. In 1921, China produced nine-tenths of the world's opium.[8]

Sun soon fell out with his warlords. To survive, his Nationalist Party joined forces with the Communists but he still raised money from the sale of opium. The 1924 International Opium Conference in Geneva noted that Indian opium was 'sold to a company in Canton to which an opium monopoly had been granted by Sun Yat-Sen's government'.[9] The ends were justifying the means.

After Sun's death in 1925, his protégé and commander-in-chief Chiang Kai-Shek took over. From Canton, Chiang's Nationalists marched northwards with the Communists to stamp out warlord power and to reunite China. In 1927, they reclaimed Shanghai together.

Chiang moved the capital of China from Peking to Nanking to mark a fresh start. Then he turned on his allies. His brutal three-week campaign, during which thousands of Communists disappeared, presumed murdered, is now known as the Shanghai Massacre.

It was a confusing time to be Chinese. Once, all Chinese were united against the foreigner Manchus. Now, Chinese could be against Chinese. You were a supporter of the Communists, or the Kuomintang Nationalists, or neither. Who was truly Chinese? Answering the question had become complicated. Then the Japanese made it easier.

When Japan modernized in the late nineteenth century, its population grew so rapidly that it ran out of agricultural land. But its real economic problems began after the Great Kanto Earthquake in 1923 and the Great Depression in 1929. Millions became unemployed.[10]

In 1931, a branch of the Imperial Japanese Army stationed in northeastern China, on territory won from Russia in war, decided that it could instantly solve its country's problems by making a land grab in Manchuria. This elite division, called the Kwantung Army, broke out of its delimited area to invade the whole of Manchuria, recklessly infringing on Chinese sovereignty without Tokyo's consent. (The next year, when Japanese prime minister Inukai Tsuyoshi refused to recognize the state of Manchukuo created by this army, officers of the armed forces shot and killed him at point-blank range.)

The occupation of Manchuria took place in September 1931, just months before Fanny's arrival in Hong Kong. There had been outrage in China at this invasion. The boycott of Japanese goods that followed was so effective, Japanese exports to China fell by 40 per cent.[11] Japan's violation of China's sovereignty is impossible to ignore and everyone still talks about it on the campus. Fanny is learning that Chinese politics live and breathe here in Hong Kong, whereas in Singapore they were simply too far away for it to feel real. (There are no local politics in Singapore. The British administrators prefer it that way.)

'But why do the Japanese want Manchuria?' Fanny asks. 'There's nothing there.'

The waiter has just filled their porcelain teapot with more hot water, spilling some on the table. Chen frowns slightly as he calls the waiter back to wipe it with a cloth.

'Who told you that?' he asks, helping her to more dumplings. She eats so little. He needs to feed her up. 'Manchuria has coal and plenty of land, which the Japanese want. They have too many people on their islands. They want to move them to Manchuria.'

Both Chen and Fanny turn to look at their waiter, who's just dropped a tray of teacups.

Chen puts his chopsticks down. 'A friend of mine went to south Manchuria last year – you know, the bit the Japanese took over from Russia twenty-five years ago. He says you should see what they've done in Dalian! It was nothing when the Japanese moved in but they built the town brick by brick from plans the Russians left behind.[12] Now it is like Shanghai. There are grand buildings in the European style, and broad avenues lined with acacia trees.[13] It is more modern than many parts of Japan or China. They had gas lighting twenty years ago! *And* electrified tramways. There is even heating in their hotels.'[14]

He is suddenly grave: 'The Japanese are extremely capable. That is why they are so dangerous.'

By the end of December, the anti-Japanese boycott in Shanghai had become massive and confused. There were fights between Chinese protestors and the Japanese military based in the Shanghai International Settlement. In the middle of January 1932, weeks into Fanny's first term, five Japanese monks were assaulted in Shanghai, one of them so severely that he died of his injuries.

The Japanese demanded an apology and compensation from Shanghai's municipal authority, though it was becoming clear that members of the Japanese military had instigated the fracas themselves, paying Chinese hoodlums to ambush the monks.[15] Nonetheless, the Shanghai council agreed to all the demands.

Of course this did nothing to appease the Japanese. The very next day they bombed Shanghai. They did not stop.

20

Fanny had been at university for less than a month when the Japanese armed forces invaded China.

Not for the first time, my great-grandfather watched his plans disintegrate. There might be more than 1,000 kilometres between Shanghai and Hong Kong, but in business the two cities were twinned. The Hong Kong stock market collapsed.[1]

Japanese planes bombed the defenceless civilians of crowded Chapei in Shanghai intensively. The ferocity was unprecedented. No civilian city on earth had ever been attacked like this before.[2] There were simply no words to describe it. The phrase 'carpet bombing' had not yet been invented to evoke this 'rehearsal for what lay ahead in Guernica, Coventry, Dresden, Hiroshima, Vietnam, Cambodia'.[3]

Even today, some historians skirt around the word 'war'. Japanese communiqués of the time preferred the word 'incident'. But it was war.

The Japanese marched their troops into Shanghai, sailed their navy into its harbour and expected to take Shanghai in days. But to everyone's surprise, the Chinese turned out to be intractable. The Japanese sent more troops into the city, more planes, crowded the harbour with ships. By the end of February 1932, Japan had 80,000 troops, 300 planes and 80 warships in Shanghai.[4] Unlucky Shanghainese who ran into the Japanese were bayoneted, shot or burned alive. The corpses of civilians stacked up high to block the alleys of the city.[5]

Suddenly the question 'Who is a true Chinese?' was no longer difficult to answer. It was any Chinese.

'The situation is getting serious,' Chen admits cautiously. He doesn't want to frighten Fanny. He's only known her for weeks but he feels protective of her. He likes her intelligence and independence, but she also seems vulnerable. They meet nearly every day. They sit outdoors to have their lunch or he walks her back to her hall of residence. Today he has brought Fanny to where there is the best view of the sea from their university. A panorama of islands spills out towards Lantau.

'You've never been there? I'll take you. Lantau is a beautiful island. It has a Buddhist monastery which we can visit. When you stand in its courtyard, you see only green hills around you. So peaceful.' Chen closes his eyes and breathes in deeply, as if he were there now. Fanny gazes at him. His eyes are still closed when he says, 'I am thinking wonderful things,' and when he opens them he looks directly at her.

News of Shanghai's plight consumed Hong Kong. If Shanghai should fall, what then? Fanny would have heard the rumours, whispered, of widespread rape. In fact, it was in Shanghai that officers of the Japanese armed forces were so disturbed by the actions of their men that they came up with the idea of 'comfort women' for the first time: prostitutes were brought into the city to a 'station'.[6] (Later, during the Second World War, when subsequent stations ran out of prostitutes, local girls as young as thirteen would be kidnapped for Japanese soldiers to use.)[7]

The war continued into March. With thousands of casualties on both sides, neither had much appetite for carrying on. Representatives from the League of Nations were allowed into Shanghai to broker a ceasefire. The Shanghai Ceasefire Agreement was signed in May. Life on the campus in Hong Kong returned to normal.

The students have their mid-year examinations. Fanny is wrestling with Emerson. Chen teases her.

'Your Ah-Meh-Song,' he laughs, 'he sounds a very lonely sort of man! He says you must rely only on yourself, which is the opposite of what traditional Chinese believe. Even I have to agree with the traditionalists that when we are born we are a part of our family, and our family is a part of our clan, and our clan is part of our country . . . you can never be alone! We are like streams that feed rivers and oceans; we cannot help but be part of the sea.' His perfect Cantonese phrases sound like poetry.

When he laughs, his teeth are white and even. When his face creases into a smile, his eyes shine.

Fanny sits four papers: English, History, Geography and Logic. History is her strongest subject; Logic is her weakest. She passes every paper except Logic.

The weather is perfect in October. The skies are blue, but the heat has passed. Late spikes of white ginger lily are still on sale in the market, sending their fragrance into the air. Fanny stops to buy a few stalks, to breathe in the flowers' spicy scent as she walks back to her hostel with Chen.

Chen asks: 'I know what I want in a wife, but what does a girl look for in a husband?' As usual he uses his teasing voice.

'Constancy,' Fanny says with some feeling, thinking of Virtue and her husband's mistress. 'Kindness.'

'But girls want riches too, don't they? Success?' He is smiling.

'Not a girl with a true heart.'

He looks at her. 'Ah, that's you, Fah-nee.'

'Oh, that's right,' she replies lightly. 'I am very steadfast. As you know I made a vow not to marry, which I will keep.'

'But that's a kind of girl's vow! It means nothing!' Chen is shocked.

Fanny struggles to keep calm. 'I took an oath before coming here. I know what that means.'

'It was not a promise to anyone,' Chen argues. 'Only to yourself. No one would blame you now if you change your mind.'

'But I won't change my mind.'

'To carry on would be pure superstition, Fah-nee. I expected more of you!' He is angry. She realizes suddenly that it matters what he thinks, but it is too late. She had promised to make a sacrifice, and that is the stronger claim.

'But it's my duty to keep my word!' she insists.

'Duty!' Chen exclaims. 'Isn't it also your duty to marry? Might a man like me not need your steadfast heart to guide him, to help bring up honourable children?' They both flush at his outburst. They walk the rest of the way in silence.

Fanny takes her end-of-year examinations. This time she passes Logic easily but she fails English, by five points.

Dr Cunich at the University of Hong Kong was very kind. He told me that Fanny was not the only student in her year to fail. He thought that there was every chance that she would have passed if she had sat her papers again the following year. Two of the girls on her course took an extra year to graduate.

But Fanny did not resit. Instead, she left her studies and returned to Singapore with her father after only a year at the university. Something had happened to make them hurry back.

Had Law fallen ill? He was nearly sixty-eight.

Were father and daughter worried that Japan might start another war?

Or was Fanny troubled by her affection for a young man, and by his attentiveness? She had believed that a spinster-hood oath would stop men from falling in love with her, or her with them. But emotions are unbidden. They always have the capacity to surprise.

My mother never talked about Fanny's year in Hong Kong without adding, 'There was a young man.' She intimated that they had had feelings for each other but she could not or would not tell me more. I understand now that this was due to the gravity of Fanny's vow. She was forbidden to have any feelings for a man.

My grandmother Virtue would have empathized strongly with her sister Fanny's situation because of its resemblance to the story of the Butterfly Lovers that Virtue cherished: two students fall in love but cannot marry. In the story the girl has been pledged to another; in Fanny's case, it was she who had made the pledge.

But the reason for Fanny and her father's return to Singapore may be far more prosaic – though to me still poignant. My great-grandfather's financial affairs were finally falling apart.

When Law took Fanny to Hong Kong with such hope at the end of 1931, he could not have anticipated that its economy would go into reverse just as they arrived. Both Britain and Japan had left the gold standard by December.[8] As their currencies depreciated, Hong Kong became expensive. The surge of trade in Hong Kong's favour began to end.

In Singapore, the Straits dollar followed sterling downwards. Law's money was suddenly worth a lot less in Hong Kong. The whole sojourn was costing more than he expected. At the same time, the mood in Hong Kong had changed, first with the war in Shanghai, then with the growing trade imbalance. It was no longer optimistic. His hope of finding investors for his Malayan businesses was drying up. Worst of all, the situation in Singapore had deteriorated further. Rubber prices that had plunged by 50 per cent at the end of 1930 were another 60 per cent lower by 1932.[9] The knock-on effect of this on other businesses was colossal.

Law had to rush home to see if he could save his investments. He was running out of money. He could not afford the expense of an additional year for Fanny after her poor marks. If Fanny had allowed herself to be distracted from her studies, that was too bad. She had had her chance. It was time to head back.

21

A little while after Fanny and Law returned to Singapore in 1933, a letter arrived from their friends in Hong Kong to say that their son had left for America. He had met a Chinese-American heiress. They were going to be married.

'Nothing can bring you peace but yourself. Nothing can bring you peace but the triumph of principles.'[1] Fanny still had her copy of Emerson's essays. It would have to help her to carry on.

She had to shrug off the tittering and the gossip behind her back, the secret nudges of those who thought that she had over-reached herself by going to university. She had failed her first year! She had fallen as she deserved. Why did she think she could be a pioneer of her sex?

It was a sobering time to be back in Singapore, which was waist-deep in a slump. Its merchant millionaires (Chinese, Indian, Arab) had lost their fortunes, the Chinese especially with their interlocked system of credit based on kinship and trust. The credit had dried up. The property market had crashed. Bankruptcies were up by 60 per cent.[2] Fanny must have worried that, without a proper qualification, she would not find a teaching job.

There was an explosion of Chinese beggars on the streets, most of them surprisingly strong and young, disgorged from the tin mines of Malaya. Thousands slept rough.[3]

There were Englishwomen where you wouldn't once have seen them, in Asian wet markets where the lanes were dirty and flies speckled the carcasses of animals but the prices were lower. They should have sent their amahs, only those were long gone.[4] Their own countrywomen had little sympathy for them. They let the side down by shopping with the 'natives'.

Outside the Raffles, unshaven white men begged for cigarettes. Rubber plantations had sacked a third of their European planters,[5] along with three-quarters of their Indian labourers. These British planters, unemployed, looked and behaved like tramps. They embarrassed other white men on the island. Soon a fund would be set up to round them up and ship them home.[6]

There were Eurasian and Straits Chinese men, former civil service clerks, who waited outside their old offices each day, looking purposeful in pressed white shirts. (They looked shabbier and less hopeful week after jobless week.) Such men resented Fanny, an Asian single woman, competing with them for work when they had wives and children to support. But Fanny had dependants too. She had to take her sister and her sister's children out of their father's house as soon as she could. She had to fulfil the vow that she made two years before, except now with greater urgency: her father could no longer support his daughters.

Fanny grasped her future with resolve. There was no role model in her family for her to follow. She was completely on her own. She would have to be the first woman in the history of her clan to look for work in a profession. Remarkably, she found something. Teacher-training classes had been suspended in Singapore, another casualty of the Depression.[7] There were now fewer qualified teachers. Fanny's year in Hong Kong was of value after all.

A boys' school that had just replaced its headmaster with

a headmistress, Mrs Waddell, offered Fanny a post. It was
6 kilometres from the centre of town, in the rural suburb of
Geylang. This was where Malay fishermen were resettled by
the British in the nineteenth century and it had an unhealthy
climate. The Arab landowners who came later tried to sub-
due this with fields of lemongrass. Citronella puts off the
mosquitoes that carry dengue and malaria. After harvesting,
the grass was put through mills known in Malay as *kilang*,
which may have given the area its name.

Lemon grass was eventually replaced by coconut and rubber, far more lucrative, and the Chinese moved in. Houses
were built for them off the main road in residential terraces
called *lorongs*, the Malay word for 'lane'. It is an insight into
how utterly peripheral Geylang was to the British of the time
that most of these lanes are marked just with numbers. But
by the 1930s the population here had grown large enough for
the colony's administrators to feel they needed their own
school.

The Geylang English School was on Lorong 23. Fanny's
house, most likely provided by the school, was on Lorong 24.
She lived there with Virtue, Violet, Peter and Florence.

The house is still there, an entire cultural voyage away
from their home in Chinatown. In Cantonment Road, the
brick façade of their old family home is measured and
restrained. Here in Geylang it is covered by exuberant plas-
terwork, wreathed in decorative mouldings. Malay and
Chinese features have been combined and happily grafted
on to European rootstock. Number 12 on Lorong 24 is not
a big house, but it has pilasters enough to satisfy anyone,
ornate capitals and festoons of plaster fruit and flowers. It is
rather pretty.

Fanny and Virtue would have been excited yet nervous to

be leaving their father's house in Cantonment Road, away from his protection. Law probably felt miserable at the departure of the daughters he adored. But this was what they had worked towards all these years. They would have recognized that.

In particular, my grandmother would have wanted to believe that her sister's dream of financial independence really could come true. What alternative did she have? I suspect she scarcely imagined that it would happen, that the day would arrive when Fanny would present her with their own house.

Fanny was only twenty-six when they moved. Virtue was thirty-nine, Violet was sixteen, Peter fourteen, and Florence twelve. Their neighbours would have wondered at this new family of women and a boy. They must have wondered even more to discover that the head of the house was a very young woman – practically only a girl. This was not the norm. Among Chinese families in Singapore, it was unheard of.

It seemed natural that they should settle quickly into their new lives. It was no longer remarkable to find that Peter could have his own bedroom, or that the bathroom was completely their own, or that they could arrange the furniture exactly as they pleased.

Virtue managed the household as she had always done with her father, to leave Fanny free to adjust to her completely new life as a professional woman.

I imagine Fanny sitting at a round kitchen table with her two nieces and her nephew supervising their homework in the afternoons while she does her marking: a small, beautiful young woman, very serious.

Despite just having started her teaching career, Fanny was already planning Violet's future.

*

'Vi, if you're really not interested in medicine, I think you should change schools.'

'Why?' Violet looks up from her schoolwork in surprise.

Virtue is cleaning the kitchen floor around them with a bucket of water and a rag. Virtue believes it is important that her daughters have as much time for studying as her son. It is what Fanny has impressed on her. Peter, always quick, has finished his assignments and is in the front garden planting a small pomegranate for his mother. The pomegranate symbolizes family happiness as well as abundance.

'The second language at your Methodist school is Latin, which is only helpful if you're studying medicine.' Fanny picks up another exercise book from the unmarked pile on her right, and opens it. 'You may as well learn French at the Convent of the Holy Infant Jesus.'

'You want me to switch schools now?' Violet tugs unhappily at her hair. 'I'd have to start all over again for the Senior Cambridge examination . . . *and* I have to supervise Flo's homework and also tidy the house.'

Both Fanny and Virtue know exactly where Violet is going with this. Fanny says: 'You'll have plenty of time for your lessons.'

Virtue adds: 'Your little sister already helps me more than you do with the housework. She swept this floor before I started cleaning it.'

'I did!' young Florence says jauntily. She's just joined the Methodist Girls' School at Geylang. She doesn't like lessons much. She prefers helping her mother.

Law decided to move too, out of the known and civilized milieu of Chinatown into another house somewhere in the wilderness of Geylang. Perhaps he wanted to be near his daughters, to keep a watchful eye over them. His protectiveness was sharpened by necessity. His circumstances had changed. If he owned his house in Cantonment Road, he probably had to sell it; if he had rented the house, it would help that in Geylang he paid less rent.

However, in making this transfer from town to suburb, he had to endure the break-up of his extended family, so precious to the Chinese. In Cantonment Road, his sons and their families had lived with him. Now, although his younger son Liang – my uncle Bernard's father – followed him to Geylang with his wife, his elder son Cheng-Wah decided to remain behind in Chinatown.

Cheng-Wah had gone to college in Nanking at an exhilarating time to be in China. He had been present at the fall of the great Manchu dynasty in 1911. He was briefly part of the Chinese republic under Dr Sun Yat-Sen. Sun's provisional government had been in Nanking itself. He was inspired by Dr Sun's ideas.

Then Dr Sun gave up his post to Yuan Shi-Kai, a militarist. The two began to clash until Sun was once again exiled to Japan, in 1913, the same year that Cheng-Wah returned to Singapore.

Cheng-Wah started teaching at his former school, Yeung Ching, the island's oldest Chinese primary school. Its headmaster, Soong Sum, was a China loyalist and activist. In 1915, Soong organized a disruptive boycott of Japanese goods in the colony. This was to protest against Japan sailing eleven warships up the Yangtse and issuing China with a menacing secret list of 'Twenty-one Demands,' including the right to occupy Shantung Province. Four years later, in 1919, when the Treaty of Versailles handed Shantung to Japan,[8] another boycott was mobilized in Singapore.

These were violent rallies. They involved physical threats and arson and people were killed. In 1915, the Japanese residents of Singapore were so alarmed, they locked themselves in an exhibition hall and refused to come out. In 1919, martial law was declared during the riots that preceded the boycott. The police had to set up a Special Branch to cope.[9] When the demonstrations ended in August, Cheng-Wah's headmaster was arrested by the British and deported,[10] but not before he must have made a profound impression on Cheng-Wah.

Law takes his son aside. 'Be careful,' he says. 'You are lucky that our Governor is not really interested in the Chinese or he might have made more of an example of you all.'

'All I did was distribute leaflets,' Cheng-Wah protests, 'they can't deport you for that! But yes, we've been lucky. The Governor is so preoccupied with Malay affairs in the peninsula that the Kuomintang can open Chinese schools down here on our island with no interference from the police. Our schools are small, it's true, but trees grow from seeds. Our textbooks teach our children to love their motherland.'

Law looks at his son through narrowed eyes. 'Things may not always remain the same.'

It would be a decade before Law's prediction came true. In 1930, a new Governor arrived in Singapore who was the former Governor of Hong Kong. Cecil Clementi was a scholar of Chinese.

The Chinese Protectorate was now called the Department of Chinese Affairs, but Law still had his contacts there. Its clerks told him that Clementi should be taken seriously.

'Watch out for this one,' Law warns his son. 'This governor

Severed heads, stained with carmine, collect in the foreground: 'Beheading Chinese troops who had committed atrocities', print by Utagawa Kunimasa V (1894).

Japanese officers are in European uniform, have nearly Caucasian features, and look heroic: 'Great victory at Pyongyang', print by Yōsai (Watanabe) Nobukazu (1894).

L–R: Peter, Violet, Florence, with their mother, Virtue.

Virtue moved back to her father's house on Cantonment Road with her children. It was considered bad luck for her father to take back a married daughter.

L–R: Fanny, Law, Virtue, Annie, Law's concubine Zhang.

A frail-looking Law (*seated*) and his family before his final return to Canton. (See page 183 for a full list of names.)

Univ. No. .... Name .... *Fanny Law* 羅芳芳

BIRTH: Place ..... *Canton* .... Date, *15/ 8 /1907* .... Nationality, *Chinese*

Parent or Guardian .... *Law Kwan Yee* ....

Home Address ..... *268 Lockhart Rd. H.K.*

Local Guardian ..... *Law Kwan Yee* ....

Address of same .... *268 Lockhart Rd.*

Previous Education *Methodist Girls'* .... (Stamped

.... *School, Singapore* ....

Matric. Exam. (of equivalent) .... / /19

Equivalent .... *Senior Cambridge* ....

Registered .... *4/ / /19 32* Hall .... *St. Stephens*

Scholarships ....

Degree Examinations .... First / /19 . Second / 19 .

Third / /19 . Fourth / 19 .

Graduation .... / 19 ....

Dean's comments and Signature

Subsequent career.

Fanny's student file from the University of Hong Kong.

Fanny's photograph from her university file.

Fanny's signature on the inside cover of one of her books, kept by her nephew Peter – the smudge is from later years.

Fanny leaning protectively over her father – probably taken in Hong Kong sometime between 1931 and 1935.

Fanny's watch: its bracelet is so small that it could now, in our time of relative peace and plenty, only fit a child.

81 Tiong Poh Road – after Law's death, Fanny moved with her family to this block in Tiong Bahru during the Second World War. They occupied the top-floor flat where she died.

Fanny is on the far left by Law's bier. Virtue is next to her.

Our only photograph of Fanny (*left*) and Virtue on their own.

Cheng-Wah's unprepossessing school is in the middle of the picture (next to the house with washing hanging from a bamboo pole thrust out of an upper window). You can just make out the Chinese characters on the sign placed under the upper window of Cheng-Wah's house: 'Heong Jo School'.

2020年10月15日 星期四　联合早报　 f ⚑ 🐦 📷 zaobaosg

一位被遗忘的抗日分子

罗澄华校长日治蒙难

1942年，香祖学校校长罗澄华因为藏有用来抗日筹款的印花图片被日军拘捕，过后被日军杀害。

缤纷史探

何乃强／文图

1942年2月15日，经过八天的顽强抵抗后，新加坡还是被日本军占领。陷落后一连串抗日分子大逮捕，随后是一连串杀日分子大逮捕，以及长达15天的检证大屠杀，估计三四万（有说超过五万）华裔年轻知识分子，被押上卡车，送到海边等地一一被枪杀。很多无辜的年轻华人，莫名其妙被枪，从此一去不回，多少家庭被毁。养正学校有不少人，如校董梅启璇、原校长张勉之，就是在这时期被杀害，其中还有一位前教师罗澄华（1891~1942）。

英电邮寻找曾叔公资料

2017年，我接到养正校友会转给我一封来自英国林碧霞女士（Mrs Teresa Seaward）的电邮，托我寻找她的曾叔祖父（曾叔公）罗澄华在死亡的资料。原来系资料，正在为编写她的家族史，希望从校友会那里，能够获得罗澄华更多的资料。

10年前，我在撰写《前养正纪事1905~1987》的时候，所读到的参考

资料中，罗澄华的名字曾在我眼前出现过一两次。当时对于有关罗澄华的事迹，我没多加留意，只当他是养正众教职员中一名老师。

受林碧霞所托，过去三年，我搜集、查阅和罗澄华有关的资料。找到一篇养正校友，前（南洋商报）记者洪锦棠（笔名本地姜，1906~1982）写的《永远不能忘记的母校》，收录在1956年，养正学校出版的《养正学校金禧纪念刊》。文中记载他是在1913年进入养正读书，当时罗澄华是他的班主任和教导他普通话（华语）的老师。

开办私塾"香祖学校"

我也找到一篇刊登在1978年7月6日（星洲日报）第16版的访谈，是养正前老师梁志生（笔名梁山，1912~1987）执笔，题为《养正学堂往和律》的文章，才知道罗澄华较多的史料。为此我询问和本地网上会馆（冈州也问新会）有超过半世纪渊源的退休资深记者，金国瑶笔中文区如柏为我查证。从他馆藏的一本1925年编印的冈州会馆筹建影会议大厦的征信录影印本所载，赫然发现"名人罗澄华祖捐三十元"，以及在金册开幕礼上，罗澄华上台致辞短祝贺词，

1927）时的学生，也是罗澄华的学生。

罗澄华没有留下个人照。给蕭老师留下深刻的印象是：蕭短髭，出口开声，轻帽不离身，有"洋学者风度"。我找到一张在上世纪20年代，何剑吴校长和养正全体教职员合照，里面就有蕭老师所描述的人物。那是罗澄华强有力的印证据。这张照片是罗澄华在过世界留下的容貌与身影。

推算一下，罗老师在养正当老师大约15年，他在上世纪20年代末离职，在身边由（现在的必麒麟街上段）开办私塾"香祖学校"兼任校长。

原以为罗澄华是广东香山（中山）人，因为他的学校取"香祖"命名，以为香祖取自"香山先祖"之意。但林碧霞确实，罗澄华原籍广东新会。（冈州也问新会）有超过半世纪渊源证明罗澄华的籍贯无误。

藏花卉图片被捕

罗澄华金子毕业于南京暨南中学高中。他有一个比他小五岁的弟弟罗澄亮（1896~1945），也是养正校友。澄亮在日治时期被日军拘捕尸所挑打，光复前后获释。不久后，因曾养不良加上旧伤不愈愈死。他的35岁妹因惧怕被日军污辱，自寻短见。罗家兄妹的悲惨命运，令人哀痛。

1942年罗澄华因为藏有印上花卉的图片被日军拘捕。这些图片是抗日分子用来筹款，作为抵抗日军活动经费。根据刊登在（昭南日报）警备司令宫所发布的新闻，日军在1942年2月21及22日，检决对些参加抗日运动、被视为敌尼之徒。罗澄华与梅启璇同为抗日同志（同是广惠肇帮），或被人告密出卖，则不得而知。罗澄华因抗日而不幸身陷囹圄，相信是在这两天被杀害的。

今年罗澄华已经离世75年，我这后辈搜找，有幸者询出这一位几乎被人遗忘的抗日分子的曾叔公，为他作历史补遗。他若是泉下有知，应该可以瞑目矣。

Cheng-Liang, referred to as 'Liang' in the book. He is Law's younger son and Cheng-Wah's younger brother.

Liang with his hands on Bernard's shoulders; his wife is holding their younger son, Leonard.

Bernard with his father, Liang. It was Bernard who told me about the Law family genealogy.

speaks Cantonese and reads Chinese. Not much is going to get past him.'

For starters, Clementi closed all the branch offices of the Kuomintang in Singapore.[11] He worried that the Kuomintang on this island could turn easily from being pro-China to anti-Britain. Then he focused his attention on Kuomintang influence in the schools.

By then, Cheng-Wah had already left Yeung Ching to set up his own small school. (Yeung Ching had become too closely scrutinized by the British to be comfortable.) Even so, he would have to be careful. He was teaching from books provided by the Nationalist Party in China, filled with Kuomintang propaganda.

Cheng-Wah decided not to follow his father to Geylang. Geylang had a big Malay population and few Chinese schools and his work would be visible there. He would remain in crowded Chinatown where he could operate unnoticed by the British.

Cheng-Wah moved his family of four into a room above his school in Upper Pickering Street with its one classroom for only ten to twenty students. He made very little money and life was extremely hard, but it was what he wanted.

In its own way, his modest Heong Jo[12] School was building a reputation for excellence. The parents of his pupils reported admiringly that if your sons were stupid, Law Cheng-Wah beat them till they grew clever.

22

Singapore was coming out of the Depression by 1934, but more men took their own lives then than before. Sometimes, they murdered their families first.[1] The final sprint requires the greatest will. My great-grandfather's had run out.

You can tell when you compare the photographs from 1931 and 1935. In the earlier one, he is clearly in command though at his ease, reclined on a carved and padded black-wood chair. Four years later and he has so diminished that he looks like a supplicant to his former self, the formidable man in the previous photograph. What happened? Illness? Heartache? The full-blown tragedy of financial wipe-out?

Opium may have been a factor in this decay, sought more and more for consolation or forgetting. The words 'opium addict' look very stark on a page but that is what he had become – with the assistance of the British. The colonial administration sold it nearly everywhere, in packages stamped with the words 'Monopoly Opium' in red.

Law would never have considered himself an addict with all that it implied: disintegration, poverty, the body of a cadaver with only an awful cough to show he was alive. But Law had shrivelled, like a phantom forced to manifest every ravage of the past four years. These were deep. He had lost nearly everything that he had fought so painfully to achieve. And he was tortured by the thought that he might die in Singapore, cast out forever in the Nanyang.

He had reassured himself again and again in his preface to

the Law genealogy: 'We are now sojourning in foreign countries. This is only temporary, not forever . . . one day we will return and trace the home village and lineage.' He had been homesick nearly all his life.

As an intelligent man, he would have done a quick reckoning: he was going to be seventy, a fitting age for any Chinese of that generation. The tally was sufficient. He had lived to be old. His life in a British colony was drawing to a close. The time had come for him to go home to die. If he did not leave for China soon, he might never make it.

Law sailed for his homeland in the spring of 1935 after celebrating his seventieth birthday. He was leaving behind all his children and grandchildren, his concubine, his brother, the graves of his wife and his daughter, everyone he had held dear for fifty years. The pull to return was that strong.

To delay a little the grief of parting, Law's two remaining daughters and most of his grandchildren travelled with him in the second half of April during school Easter holidays, a party of ten. His sons were unable to follow. Cheng-Wah had his Chinese school to run (no Easter holidays for them) and Liang had joined the Police CID. You couldn't come and go as you pleased.

The grandchildren who joined Law's excursion were Cheng-Wah's three children Heng-Nam, Yin-Yue and Annie (now eight years old); Virtue's two eldest, my mother Violet and her brother Peter (Florence, fourteen, stayed behind); and Orchid's two eldest, Pak-Leong and Hou-Yin (leaving their youngest brother Pak-Hung, sixteen). Liang's son Bernard was less than two years old, and his younger son was not born yet.

As for Law's concubine Zhang, she had no desire to see China again. She was installed by Law at her request in an ashram run by Buddhist nuns. Zhang was forty-one years old. Law paid for her to be taken care of until her death.

Hong Kong is very different from the last time that they were there, and not just because of a new bank building, very tall, that now dominates the waterfront. The people seem less happy, more anxious.

America is boosting the price of silver to help its own producers and Hong Kong has become expensive on the silver standard. Its trade has halved since 1931;[2] its property market has disintegrated. There are beggars everywhere, filthy-looking, aggressive, often clutching babies and children whom they thrust in front of you. In restaurants, the food can taste stale, unsold from previous days, and the rickshaw men who harass passers-by look thin and gaunt rather than lean and muscular.

The Law family is overjoyed, however, to be joined by the woman who took Orchid's place after she died. The second Mrs Lye is in Kowloon with her young children to visit her parents. Her grown-up stepchildren, Orchid's son Pak-Leong and daughter Hou-Yin, are already part of Law's party. Law, Virtue and Fanny have kept close to them all these years. My mother loved her cousin Hou-Yin like a sister.

Now the group is fourteen-strong and the day passes in a blur. They take the Peak Tram to the top to admire the view of Victoria Harbour; they go back down to board the Star Ferry to Kowloon to shop. They eat and they chat. Sometime during their day together someone spots a photographic studio and they troop in, a whirlwind of energy and noise. The photographer is very patient.

In the photograph, Virtue and Fanny pretend that their circle of three sisters is complete. No memory of premature death need sully their afternoon. A charm has brought them together. They have with them the woman who married Orchid's widower and who replaces Orchid for them too. They have taught their children to call her 'Third Aunt', which was Orchid's title in their family, and they embrace her children as if they were Orchid's own. Her two young sons and little daughter are placed carefully next to Law as if he were their grandfather.

Orchid's own children stand at the back with the other adults. Hou-Yin is on the far right with her arm around my mother. Her eldest brother Pak-Leong is on the far left, next

Standing, back row, left to right: **Lye** *Pak-Leong (Orchid's elder son),* **Law** *Yin-Yue (Cheng-Wah's elder daughter),* **Law** *Heng-Nam (Cheng-Wah's son), Peter* **Chang** *(Virtue's son – he later adopted the spelling* **Tsang** *for his surname), Fanny* **Law***, Virtue (***Law** *Mong-Han, formerly Mrs Gilbert* **Chang***), Mrs* **Lye** *Lin-Ching or 'Third Aunt' (Orchid's successor),* **Lye** *Hou-Yin (Orchid's daughter), Violet* **Chang** *(Virtue's elder daughter). Standing, middle row, left to right: Angelina* **Law** *(Cheng-Wah's younger daughter),* **Lye** *Hou-Seong (Third Aunt's daughter). Sitting, left to right:* **Lye** *Pak-Ming, Grandfather* **Law** *Quan-Yee,* **Lye** *Pak-Yan (the two boys are Third Aunt's sons). Surnames are in* **bold***.*

to Yin-Yue. These two first cousins are secretly in love. Yin-Yue's father Cheng-Wah and Pak-Leong's late mother Orchid were brother and sister. They do not share the same surname, but their union is frowned upon by very traditional Chinese.

As for Law, he eluded death in China from starvation and he eluded death in the tropics from malaria, tuberculosis, typhoid, any of the vexatious diseases of the humid south that had claimed so many lives, including his wife's. But in the photograph he doesn't look triumphant. He looks worn out. He has had to fight to live this long, to have this chance to return home.

From Hong Kong, they set off on the Kowloon–Canton railway for the Law ancestral home, having said their good-byes to Third Aunt.

At last they arrive in Law's village in the Canton Delta. Is it as marvellous as he described? They stay with extended family in an ancient house with a large inner courtyard. The lavatories are disconcertingly backward and a smell of manure hangs over everything.

Here is a kind of agricultural *samsara*. Mulberry trees are grown around the ponds for leaves that silkworms eat, and for shade liked by the pigs and chickens that snuffle and peck under them; silkworms and pigs and chickens produce waste that go into the ponds to make plankton that feed the fish; fish waste and silt are dredged from the ponds to fertilize the mulberry trees . . . on and on in a virtuous loop where every-thing is recycled to be reborn as new plants, new fish, another generation of pigs and chickens and humans.

The warmth of their welcome from the Law clan is tre-mendous and the cooking is as satisfying as their grandfather had described – one bite takes you back to where the carp swim and where the chickens pick their way around the green. Nearly everything is prepared with ginger and chives that smell of sweet earth. Their meals always end with fruit. The loquats and plums taste as if the landscape around them has melted into honey.

The final farewell is difficult when his grandchildren leave with Fanny at the end of the school Easter holidays. (Virtue may have stayed on a little longer.) The plan is for Fanny and Virtue to visit their father regularly from Singapore, but his grandchildren know that they will probably never see him again.

Having settled into his Canton village, Law is perhaps impatient to cast off his down-filled silk jacket in the early summer. He has been away so long that he will have forgotten the seasonal 'plum rains', named for the little yellow Chinese plums that ripen at this time. The rains bring cold bursts to the south coast of China even in June. Old farmers know not to take the weather for granted till after the Dragon Boat Festival.

Law is more used to the tropical heat than he likes to admit. His lungs are weakened by years of opium-smoking. He finds it unexpectedly difficult to cope with the cold and the damp.

He does not manage even to see through the summer. Before the end of August, he is dead.

23

Fanny and Virtue are back in China far sooner than they had expected. It is the late summer of 1935, barely half a year since Law's return. This time they have their brothers Cheng-Wah and Liang with them, to bury their father. But the sisters take charge. They spend all the money their father left them on the grandest funeral that they can buy.

There are nearly three weeks of formal mourning, filtered through ritual and ceremony. The burning of incense and funerary offerings seems endless, and monks chant through the day and night. In the background, the noise of professional mourners is constant. They trill and wail from a catalogue of codified laments[1] to broadcast the news that a man who was many things has died: a deeply honoured parent; a much-loved father; a man who was once important, an official interpreter in the British Straits Settlements.

All this is expensive, but filial. It is how to reach through the curtain of death to comfort your own.

My cousin Susan in Singapore – my mother's brother Peter's daughter – found an old photograph of the funeral. Fanny and Virtue are on a street, standing next to a heavily decorated bier. They are dressed for profound grieving in long white gowns, their heads covered with white hoods. They wear unhemmed sackcloth tunics over their robes, tied at the waist with a white sash. They look miserable. Even in the small, blurred image, you can see that Fanny's eyes are puffy from crying.

Fanny, far left; Virtue is to her left.

They arrive back in Singapore with only their father's opium pipes as keepsakes, much to the chagrin of their sisters-in-law who, anxious in lean times, were waiting in hope for property of value.

This small coda and the photo from his funeral end the story of my great-grandfather. It has grown beyond all expectation (alas, the cookbook has not). When I started on my family history, I had only a name and a fortunate guess that an old man in a photograph might be seventy years old. Yet it had been enough to give a working date for his birth and to lead me to the calamitous nineteenth-century famine that drove men from their homes. It felt little short of miraculous to then locate him in the archives of the British in Singapore. His life from seventeen to seventy is complete.

But I found I could not stop. I had to follow Fanny's story to see where it might lead, perhaps to know the woman in the photograph. And the invisible history that flows around us every day was pushing me on. My research was propelling me forward to end not here but seven years later in 1942, when world war would erupt in the Pacific.

It was the destination of my family. History would sweep on, taking with it Fanny, the interpreter's daughter.

24

A year after the death of my great-grandfather, on a freezing February night in 1936 far from Singapore, officers of the Imperial Japanese Army broke into a house in Tokyo and murdered an old man in his sleep. They riddled his body with bullets, then slashed it with a sword.

Takahashi Korekiyo was the cabinet minister in Japan who single-handedly saved his country from economic obliteration after a devastating earthquake was followed by the 1929 Depression that almost brought down America.

He was made finance minister in December 1931, months after a maverick wing of the Imperial Japanese Army invaded Manchuria. He was seventy-seven years old, but with the boldness of a man half his age he instantly took Japan off the gold standard, devalued the yen, reduced the Bank of Japan's prime rate, and printed money to spend on building projects.[1] These were unprecedented policies. Keynes's *General Theory of Employment, Interest and Money* would not be published for another four years.

Takahashi's measures worked at once. Fatally, he also bankrolled a surge in military spending even though the Japanese army was growing uncontrollable. It had invaded Manchuria without permission from Tokyo just months before Takahashi's appointment. The next year, it would assassinate his prime minister when he refused to endorse this army's puppet state in Manchuria.

But when Takahashi first took over at the finance

ministry, expanding the army and the navy seemed to solve at a stroke the need to be reflationary with the problem of unemployed young men. By 1935, the Japanese armed forces accounted for nearly half the national budget.[2] When Taka-hashi then tried to rein them back, it was too late. The military had grown too powerful to stop.

On the same night in 1936 that the officers killed Taka-hashi, their co-conspirators murdered two other cabinet ministers and bombed the Bank of Japan. The Tokyo corres-pondent for *The Times* called this 'government by assassination'.[3] A new cabinet was formed in March. It was virtually hand-picked by the military with its certainty that imperialism alone could solve all Japan's problems – its growing population, its shortage of space, its lack of the mineral resources needed for wealth.

In October, this cabinet had the temerity to issue orders to Chiang Kai-Shek's government in China.[4] Its Japanese militarists seemed to think their desires needed only to be announced unilaterally to be accepted, and took dangerous offence if they were not.

'Can you believe it?' Cheng-Wah flings his Chinese newspaper on the restaurant table as he pulls out the stool next to Fanny's. They meet occasionally for dim sum on a Sunday morning, after Fanny has been to church. He rather likes catching up with his youngest sister. His wife is not very interested in pol-itics, nor his other sister Virtue, but Fanny will listen.

'Japan wants autonomy in five of our provinces where its consulates won't have to answer to our Chinese government. And then, as if it's not already plain what Japan really wants, it dares demand that its troops be allowed all over China, supposedly to help fight the Communists!'

'I know,' Fanny says gently, 'the English newspapers have reported it too. Just as well that the Chinese government publicized these supposedly confidential demands to the world.'

'It's embarrassed the Japanese to no end,' Cheng-Wah agrees.

There was immense alarm in China over these decrees and disbelief that Chiang Kai-Shek could ignore this threat from Japan. His Kuomintang troops were still only fighting Chinese Communists. In December, extraordinarily, Chiang was kidnapped by a patriotic former warlord and held for thirteen days until he agreed to a truce with the Communists, succumbing finally to the popular wish of his countrymen that all China be united against Japan.

This was not an outcome that Japan had expected. Suddenly it was facing a larger and less digestible prey. It would have to move faster.

In April of the following year, 1937, Fanny and Virtue visit their father's grave in Canton. (Violet, twenty years old, has been left in charge of Peter and Florence in Geylang.) When they stop in Hong Kong, they go to a photo studio. It was what their father had always done: marked their visits to this colony with a photograph.

This arresting photograph is the only one of my grandmother and Fanny on their own, two sisters who loved each other so much. Virtue looks composed if sad, but there is a seascape of feelings on Fanny's face: her head is again tilted though not beseeching this time as much as emphatic. Those lips look about to part as she stares across years, and generations, to tell us something – I'm sure of it – but what?

Fanny, left; Virtue, right.

The newspapers in Canton report that the Japanese military has been troublesome in north China. Its soldiers in Manchuria, near the suburbs of Peking, practise army manoeuvres that unnerve the residents. While Peking is no longer the capital of China – moved to Nanking after Chiang Kai-Shek came to power ten years before – it still resonates in the popular imagination.

In July, after Virtue and Fanny have returned to Singapore, the Japanese storm Peking.

'Japan has invaded China!' Cheng-Wah is breathless. He has hurried to his sisters in Geylang with the news, all the way from Chinatown. 'Peking and Tientsin are in the hands of the Japanese!'

'Are you sure?' Virtue asks as Fanny tries to calm her brother down: 'When we were in Canton we read that the Japanese like performing army exercises.'

'Listen!' Cheng-Wah almost bellows at his sisters. He needs them to know how this is different, how this might be a watershed. He has no idea where it might end or why his heart pounds with such foreboding. But he finds it impossible to articulate this fear.

He manages only to say: 'They'll go for Shanghai next.'

25

On Valentine's Day in 1938, the British open their brand-new naval base in Singapore. It is the most modern in the region, equal to any in the world. There is no larger drydock anywhere else. Eleven thousand guests attend the ceremony.[1]

The whole island is treated to a dazzling military display. Fighter planes roar overhead as guns boom in the distance. The Americans send friendly warships into the harbour. In the evening, searchlights etch bright arcs in the night sky. [2] The invisible enemy, never named, is Japan. Its imperial ambitions worry other imperialists.[3]

Peter, nineteen, is at the Esplanade with his sisters and their cousins Pak-Leong and Yin-Yue to enjoy the military entertainments. The girls cover their ears when planes fly over them. The boys laugh. They finally get home after struggling through the crowds and queueing for the bus, but Peter is still full of animation.

'You should have seen the planes!' he tells Fanny and his mother Virtue. 'The girls hated the noise but they were really impressive.'

'You won't find a real war impressive,' Fanny corrects him.

Peter tries to look contrite but when he catches his sister Florence's eye, he winks.

Japan had been an ally of Britain's in the First World War and the Anglo-Japanese Alliance had held for twenty years. But the world had changed during the Great War and it was

America that Britain now needed as an ally. However, the Americans and the Japanese didn't get on. They were rivals in the Pacific. In 1919, when Japan had proposed a racial equality clause in the Treaty of Versailles, America had blocked it.

Japan had wanted its citizens treated the same as white European immigrants to the US but Australia opposed the idea, knowing that it would derail its White Australia Policy. The Australian Prime Minister William Morris Hughes managed to get on side not only others in the British contingent, but President Woodrow Wilson.

In the voting, when racial equality won a clear majority with the support of France and Italy, it was rejected by President Wilson. He decided that, after all, unanimity (not merely a majority) was required. Instead, Shantung province was taken from China and given to Japan as a sop.

In 1921, under pressure from America, Britain ended its naval partnership with Japan. It was replaced by a Four-Power Treaty that included America and France, and left Japan feeling sidelined and insecure.[4] When the idea of a naval base at Singapore was raised in 1923, Japan protested. It saw this as a threat even though it was illogical to think that if Britain planned to attack Japan at all (presumably on behalf of America), it would be from Singapore rather than Hong Kong, which was 1,500 miles nearer.[5] Nevertheless, the plans were quietly shelved. Many British politicians still felt guilty that they had dropped an old ally.

Construction did finally begin in 1928 but it was dogged by delays and ended up taking ten years.

Now those voices once raised in Britain on behalf of Japan were silent. It had invaded Peking in July 1937. By December, it had captured China's capital, Nanking. What the Japanese did there shocked everyone.

Since 1906, a division of the Imperial Japanese Army had been based in north China to protect the territory that was gained from war with Russia. Few people realized that this division, the Kwantung Army, was contaminated by a distorted samurai code that treated the conquered with dangerous contempt.

This army was also infected with a command doctrine that had been revised to pass down control from division to regiment to company.[6] This meant that power vested completely with the captain of a company, who did not have to report back up the line the brutal rape and murder of civilians or, indeed, the brutality of officers to their own men.[7]

In Nanking, corrupted morals and the habitual delegation of authority combined with the desire to subjugate.[8] The result was toxic.

European and American missionaries in Nanking witnessed indescribable depravity and their reports were beginning to find their way to newspapers around the world. It was not easy getting word out. A journalist for Reuters was stopped by Japanese soldiers when he took his account to the Shanghai telegraph office. He managed, just, to post it to Singapore instead. In it he confided that 'the scenes of horror being perpetrated in Nanking following the occupation by victorious Japanese forces' were not a temporary madness aroused by 'bloodlust' in battle, but something darker that had continued uncontrolled. [9]

What marked these war crimes apart from others was their scale. The International Military Tribunal for the Far East estimated later that twenty thousand women were raped in Nanking alone. These assaults spared no one, neither the elderly nor the young – as if the capital of the Chinese republic had to be crushed symbolically through its women.[10] The

Daily Telegraph reported in London at the end of January that children were being bayoneted and eleven-year-old girls raped.[11]

The soldiers nearly always killed those they raped, sometimes with unimaginable cruelty. What the people of Nanking remember is indelibly horrifying, almost impossible to read. But there are testimonies from the soldiers themselves. A Japanese war veteran told the writer Hiroko Sherwin of the young Chinese mother that his officer raped and then threw down a well; her crying toddler who followed to tumble in after her; the hand grenade that his officer told him to fling in after them.[12]

There is the International Military Tribunal for the Far East:

'At [. . .] we captured a family of four. We played with the daughter as we would with a harlot. But as the parents insisted that we return the daughter to them we killed them. We played with the daughter as before until the unit's departure and then we killed her.'[13]

The tribunal's files also have on record a Japanese company commander's instruction: 'Either pay them money or kill them in some obscure place after you have finished.'[14]

Except the women of Nanking were not hidden in obscure places. They were murdered in plain sight, sprawled on the street, naked from the waist down, with their legs still apart, frozen by rigor mortis, captured for a second time in photographs.[15]

Fanny's brother Cheng-Wah learns about these abominations from his Kuomintang connections in China but he cannot bear to repeat them to his sisters or to his wife. They will have to learn about them from the Singapore newspapers.

The English press is always more restrained than the Chinese, but even the *Straits Times* writes: 'The streets are strewn with numberless corpses, among them being the naked bodies of hundreds of young women. Many of these bear bayonet wounds and have been assaulted.'[16]

What Fanny reads sends a chill through her. She asks Virtue in an undertone, careful that her nieces should not hear (Violet is twenty-one; Florence is seventeen): 'Can men really be so wicked?'

Virtue's face is grim when she replies: 'Beasts would not do what they do.'

26

In October 1938, Japan invades Canton where Law was born and where he is buried. With Canton in Japanese hands, Fanny and Virtue cannot visit their father's grave. It breaks their hearts not to carry out the rites of ancestor worship that are required at his burial place – Fanny's Christian thinking stops where her Confucian certainties begin.

She has become more serious. She misses her father. He had loved her unreservedly and expressed both courage and imagination in supporting her dreams. She had lost him when he moved to Canton and lost him again when he died so soon after. She is losing him a third time now that travelling to Canton is out of the question. She tries to keep his memory alive by clinging tighter to the Confucian ideals that he had cherished (even if he was not always able to fulfil them himself).

In her eighties, my mother was waiting one day at the doctor's clinic when another old lady walked in. My mother looked up. 'Esther!' she exclaimed. 'Violet!' the lady answered. They had been neighbours in Geylang before the Second World War. My mother had taught the younger Esther to dance. They had not met in more than sixty years but they recognized each other instantly.

I was introduced to Esther and her daughter Rosemary later, on a visit to Singapore to see my mother. They took me to where Fanny had lived in Geylang. Esther said that on their street, they hardly ever saw Fanny. She kept to herself, following a particular tradition of female conduct that was considered correct in China. Confucius believed that women should be modest as well as chaste and loyal. In the sixteenth century, such female rectitude reached an apotheosis.

A cult emerged in imperial China where widows or girls whose fiancés had died refused to marry other men. If threatened with rape or forced to marry against their will, they killed themselves. They were called 'chaste widows' or 'faithful maidens' and they were acclaimed as role models,[1] upholding community honour.[2] Public arches or shrines were built in their memory, inscribed with their stories.[3]

By the late Ming dynasty in the seventeenth century, their extreme fidelity had become a metaphor for loyalty to the state and their martyrdom resonated strongly with the gentry in a time of crisis – when the Chinese Ming dynasty collapsed, courtiers and their families killed themselves in allegiance to their Emperor.

The Manchus who took over from the Ming carried on promoting the cult of chastity into the twentieth century,[4] eager to show that they understood and accepted Chinese culture. Imperial awards were given based on merit, keeping local bureaucrats busy. Seeking out women of virtue to verify their stories wasn't easy. Unlike sworn spinsters, who were noisy and sociable (unmarried from self-interest rather than moral choice), these ladies were reclusive. One faithful maiden was so solitary, not even her family was allowed near. She never left her room and had food passed to her in a basket through her window.[5]

Fanny is private. When she gets home from school she goes straight indoors. She doesn't linger outside. Stepping into the relative cool of her house after the hot walk back in the bright afternoon, she immediately relaxes. Virtue always brings her a glass of water. Then she rests before working, listening out for Violet, Peter and Florence as each comes in from visiting friends or from school.

Virtue never lets her help prepare the evening meal or do very much else around the house. Fanny is at her most content when she sits at supper with the children she has helped bring up, though you would never guess it from her face. She keeps a carefully severe exterior and admonishes, advises or adjures, whichever is the appropriate response to the stories that these vibrant young people tell – Violet, now twenty-one, Peter, nineteen, and Florence, seventeen.

Later, when I asked my mother or her cousins to describe their aunt Fanny, the adjectives that always came up were 'strict' or 'stern'. The charming girl at university had become defined by her responsibilities. She was now the head of their household, a role that was once her father's. Virtue consulted her on everything and trusted her judgement implicitly. It must have felt like a weight.

Fanny is only thirty-one, but she dresses in sober colours. It is proper that she does not wear anything bright. In spite of trying to appear as plain as possible, she is still striking to look at. She gives the impression of being tall when she is tiny, little over 5 feet. She wears a slim gold watch on her left wrist and sometimes a light wrap around her shoulders. The neighbours who catch a glimpse of her describe her as 'elegant'.

27

Fanny still has the one close friend, Nyong. She helps run her brother-in-law's tailoring business. Seng-Choy is very well connected, one of the few Chinese in the colony to be a member of its municipal commission.[1] His 'Wing Loong Merchant Tailors' on High Street has a large European clientele. His workmen can run up a full dress suit, of which he is very proud.

Seng-Choy owns a holiday house by the sea in Changi on a coastal road named after his business, Wing Loong Road. Changi's coconut plantations were cleared in 1926 to make way for the Royal Air Force, and a little village has sprung up to provision the families of the RAF. The picturesque beaches nearby have become popular for second homes. A prison and more barracks have been added as part of Singapore's coastal defence.

Fanny sometimes visits the Changi house with Nyong. Like other seaside bungalows in Singapore, it would have had a garden of coarse grass and ixora, whose tightly packed blooms provide protection from the salt air.

The two friends like to sit at the top of the beach under a canopy of sea hibiscus trees. Ants fall giddily from the heart-shaped leaves and papery yellow flowers, stomachs heavy with sap. What might they have talked about, shading their eyes from the blue flare off a flat sea?

In February 1939, Japan invades Hainan Island off the south coast of China. Hainan is only a hop from Vietnam and the rest of Southeast Asia, though few people paid heed apart from Chiang Kai-Shek. His wartime capital of Chung-king in China is bombed every day by the Japanese but he still finds time for a press conference to warn against Japan's 'inordinate ambition' and to predict that by taking Hainan, Japan is 'sowing the seeds for a war in the Pacific', even 'incit-ing a world war'.[2] Nanking is already last year's news, though it has not been forgotten. Can any woman forget?

'Did you know that in China they built bridges for women who were virgins?' Fanny asks.

'What?' Nyong laughs. 'Old spinsters like us?' They are both thirty-two.

'No, no, girls who killed themselves to avoid being raped, or if they had to marry another man if their fiancés had died.'

'And they built bridges for them?' Nyong sounds incredulous.

'In China, it wasn't always wrong to kill yourself. Some-times it was honourable – when it was to protect your chastity, or out of loyalty, or even to express regret. The last Ming Emperor killed himself when he lost his empire . . . then his loyal ministers and wives did the same.'

Nyong grimaces.

Fanny carries on: 'We remember them now as heroes.'

In April, Japan occupies the Spratly Islands just north of British Borneo, deeper into Southeast Asia. Is it merely mischief-making or is it putting building blocks in place?

No one worries about Japan when, five months later, Ger-many attacks Poland with no warning. The making of history, so often unseeable, is sometimes crystal clear. Britons the world over are electrified by the news two days later that their country has declared war on Germany.

For the moment it is a phoney war with the announcement of war made but fighting not yet begun; however, in Singapore the Malaya Patriotic Fund is organized at once in aid of Britain. Its women become indefatigable in fundraising. The Arab ladies throw lunch parties, the Chinese *tai tais* host tea dances. Miss Rosemary Dant plays the cello. At Mrs Baxter's film premiere of *Lady Hamilton*, Mrs Elder looks after the programmes, Mrs Baker and Mrs Scrimgeour manage the tickets, and Mrs Knuffman runs the bar.[3] Lady Thomas leads a band of women to make clothing for men at the front. Her husband the Governor's own pyjamas are used as a pattern.

The expectation of war in Europe turns out to be good for Singapore. Rubber prices climb in 1940.[4] The city hums with bullock carts, hundreds of rickshaws, thousands of motorcars, even more bicycles. They contend with each other and the trolleybuses for mastery of the roads.

Life has become much more comfortable for those who can afford it. The Cold Storage Company sells fresh meat from Australia, fresh milk, ice cream, and locally brewed Tiger Beer. Robinson and Co. satisfy all other needs from hats and perambulators to canteens of silver cutlery. Its cocktail dresses are from Paris. More Englishwomen are persuaded to live in the colony than ever before when only a few years earlier, there was just one European woman to every fifty bachelors.[5]

Englishmen delight in the greater presence of their countrywomen even if they seem intent on replicating suburbia, 'usually Surbiton'.[6] Lunches have to be hosted, lunch menus devised, personal recipes entrusted to local magazines, most memorably one for 'Grenadilla Appetiser': put in a glass alternate layers of sherry and the pulp and seed from a green passion fruit and 'swallow in one mouthful'.[7] Mrs Kinsey recommends fowl kedgeree for luncheon, to be eaten with spoon and fork 'as with curry'.

There are servant problems for women who have never had servants. Mrs Barbara Goodwick is especially exercised by her gardener, who seems to require salary advances for all religious festivals (Christian, Hindu, Muslim and Buddhist), not just his own.

The actress Marie Ney has arrived in Singapore, a star of Hitchcock's *Jamaica Inn* who has acted with Redgrave and Thorndike at the Old Vic in London. She is raising money for the Malaya Patriotic Fund at the Victoria Theatre with a three-hour enactment of nine Shakespearean heroines – Viola, Ophelia, Beatrice and Queen Katherine, among others. This was possibly eight more than her British audience could digest. They do love a bit of Noël Coward. The reviewer at the *Singapore Free Press* is very gallant: 'Miss Ney had obviously gone to a very great deal of trouble to arrange and rehearse her programme . . .'[8]

I discovered Marie in an old magazine of the Association of British Malaya, once a powerful lobby for the colony's wealthy merchants. She had an interesting rather than a beautiful face but I was struck by her because she was nearly the same age as my grandmother at the time – both in their forties – and yet her life could not have been more different from Virtue's nor, indeed, Fanny's.

Marie had married late, at the age of thirty-five, to a rich and dashing Malayan planter, Thomas Menzies. Already, her life had diverged irrevocably from Virtue's. Which wealthy

Chinese man would marry a woman over twenty-five, and an actress? Menzies also accepted that his wife should be in London to nurture her career while he lived in Malaya. Only Britain's declaration of war made him feel that Marie was safer by his side, even if there was still no actual fighting.

In May, the month after Marie's performance of the Shakespeare heroines, there is a Blitzkrieg on the Netherlands and France. The phoney war is over. With real war there begins a game of follow-the-leader with Japan always acting just after a German escalation of the European war. When the Battle of Britain is initiated in July, and the Blitz on British cities in September, first Japan occupies the airfields of northern Indochina, then it moves in on the region.

By the end of 1940, Japan is firmly in French Indochina and therefore Southeast Asia. It controls north Vietnam.

But as Hitler has extended the European war to Africa, the anxiety is over Germany not Japan even after it joins the Germans and Italians in a tripartite pact. Japan hasn't declared war on Britain. It is still possible to think it wants north Vietnam only to stop arms being smuggled into China.

In Fanny's and Virtue's gentle Geylang household, no one is worrying about the Japanese in Indochina. A skirmish of a different sort is being instigated: Violet, twenty-four and unmarried, has turned up with a baby.

28

The baby is not her own but this makes it barely less shocking for Violet's chaste, mostly female family, because she wants to keep it.

Fanny is marking schoolwork in the kitchen and Virtue is washing green leafy *choi sum* ahead of the evening's supper when Violet arrives home by rickshaw with a baby.[1] She tells the older women airily that if they don't want the infant she'll go straight to her grandmother, her father Chang's mother, who has agreed to look after the baby if they won't have her in the house.

Fanny is furious. She understands this is not just an act of rebellion on her niece's part but her condition for a truce.

Fanny still teaches in Geylang to support her older sister Virtue. It is now the spring of 1941 and Virtue has lived these last eight years in circumstances beyond what she once imagined possible. She lodges in a fine small house with a little garden at the front where she has planted jasmine and pomegranate. Her three children have had the unalloyed luxury of full-time education.

Peter, twenty-two, has finished at the Raffles College and is hoping to study engineering. Violet, twenty-four, and Florence, twenty, were each taught in English right through secondary school. This means that neither is fixed to the necessity of marriage. Respectable employment is an alternative. Violet went to secretarial college and Florence is a typist.

It was Fanny who made this possible. She gave Virtue hope in place of despair when she decided, eighteen years before as a sixteen-year old girl, that she would take a vow of spinsterhood in order to support her older sister.

Therefore, Virtue has shown her gratitude to Fanny with a significant gift: my mother Violet. She has 'given' her eldest daughter to Fanny, with the unspoken presumption that Violet too will never marry.

I found this out only a year or two before my mother died, when I was talking to her friend Daisy, who was Nyong's niece. Daisy was as close to my mother as her aunt had been to Fanny.

'Did your mother never mention . . . ?' Her eyes had searched my face. 'Ah, I suppose she wouldn't have. Sworn spinsters like Fanny often adopted unwanted young girls to bring up to be like them, to care for them when they grew old. These foster girls also looked after the spinsters' spirit tablets after they died. Your mother was promised to her aunt. I don't think she was expected to marry.'

I must have looked confused because Daisy explained: 'If she married she couldn't have looked after her aunt or kept her memory alive after she died. I don't suppose Fanny worried about spirit tablets as she was supposed to be Christian, but she wouldn't want to be forgotten or to have her grave neglected.'

To begin with, as Violet was neither an orphan nor a cast-off, she simply thought that she was someone in whose future her aunt took a particular interest. Though she loved nothing more than playing with those cousins who also lived with their grandfather, she also liked being singled out when she turned nine to go to school with her young aunt, especially when they went at first in a carriage owned by Fanny's friend.

But then her mother Virtue learned from Fanny how education was important, and even more important for a girl whose vocation was perhaps not to marry and who would have to be self-reliant.

Virtue beat Violet's legs with a rattan cane if she did not come within the top three of her class of forty at primary school. (The headstrong Law sisters had been allowed by a loving father to think they might always be right.) This was to instil in Violet the importance of excelling at her studies. 'You could lose a mountain of gold,' Virtue said, 'but no one can take your education from you.' Violet never understood why this was so vital for her.

Violet looks up when she hears giggling and sees a tangle of legs disappear out of the front door. They belong to Peter and Florence and their cousins. 'Concentrate,' her young aunt Fanny says, tapping her finger on Violet's open book. 'When you finish you can go and play.' She looks at Violet's mournful face. She says, 'You have to work harder because you are cleverer,' as if that could console her.

Fanny and Virtue placed great hope in Violet as she began to do well, later allowing themselves to dream that she might one day be among the scattering of girls in the colony to study medicine or to have a university degree. They learned from what Fanny had accomplished with just a year at university that they could aim high. Fanny's career was the baseline, but if Violet worked hard she could be more than a woman of independent means. She could bring distinction to her family.

The only impediment to their plan was a certain idleness in their protégée and a rather too flat nose with large nostrils, to which Chinese physiognomists worryingly ascribed the attributes of extravagance and self-indulgence. This became more evident as Violet turned into a young woman in Geylang.

She loved eating well. If she was given something at dinner that she didn't like, she would empty a glass of water into her bowl of rice and eat that as a protest. She loved fashion. She spent far too much time looking at pictures of cheongsams in the very latest Shanghai or Hong Kong styles. She was extremely sociable. She was teaching her young neighbour Esther the foxtrot.

Therefore, despite those regular beatings when she was a child, Violet turned out not to have the aptitude (or the inclination) to study at the colony's college of medicine. This was unfortunate. She had not managed to win a scholarship to a university abroad and there was still no university in Singapore or Malaya. It was beyond Fanny's resources to send Violet to Hong Kong.

Fanny decided, pragmatically, that her niece could then do worse than be a secretary instead. She had Violet moved in her final year at secondary school from the Methodist Girls' – where the second language was Latin – to the Convent of the Holy Infant Jesus, where it was French. 'What's the use of a dead language?' Fanny asked, of no one in particular.

Violet finished her Senior Cambridge examinations with a creditable clutch of results and qualified at secretarial college. But then she heard that her good friend Nan and her sister, two outgoing Straits Chinese girls, had joined a maternity hospital as trainee nurses. They said it was convivial. It sounded more fun than working in an office. Violet thought that she might follow them.

'Are you sure, Vi?' her aunt asks drily: 'It seems to me you've only got time for dancing.' But Fanny accepts that nursing is a genteel enough occupation for a young woman, though she had once hoped her niece might be the doctor.

Violet was attached to a free maternity hospital near Serangoon Road, training under British nurses. She loved the company of the other trainees. She adored Christmas, when the wards were decorated with tinsel and the young Asian nurses were treated to a feast of tinned consommé, roast chicken, sausages, ham and tinned asparagus. Matron served fruit punch with more than a splash of gin to get them all dancing.

But she didn't much enjoy the actual work.

Violet left the hospital after less than a year. It was one thing not to like the sight of blood, another not to like dirty nappies either. Matron had to scold her before she would change a baby.

Fanny sits down with her niece. She is going to be practical. 'The best thing, Vi, would be to join the government service. It has the best pensions.' She notes the wash of boredom over Violet's face and adds: 'That doesn't seem important now when you are young, but it will take care of you in your old age.'

Violet did listen to her aunt and found work at the Ministry of Finance as a secretary (one day she would be the first Asian supervisor of its statistics department). It might be boring but at least your hands were kept clean.

Fanny had been patient with her niece's vacillations, but her expectations were hardening. She needed Violet to be more serious. She would never force her into spinsterhood but it was what she hoped that Violet would choose. Romance and marriage were over-rated. Virtue's husband had another woman; Orchid's had been troublesome. Love could only disappoint: she had experienced this for herself. You might love a man forever from afar, but he would quickly move on. Fanny embraced her role as Violet's guardian. She wanted to wrap her niece in a protective film of cynicism.

She disapproved of the occasional young men who called at their home in Geylang to see Violet. There was never a young man whom Fanny and Virtue felt quite good enough. They saw off these gallants quickly with their *froideur*. It was becoming very plain that the sisters had mapped out a future for Violet that did not feature marriage.

Violet had always known that she would be responsible for her aunt when she grew old, but it was never quite spelled out to her that she must be celibate too. She was only now appreciating with force that to be her aunt's ward was also to be her apprentice in spinsterhood.[2] Her aunt revered it as a calling. She wanted Violet to value chastity as she did. She believed that she was passing on a merit.

Violet fought against this for some time but the steady grind of expectation made her decide that it was hopeless to hold out against her mother and her aunt. It was especially difficult to repudiate her mother, who felt that only Violet could repay the debt of gratitude their family owed to Fanny. If not for Fanny, where would they be now? But Violet was not giving up without a fight.

*

'Vi, you must come quickly!' Her friend Nan is on the telephone from the hospital. 'I'm keeping the baby for you but as she's so pretty, the *ayah* wants her too. If this cleaner takes her, I don't know what will happen to this poor baby. The *ayah* already has more children of her own than she can manage.'

Before Violet stopped training at the maternity hospital, she had asked her nursing friends to let her know at once if a healthy baby girl should be discarded in the wards. This was still common practice among desperate, poor Chinese. Her mother and her aunt would have to accommodate her on this at least. Even if she was not to marry, Violet wanted a daughter of her own.

She has just brought home a beautiful little newborn with a thick mop of black hair. Violet loved her on sight.

Fanny is incandescent: 'Is your mother's life so easy that she needs to look after a baby too?'

It is Virtue who makes the peace, though in her own inimitable way. She scolds Violet in Cantonese: 'You can't adopt the baby! What will people say? *I* will be her mother.'

At first, they simply call the tiny girl 'Jade' in Cantonese. Then Fanny relents. She picks an English name for the baby – Eunice, which means 'good victory'. Does it express her hope for both the war in China and the war in Europe? It seems onerous for such a little thing, though it could have been auspicious. Only, it is too late.

29

Fanny's household is willingly caught up in an infant's web of feedings, baths, cries and smiles, though it is mainly Virtue who looks after the baby. Violet works full time at the Ministry of Finance but Fanny sometimes helps with the expense of baby clothes and milk powder.

Fanny can sometimes be persuaded to keep her sister or her nieces company shopping in the centre of town even though she doesn't like crowds. She is struck by the number of European men in military uniform on the buses and on the street.[1] Churchill has been pouring British and Allied troops into Singapore since February, to ease Australia's and New Zealand's fears over Japan.[2] (Except the troops are a mirage. There aren't real tanks or battleships or aircraft carriers behind them – just a few near-obsolete planes and, to be discovered too late, the wrong type of gun.)[3]

Everyone knows the English are polite. They queue and hate to make a fuss. They never complain in a restaurant.

The Japanese are also polite, which is why the English like to think the best of them, even if they are now German allies.

But the Aussies and the Kiwis are not so polite. They dare to suggest that Japan might want to invade them. They say that their countries are already experiencing a 'pacific invasion' of the Japanese through migration.[4] Australia and New Zealand have pressed Britain for years to fortify Singapore. Only Singapore stands between them and 'the Japs'.

It is true that Japan is in a protracted campaign that it cannot afford, and that it may therefore be looking at the resources of others with more than just envy. It had expected to conquer China in weeks when it invaded at the end of 1937. It is now 1941. The war is depleting Japan's reserves of oil and alienating the US, on which it depends for more oil.[5] It feels like a steady slide into a black hole.

The Japanese are terrified that, with no mineral wealth of their own, they are permanently vulnerable to the machinations of the West and especially of Russia, with its hot breath on Japan's northern flank.

But how to proceed? The army and the navy cannot agree on whether to head north to beat back Russia, or south to help themselves to the riches of Southeast Asia.[6] Soldiers are trained in secret on tropical Hainan island for jungle warfare, just in case.

In Singapore, there are no plans for jungle training. Instead, troops are free to enjoy the delights of the city. Newly arrived officers are sometimes shocked by this 'soft living'.[7] Peter reports to his family that there were throngs of European soldiers at the amusement park where he was the previous night with friends.

There are three 'Worlds' in Singapore – the Great World, the New World, and the Gay World. They are leisure grounds like those in Shanghai with every type of entertainment from food stalls to restaurants, street jugglers to cabarets, Chinese opera, cinemas . . .

'We almost couldn't move for British and Australian servicemen,' Peter says, 'especially at the shooting galleries. They were really good!'[8]

Fanny listens carefully, not yet sure what to do with the information.

While the troops contentedly spend their money in the 'Worlds', their officers go elsewhere.

The rash of dashing men in officer uniforms has, dare one say, turned the island festive. Ever since the Grand Hotel de l'Europe closed, the Raffles Hotel is where smart Europeans meet to be sociable. Its curry tiffin lunches are extremely popular. In the evenings, you can dine on its lawn under the stars and the traveller's palms. There is a cabaret every night except Sunday. It is always full, despite a strict 'officers only' policy.

The Raffles has what it calls the 'coolest ballroom in the East', a boast meant to be taken literally.[9] The dance floor has been relocated outdoors on to the verandah overlooking Beach Road, where night breezes blow. The hoi polloi gather at its gates for a glimpse of fair-skinned women, shoulders bared, in the dancing embrace of their men.[10]

Europeans still make up only 4 per cent of the people of Singapore. There are now more than six hundred thousand non-Europeans or 'Asiatics', as the British like to call them, mainly Chinese. They crowd the food stalls along the dusty lanes of Little India and Chinatown, Sultan Street and Mosque Street, where Indian, Chinese and Malay chefs cook outdoors over brightly burning firewood.

Happily, smoke from the sticks of satay grilling on Beach Road don't reach the open ballroom of the Raffles, where a saxophone is stretching lazily for a high note. The band is one of many from Europe chancing their luck in the fashionable cities of the East. It will stop playing if a gentleman approaches the dance floor not in full evening dress.[11]

But snobbery is merely a fear of disorder. The Far East is simply too exotic. The invitation to abandon lurks in everything: the bright colours, the heat, the storms. The heavy scent of frangipani and gardenia combine at night to make ungovernable senses come alive.

No one thinks the soldiers crowding the island could suggest impending danger. On the contrary, they are the reason to feel confident. The colonial government encourages this impression. Singapore is still a 'little spot of paradise',[12] and everything carries on as normal.

The Geylang English School has its sports day in May. Fanny helps her fellow teachers to run it. She has taught at the school for eight years now and is a respected colleague. When Mrs Waddell left three years ago the headmaster who replaced her, Mr Low, decided that sports day should now be known as 'annual athletic sports' and be more competitive. Fanny is sorry that the egg and spoon, sack, potato and wheelbarrow races of previous years have mostly gone.

In June 1941, Germany invades Russia. At a stroke, it has removed Russia's threat to Japan. Japan quietly launches its 'southward advance'.[13] This is unfortunate for Singapore, expected to safeguard the mineral wealth of Malaya and the Dutch East Indies, but the Singapore newspapers seem unaware of this setback. Instead, they deride Japan's 'dilemma' – it is in a tripartite pact with Germany and Italy, but it also recently signed a treaty with Russia.[14] Its plans in Southeast Asia must surely be in disarray. Reading this, Fanny feels a surge of relief.

But in July, by threatening war, Japan forces what is now Vichy Indochina to hand over its airbases in the south near Saigon. It instantly crosses an important line. It is not widely known that Japan's land-based bombers have a much longer range than in the West.[15] Singapore is now comfortably within striking distance of its bombers.[16]

If the presence of Japan in Southeast Asia makes anyone

uneasy, they can be easily soothed by repeating what every-one thinks they know about the Japanese: they are incapable of attending to more than one thing at a time. They have a war in China. They can't possibly manage war anywhere else.

Only America is not so complacent. It is sensitive to the security of its colony in the Philippines. It retaliates immediately.

'That will teach the Japanese!' Liang waves a copy of the *Straits Times* triumphantly in front of Fanny and Virtue the moment he walks through their front door. 'They thought they could bully the French in Indochina but America has called their bluff!'

Virtue goes to the kitchen at once to fetch him a glass of home-made barley water while Fanny sits him down in their front room. It's a mercy to Virtue that she can leave either of her brothers with Fanny when they want a long discussion of the news. *She* doesn't have time to listen. There's too much to do while baby Eunice has her nap.

Liang visits his sisters at least once a week. It is no effort to keep an eye on them since he also lives in Geylang. His older brother Cheng-Wah is in Chinatown, an inconvenient distance away, and is always busy with his school.

'What do you think Britain will do?' Fanny asks, interested, though she can't help smiling at Virtue's hastily departing figure.

'Haven't you heard?' Liang gets up with excitement and is practically dancing around. 'Now that America has stopped exporting oil to Japan, the British and the Dutch are going to do the same! With no oil, Japan will have to back out of its war in China!'

*

Japan is taken completely by surprise that America should react to its annexations in Indochina with an oil embargo. It calculates that, without oil, it could collapse in two years.[17] But, far from caving in to American pressure to withdraw from Indochina, it secretly progresses plans to spread war – though with various intelligence forces at work, this is not always *so* secret.

By September, the *Singapore Free Press and Mercantile Advertiser* is writing openly that it will only be months, if not weeks, before Japan completes its bases in Indochina to make her next move – and this could be to bomb Singapore.[18]

But the residents of Singapore are not alarmed. Not everyone reads the *Singapore Free Press*. Not everyone agrees with it, though Fanny asks her eldest brother Cheng-Wah, 'Is that possible? Should we be afraid?'

Cheng-Wah reassures her: 'Of course, anything is possible. But it is very unlikely. The government is adding to our defences all the time. Just look at the number of soldiers around!'

Fanny had asked her brother to meet her for lunch after church. It's terribly convenient – by the time she travels from Geylang to the Anglican St Andrew's Cathedral near the Esplanade, she is halfway to Chinatown and a dim sum lunch. But it's not a general discussion of politics that she'd like today. There is something else that is worrying her.

She has noticed for some time that her niece Yin-Yue and her nephew Pak-Leong are very close. It has come to the point when she must speak. She takes a sip of her tea: 'You must realize too what these two young people want. But it's not fair, Eldest Brother, to let them carry on when they can never marry.'

Cheng-Wah wrinkles his brow. 'We've warned them and

they know the difficulties. But their connection is so strong that it's uncanny, almost as if . . .' He stops. Sometimes he wonders if this is what his late sister Orchid wants. He carries on: 'When something happens so naturally, should we interfere? It's not as if it's not been allowed before – in imperial China, first cousins have married when they didn't have the same surnames.' He feels the sudden need for sustenance to face up to his youngest sister. He reaches out for a basket of hot steaming buns.

'Yes, I accept that sometimes the children of sisters did marry. But it still doesn't feel quite right that the children of a brother and a sister . . .' Fanny tails off.

Cheng-Wah helps himself to pickled sliced green chillies for his dipping sauce, a Nanyang habit, chewing all the while on a bun. His sister surprises him. She's rejected tradition in so many ways – by making a public promise not to marry (those Canton spinsters were the rebels of their time), by becoming a Christian, and then by working as a professional woman. And yet she's also deeply traditional, more than many Chinese now. He says nothing.

Fanny takes another sip of her tea and decides to carry on: 'Perhaps you should just tell them not to see each other for a while. Let them meet other people, give themselves a chance.'

'Perhaps,' Cheng-Wah says.

In the same month as its editorial on a possible air attack by Japan from Saigon, the *Singapore Free Press* also announces the arrival of Duff Cooper in Singapore. Churchill has dispatched his friend as further appeasement to the Aussies and the Kiwis. Duff Cooper is a cabinet minister. He will be Churchill's eyes and ears in the colony.

Fanny may feel encouraged that a British minister is to be

based in Singapore but otherwise it makes little impression on her. Like most of the other ordinary people on the island, the 'Asiatics', she's hardly heard of Cooper. His cabinet post, Chancellor of the Duchy of Lancaster, means nothing to her at all.

Cooper will begin his assignment by reporting on how the colony is preparing for possible war. This doesn't go down well at all with the Governor, Sir Shenton Thomas. He fears Duff Cooper may undermine his own position as constitutional head of the Straits Settlements.[19] Sir Shenton doesn't worry about war in Singapore but he worries that people will worry. Confidence is everything. He has no confidence in Cooper.

It is because of the improbability – nay, the *impossibility* of war in Malaya that Duff Cooper is accompanied by his wife.

The celebrated Lady Diana Cooper is now nearly fifty but still beautiful, and witty, though not so diverting that teacups cannot clatter disapprovingly in the staid salons of Tanglin: it was 'improper' that she had been sent out during Britain's lean war years *at public expense* to be with her husband, especially as the Coopers had apparently arrived with a hundred suitcases containing Lady Diana's 'tropical trousseau' and other essentials.[20]

Singapore may not like Lady Diana, but she loves Singapore. Their Pan American flying boat, the *Anzac Clipper*, was guided in by an escort of three bombers to land near the jetty where the head of the British Far East Command, Air Chief Marshal Sir Robert Brooke-Popham, waited with a retinue of officers. The 'whole set-up', she confides mischievously, 'entirely to my liking'.[21]

She picks gardenia 'long-stalked' from her garden. She fills their home with 'clean white rugs and Oriental jars, white cushions'. She visits Chinatown, even the streets which other Englishwomen shun, where coffin-makers shape their wood and 'native' restaurants send out intriguing new aromas – 'soya? sesame?'

She strolls through the graceful colonial town she describes as 'rococo' with its 'frail pink and robin's-egg blue arcades', wondering, is this all too delicate to last?[22]

Far from the main town, east and north of two strong-smelling rivers that join before they reach the sea – the Kallang and the Geylang – Fanny is walking back from school. When she gets home, she stops for a moment in their front garden by the pomegranate tree that Peter planted years ago. She rubs a leaf between her fingers thoughtfully. There is so much going on – a baby in the house, Pak-Leong and Yin-Yue and what might happen, and all the while the background noise of possible war. She looks at the pomegranate. It has grown but it's still quite spindly. Will it last? Could it ever hold up the fruit that it might bear?

30

Despite the Governor's adamantine faith in the absurdity of war, the Americans report in November 1941 that Japan plans to be belligerent.[1] Therefore, local journalists are encouraged to declare: 'Singapore is today more strongly defended than any island of similar size anywhere in the world'; Singapore is 'one of the safest places in the world'. It is the Gibraltar of the East.[2]

Up until recently, blackout practices were low-key, about forty minutes long, and usually when nearly everyone had gone to bed.[3]

But when the Japanese move tens of thousands of troops into their bases in Vietnam and Cambodia and gather their warships in Indochinese waters, American intelligence can no longer be ignored. In the Philippines, they can see fleets of Japanese cruisers and aircraft carriers accumulate around the Spratly Islands near British North Borneo.[4] The Prime Minister of Australia takes this information so seriously, he wants to put Australia on a war footing.[5]

On 1 December 1941, Governor Sir Shenton Thomas is forced to declare a state of emergency in Singapore and Malaya, in spite of himself. He still only half believes the threat. He eschews the building of air-raid shelters or the enforcement of full blackouts at night. These would only appear defeatist to the local population and scare them. When British troops arrive in the colony for the first time, they are mesmerized by the lights of Singapore city, so unlike 'blacked-out England'. [6]

Brooke-Popham, head of British Far East Command, busies himself handing out official platitudes. The Japanese are too afraid of the British to attack Malaya.[7] The Japanese are terribly short-sighted. If the Japanese do attack, it will be Hong Kong first and they will be so exhausted by the effort that they will be easily put down.[8]

The Law family is among the many in the colony gratefully to lap up the clichés, except for Cheng-Wah whose Kuomintang sources have been uneasy since the summer with news of Japanese activity in southern Indochina. They have also learned that training has stepped up for Singapore's volunteer force, which must mean something. The Straits Settlements Voluntary Force is made up nearly exclusively of Europeans and Eurasians.[9] Sir Shenton will not recruit Chinese. He worries that he may end up arming either the local Kuomintang or Communists for an insurrection against his government.

One of the battalions of the Voluntary Force will use Fanny's school as its headquarters while the buildings are unoccupied in December, over the Christmas holidays.[10] She hurries down to Chinatown to tell her brother this. She knows he will be interested.

'Really?' Cheng-Wah looks thoughtful. 'The VF will be in Geylang English School?'

'But they will have to move out at the end of the Christmas break,' Fanny declares, 'or we won't have a school in the New Year!'

'I think, Sister, it may all take a little longer than you imagine.' Cheng-Wah puts up a hand as she objects: 'I have no idea where your schoolboys will study, but I'm sure the authorities have a plan. You'll just have to wait for the start of January to find out.'

'But what are you suggesting?' Fanny is indignant. 'That the Japanese may actually attack us? Every day, the newspapers report that we grow stronger – and as even you have said before, you only have to look around to see that it is true. *So* many soldiers and officers!'

Her brother remains implacable that there will be some sort of scuffle somewhere with Japan, most probably out at sea, though like everyone in Singapore he is confident that the British will win.

'The Japanese may target Hong Kong first,' he concedes, 'and that will give us more time to be ready.'

Fanny is therefore elated to read that the *Prince of Wales* sailed into Singapore the very day after a state of emergency was declared. It couldn't have been better timed to lift the spirits. It's on the front pages of all the newspapers. Fanny feels a glow of pride to know that the most advanced battleship of its day is here to protect their island.

Prime Ministers Curtin in Australia and Fraser in New Zealand have been clamouring for a squadron of modern fighter planes in Singapore. Churchill, constrained by a fearsome enemy in Europe, offers a state-of-the-art battleship instead. The *Prince of Wales* is virtually brand new. It is supported by the *Repulse*, a battlecruiser, and four modern destroyers. Unfortunately, her aircraft carrier escort had run aground on its maiden voyage and there are none to spare from the war in Europe. But this is no great impediment. Churchill calculates that the effectiveness of this detachment will be in its aura of menace. He calls it 'Force Z'.

*

Violet and Florence are indifferent to battleships, probably because their brother Peter talks about them so much. Their days are filled instead with the milestones that baby Eunice tosses out every day like tricks from a conjuror's hat. She is eight months old and learning to crawl. The sisters compete to see who can get her attention to crawl to them, but she seems to recognize that Violet is the one who indulges her more. She's learned to recognize the name 'Eunice' from these girls but also the Cantonese 'Jade' from the woman who looks after her and who is teaching her to say 'Ma Ma'.

'Look, Aunt!' Violet calls out to Fanny, who has come down for supper. Fanny laughs when Violet holds out a biscuit tantalizingly to Eunice (close, but not close enough) and the baby, sitting upright on the floor, falls at once to the ground on all fours and moves towards Violet at speed.

At His Majesty's Naval Base, Singapore, there is no need to crawl for canapés at the party Admiral Sir Tom Phillips is hosting on 3 December for very select guests. Red and white awning is stretched over the decks and a band plays. The men are in formal dress, the ladies look elegant. Everyone is smiling. Toasts are drunk to victory.[11]

Lady Diana is present and hugely impressed by her host, 'four-foot-nothing and sharp as forked lightning'.[12] Tom Phillips was in fact 5 feet 2, but it was true that he had a formidable brain. By the end of the evening she has a pet name for him, 'Tuan Tom', *Tuan* being the Malay honorific for any man you want to flatter.

Tuan Tom knows better than most that his ships are vulnerable without air cover (though, like nearly everyone in the West, he is unaware of Japan's true air capability). He acknowledges that he will need help from the US Navy. He wastes no time. He flies off the very next day to meet Admiral Hart and General MacArthur in Manila, but it is already too late. On 6 December, during their third afternoon of discussions, the Americans learn that the Japanese are heading towards Thailand and Malaya with a large convoy of troopships and warships; within the hour, Admiral Phillips leaves for Singapore.[13]

He holds an urgent meeting with his Allied counterparts when he arrives on the 7th. He does not know that he has only hours before the invasion of Malaya.

The Japanese approach Malaya's northeastern coast under the cover of a winter monsoon, the same monsoon that the British thought would put their enemy off. Instead, the Japanese embrace it as their cloak of invisibility.

Just after midnight they will land not just tens of thousands of men, but tanks, artillery, bicycles, rafts – even wood for the bridges they know that they must build. Their plan is to incapacitate the British airbase at Kota Baru before securing a Thai town just north over the border. Singora is of vital importance. It has a road that crosses the Kra isthmus, the narrow stem from which the whole of peninsular Malaya dangles like a jackfruit. This road will bring the Japanese from east to west, to the main system of highways in Malaya that leads down to Singapore.

After surprising the small British garrison at Kota Baru airfield, Japan focuses its attention on the US Pacific Fleet at Pearl Harbor.[14] America must be prevented from going to Malaya's rescue.

Hours later, at 4 a.m. on 8 December 1941, Japanese pilots fly over Singapore where streetlights helpfully illuminate the night.[15] They guide the pilots as they bomb airbases and parts of the town. By morning, more Japanese bombers are on their way to Hong Kong, Guam and US targets in the Philippines.

Japan, believed to be incapable of simultaneous warfare, has just pitched the Pacific into the Second World War.

Admiral Phillips is under pressure to act fast after the bombing. It is completely against the instincts of a man like him to head for cover. It is obvious that he must sail as soon as possible towards the Japanese off the east coast of Malaya to do what he can. He leaves in the late afternoon of 8 December to head north. He has, of course, no aircraft carrier. He asks for and is told at first that fighter protection can be arranged.[16] But he learns in the night that the British are quickly losing control of their aerodromes in north Malaya. Air cover is no longer possible.

Nevertheless, he decides to carry on. He must believe that the mere sight of his squadron will scare off the Japanese. He is so confident, he has brought journalists with him.[17] Instead, he is spotted by enemy planes and on the morning of 10 December, his ships attract a swarm of Mitsubishi G3M2s.[18] They take turns to score direct hits on the *Prince of Wales* and the *Repulse*.

The crew stay at their stations, engulfed in thick smoke. They leap overboard only when ordered to abandon ship – 'God be with you' – into a sea emulsified by thick, black oil. The *Repulse* sinks first; the *Prince of Wales* fights on, desperately firing from every available gun as it lists badly to port. The admiral is clearly visible on its bridge with his captain by his side. Neither man moves. Then it goes down.[19]

A week after his triumphant arrival in Singapore, Tuan Tom is dead.

31

The bombing of Singapore stops so quickly, most people think the air raid is a drill. Fanny and her sister's family in Geylang sleep through it all in the pre-dawn darkness of 8 December 1941. Even baby Eunice. Some of the booms are so distant, they hardly register.

But as most of the civilian damage is in crowded China-town where Fanny's brother Cheng-Wah lives, she and the rest of her family soon hear about the genuine fright he has had: sixty people killed and many more injured. It could have been him! The wooden houses of Chinatown caught fire like matches.

Cheng-Wah's contacts at the Kuomintang are in a state of hyperactivity. No one predicted that the Japanese would materialize out of the war in China to fly over Singapore 3,000 kilometres away. However, the evidence is impossible to deny.

Fanny, Virtue and Liang are all in Chinatown to see Cheng-Wah and his family. 'We were woken by noise like celestial thunderclaps.' Their eldest brother looks pale. 'I thought the sky had fallen.'

'Or the earth beneath us had erupted,' his wife adds as she quietly serves them tea. She looks worn out. Virtue takes the tray of cups from her and makes her sit down. Fanny gives her a sympathetic look.

Cheng-Wah continues: 'I tried to go to where houses have

been bombed to see if I could help, but soldiers had the whole area cordoned off and wouldn't let me in.'

'Not everyone is as public-spirited as you, Eldest Brother.' Liang is shaking his head. 'There are those who just want to look. Then they spread stories that frighten people even more. Though my colleagues in the police do say there are enough body parts to fill an abattoir.'

'But how did this happen?' Fanny looks round them helplessly. 'How did the Japanese go from being no threat at all to murdering our neighbours? We were told again and again that they were too far away, too disorganized . . .' She trails off in confusion.

The others are silent.

The English-language newspapers are urged to play down events and in the following days they hardly mention anything as trivial as a bomb. As they cannot ignore it completely, they present Chinatown instead as a series of cheery vignettes: survivors swap jokes as they rake through the rubble for their belongings: a man with a heavily bandaged head waits contentedly in a queue for his lunch.

Sir Robert Brooke-Popham issues his Order of the Day: 'We are ready. We have had plenty of warning and our preparations are made and tested . . . We are confident. Our defences are strong and our weapons efficient.'[1]

Everyone believes him, especially the Governor.

But on the mainland of Malaya, a pattern is being set that will dog the British all the way south. They will be constantly surprised by the speed, intensity and sophistication of an enemy they had thought would be unprepared and ill equipped. The Japanese always arrive sooner than expected. They don't stop to draw breath. When they attack Alor Star airfield near the Thai border, the British retreat with such haste that the porridge is still warm in the officers' mess.[2] By the middle of December, all British planes have been withdrawn to Singapore.[3] The Japanese control the airfields of northern Malaya.

And the Japanese are landing tanks. The British have no tanks of their own. The British believe tanks to be unsuitable for jungle warfare. Therefore, they have no anti-tank guns.

The front pages carry a bulletin, 'BRITISH FRONTIER IN NORTH MALAYA UNBROKEN', describing the few casualties among the troops and their excellent morale.[4]

But Fanny's brother Cheng-Wah is no longer so easily reassured. The Japanese could bomb Chinatown again. The next time, his family may not be so lucky. He has found accommodation in a new housing estate, built by the British to relieve congestion in Chinatown. It is about 3 kilometres to the west of where they live.

'But what's the point of moving when it's still close to Chinatown?' Cheng-Wah's wife is unhappy at the idea of uprooting their family. 'We could be bombed there too.'

'Because the flats there are made of something new called reinforced concrete,' Cheng-Wah explains patiently. He says 'reinforced concrete' in English. He can't think of a Cantonese equivalent. 'It is very strong, so even if our neighbours are hit by bombs we won't burn as quickly as here in Chinatown in our houses made of matchwood!'

His wife will soon see and appreciate for herself the three- and four-storey blocks that are designed in the fashionably aerodynamic style known in the West as Streamline Moderne. All the flats have electricity and mains sanitation. As this is the first public housing estate in the colony, there is even an underground air-raid shelter for civilians, the only one on the island.

Not everything is perfect about this housing project of course, which is why there are still unoccupied flats. The British town planners wanted to attract the Chinese who were suffering most from overcrowding. But, in a master-stroke of cultural blindness, they built the estate on the site of a former cemetery, ignoring the genuine fear of ordinary Chinese of anything to do with the dead. It is extremely bad feng shui.

But Cheng-Wah is a modern man. He had been in Nan-king when, after a continuous history of three thousand years, imperial China had ended, to be replaced by a republic. He knows that change is possible. This is not the time for obstructive superstition.

'But it's on old burial ground!' his wife continues to object. 'And what about the name? Tiong Bahru means New Ceme-tery. It's an unlucky name for an unlucky place!'

Cheng-Wah looks at his wife and shakes his head, as if to say that she should know better than to mention something so silly. They move into a fourth-floor flat in Tiong Bahru.

Days after bombing Singapore, the Japanese cross the Kra isthmus. They are now on the west coast of Malaya, ready to take hold of the critical trunk road that the British so oblig-ingly built on this side of the peninsula. It runs from north to south straight down to Singapore.[5]

They break through the first defensive line at Jitra and force the British into retreat down Malaya. Now 'all' they have to do is to move steadily south against what they believe to be a superior enemy. Kuala Lumpur, capital of the Feder-ated Malay States, is 450 kilometres away; impregnable

Singapore, jewel of Southeast Asia, another 800 kilometres further. It must have been a daunting thought, but the Japanese infantry mount their bicycles and pedal on.

It is at least a plan. The British now have no plan at all.

'Very nice,' Liang says, admiring the modern lavatory. His sisters told him to visit their brother in Tiong Bahru and not to forget to bring a bag of eight or ten oranges with him (both lucky numbers) to wish Cheng-Wah good fortune in his new home. Virtue and Fanny, fruit-laden, had already had their tour of Cheng-Wah's flat and were full of compliments about how bright and airy it was compared to the dingy room that he had occupied in Chinatown. 'And so much more space!' they had said, one after the other, nodding approvingly. It's a distraction from worrying about the Japanese. The newspapers are full of anodyne assurances, but doubt is creeping in. The sinking of the *Prince of Wales* troubles Fanny. A clot of fear is growing inside her, which she does her best to ignore.

Cheng-Wah's wife and children have gone to the shops for various odds and ends they never knew they needed until they moved from a single room to this three-bedroom flat. They are constricted of course, as always, by Cheng-Wah's very limited budget.

Cheng-Wah sits his younger brother down for a frank talk. Liang is good at languages, like their father. He is now working for Police Special Branch as an interpreter. He may be privy to some interesting insights. Cheng-Wah is wondering if Singapore is as safe as the British say. 'Tell me, what have you heard about the situation in Malaya?'

Liang repeats what he knows: 'Apparently air cover is essential for defending Singapore, but in all these years

Britain has not sent the planes we need. We've not worried about it too much before because we thought we could rely on American help from Pearl Harbor and the Philippines . . .'

'I understand.' Cheng-Wah sighs, nodding. 'That's gone.'

'Exactly! As have our airbases in Malaya and our warships. Now everything depends on the army.' Liang lowers his voice: 'The trouble is, the army was always supposed to support the navy or the air force, not take the lead in defence. There's a suspicion they're not sure what to do next.'

'But the British far outnumber the Japanese.' Cheng-Wah frowns as he concentrates. 'They have guns and troops; they still have the upper hand?' It wasn't meant to sound like a query, but it does.

'Let's hope,' Liang replies.

32

Beautiful Penang has fallen to the Japanese!

Governor Sir Shenton Thomas and Duff Cooper tussle over whom to save. Sir Shenton orders a full news blockade but the awful truth seeps out anyway: this British settlement has been evacuated only of its Europeans.

As the Japanese complete their capture of Penang on 19 December 1941, Duff Cooper goes on radio from Singapore to assert that though 'the majority' of Penang's civilians were to be extracted as British forces retreated, it was 'obvious that the whole population could not be evacuated in the time or in the shipping which was available, and many doubtless who had their homes and families there and had lived there all their lives preferred to remain'.[1] He wishes them the best of luck.

His broadcast blows like an icy draught over the 'Asiatics' of Singapore, the British collective for the Chinese, the Indians and the Malays.

The Governor lets it be known he is appalled that evacuees were picked on the basis of race.[2]

Peter's home-made crystal receiver has been replaced by one of the ever-cheaper radios that you can now buy off the shelf, but he's still in charge of switching it on.[3] He's huddled before it now with his sisters and his aunt. (Virtue doesn't understand English and will get a translation later.)

They are shocked by what they hear.

The young people turn to Fanny. 'What do you think, Aunt?'

She is upset but she knows she mustn't show it. 'It's too early to tell. Let's see what happens in the next few days.'

'I don't believe the British only helped their own people to leave Penang!' Violet is defiant at the news. My mother did always have complete faith in the British. 'They wouldn't just leave the Chinese!'

'What makes you so sure?' asks Florence, born with my grandmother Virtue's healthy scepticism.

'It does seem to be what Mr Cooper implied,' Peter agrees with their youngest sister. 'If you listened carefully.' He is quiet for a moment; then he looks at Violet. 'So you think that in Penang, the Chinese, Indians and Malays wanted to stay for the Japanese?'

It has only been three years since 1938, when Japanese soldiers raped and massacred the civilians of Nanking in China. No one is ignorant of the horror, least of all Fanny. If Singapore should collapse, will they be abandoned too?

Duff Cooper wants martial law declared. Sir Shenton resists. The bombing of Singapore was like a lightning strike. The skies have been clear since. Newspapers must hold back the truth, for 'morale'. They publish photographs of refugees from Penang – European women and children – who are smiling and healthy and washed and who carry neatly packed luggage. They are put in hotels or housed with willing families.

The authorities are assiduous in affirming that everything is under control in 'Fortress Singapore'. These official assurances sound like guarantees. Therefore, life in the colony happily carries on.

Christmas is round the corner. Nightclubs and ballrooms are more popular than ever. The catering is good. At the Capitol and Cathay you can dine on grapefruit with maraschino, or clear oxtail soup, before a main course of English capon or lamb. At the Raffles Hotel you can order Château d'Yquem with your pudding.[4]

The Trio Granados is playing at the Seaview Hotel while at the Capitol, they have managed something of a coup: Jeanette MacDonald and Nelson Eddy, fresh from their success in Noël Coward's *Bitter Sweet*, sing to the backing of the New Moon.

On Christmas Day, the Japanese seek out Singapore's 'Asiatics' with their propaganda.[5] Flying from Penang, their pilots drop snowdrifts of paper over the island. The messages on these leaflets are laughable: 'Burn all the white devils in the sacred white flame of victory!'[6]

Everyone is cheered by Churchill's assurance to Australia that Singapore will not fall.

In Geylang, the Law sisters sit down with Peter and Florence to an 'English' lunch prepared by Violet, who cannot cook. (In later life she had to learn and cooked beautifully, only very slowly – as if embroidering flowers, her sister Florence liked to say, not as a compliment.) Just as well there is no question of a roast, as they have no oven. Virtue braises or steams or fries everything over a charcoal fire.

Violet is trying to replicate the feast that Matron served last Christmas at the maternity hospital. She went to Cold Storage, the colony's purveyor of fine European food, to buy a small cooked ham. Fanny is aghast to hear how much it cost. They sit stiffly round the table and eat it cold, with slices of white loaf, butter, and sliced cucumber and tomatoes. Baby Eunice is on Virtue's lap, chewing on a bit of bread without much interest. That night, when Virtue chops up the leftovers to stir-fry with vegetables and serve hot with steamed rice, they wolf it down.

On Boxing Day, they are all deflated by the news that Hong Kong has fallen. Then a neighbour drops by with the rumour that another prosperous Malayan town has just been captured by the Japanese, though newspaper headlines soon declaim, regarding Ipoh's defeat: 'British Withdrawal According to Plan'.[7] Ipoh is just 175 kilometres north of Kuala Lumpur.

Late on the night of 29 December, Japanese planes attempt a few more raids on Singapore, but there is minimum damage as they are seen off promptly by the British. Duff Cooper manages finally to have martial law imposed.[8]

But the colony's small community of Europeans isn't passing up this chance to celebrate their New Year's Eve (the dates are different for a Malay, Indian or Chinese New Year) even if the dancing has to be behind blackout curtains. Officers in beautifully pressed uniforms step out with girls in heels and sparkles, some of them young Queen Alexandra's nurses from the island's new British Military Hospital.

Occasionally the dancing pauses at the wail of a siren and the call of the ack-ack guns. Then the music resumes to the sound of champagne corks popping, and laughter. 'Tomorrow?' the revellers sometimes stop to ask. 'We'll think about that . . . tomorrow!' they cheerfully answer.[9] Some of these young people will never be so happy again.

On New Year's Day, the bombing of Singapore resumes. This time it doesn't stop.

33

Fanny winces as the air-raid siren starts to howl. A month ago, no one believed the Japanese could trouble Singapore. Now, in January 1942, they are all resigned to indigestion as Mitsubishi bombers fly over the island twice a day every day, at breakfast and at lunch.[1]

The bombs are aimed at Keppel Harbour or the naval base in Sembawang. Both are mercifully far from Fanny and Virtue in Geylang, though recently they've sounded nearer.

Fanny looks back wistfully on the days that passed so slowly after Christmas when her teaching duties were suspended. She understands now that monotony is tranquillity.

As Churchill wants to be sure of victory in Singapore, he has appointed a Supreme Commander to take overall charge. General Sir Archibald Wavell will head the American-British-Dutch-Australian Command. Everyone refers to it as ABDACOM, which trips off the tongue like the notes of a cha-cha. And the ineffectual Brooke-Popham has been replaced.

Except Wavell removes himself to Java and takes Brooke-Popham's successor with him.

Duff Cooper announces that Wavell's appointment has made his own redundant. The Coopers depart Singapore as the Japanese occupy Kuala Lumpur on 11 January (no fighting required, the British had left). They wait at the airport, unable to leave as bombs fall.

Lady Diana asks for a drink: 'I said, "Boy, give me a last gin-sling." Of course he thought I said "large" and got me a beer-glass full. The result was wonderful, and I survived a very trying time without a qualm.'[2]

With Duff Cooper gone and Wavell in Java, there is no longer anyone senior in Singapore besides Governor Sir Shenton Thomas and Lieutenant-General Percival, a tall, thin man with buck teeth and a toothbrush moustache. He had helped to write a paper four years before on how the Japanese might attack Singapore from the north. It was ignored.[3]

The Governor still believes that victory is possible. Lieutenant-General Percival thinks they have already lost the war.[4]

Cheng-Wah drops in on his sisters in Geylang. Virtue and Fanny fuss over their elder brother, grateful for the diversion. But he brings disturbing news: 'This morning the Japanese planes – someone counted twenty-seven! – dropped their bombs again in the middle of town.' The sisters exchange glances. They have a feeling that they know what their brother is going to say.

A top-floor flat has come vacant in New Cemetery, Tiong Bahru. No one wants to live on the top floor, not since Japanese bombs started falling daily. But Cheng-Wah insists: 'It's got to be better than where you are now.'

Geylang is uncomfortably close to the island's only civil aerodrome, Kallang Airport. The Japanese have been pounding the military bases at RAF Tengah, RAF Seletar and RAF Sembawang. It is only a matter of time before they turn their attention on Kallang. Once they start, the nearby houses of

Geylang will incinerate in a trice. Like those of bomb-ravaged Chinatown, many are built from wood.

Fanny sees the sense of what her eldest brother says and Virtue is in complete agreement, so they start to pack.

Virtue is in charge of the kitchen: the pots and pans, the bowls and chopsticks, cups and spoons. Fanny looks after the bedding. Peter is to move some of the furniture with the help of his uncle Liang – a few chairs and a table, a chest of drawers.

Fanny has paid for the hire of a small lorry, but it cannot take very much. Perhaps they only bring their mattresses with them, not the bed-frames. They certainly don't pack all their clothes. They expect to be back in a few months when the war will surely be over.

Violet and Florence take turns to look after baby Eunice and to help Virtue sweep the house to leave it tidy. They put sugar in an old milk tin and leave it by the front door with a sack of rice. The condiments (salt in an earthenware jar and soy in a bottle) will be bundled together with an assortment of things in the gunny sacks that Peter brought home. He has watered the garden. Fanny supervises and worries about the weather. It shouldn't rain but if it does, the mattresses will get soaked in the lorry's open back.

Fanny finds it unexpectedly hard to lock up her pretty house with its brick façade garlanded by plaster fruit and flowers. They have lived here for nine years. She tells the others to wait outside while she makes a final check. She walks around a last time, looking out of a bedroom window, feeling a tile on a wall, touching a cupboard that they've had to leave behind. This is where she created a home for Virtue and her children and even an unexpected baby. It's where she made their little family real (which had been a distant hope), where she kept them safe. She feels suddenly grateful. But she also feels as if she's leaving a protective shell.

The actress Marie Ney is still in Singapore. (I found her again in the journal *British Malaya*. It felt like bumping into an old friend. This time I got to hear her voice directly as she had written an article for the magazine.) Marie has joined the British Malayan Broadcasting Corporation on Caldecott Hill, where its new director of talks, fresh from Blitzed-out London, is putting on a radio play about Occupied France – ignoring bombed-out Singapore. Marie is one of its stars.

Like many Englishwomen, she has put off leaving Singapore even as the war grows impossible to ignore. Her beautiful house in the centre of town has been commandeered by the military. Australian troops camp on its wide lawns. Marie and her husband Thomas Menzies will soon have to move to a Raffles Hotel already bursting at the seams. Families bivouac in its lobbies and corridors.

The ripple of refugees that began with the fall of Penang became a tidal wave after Kuala Lumpur. They come in their hundreds of thousands, of all races. They arrive not just on boats and trains but any way they can, jammed into buses or the backs of lorries. They look terrified. Their belongings are not neatly packed.

There is nowhere to put them. While European refugees cram in the common parts of hotels, Asian refugees sleep rough on the stairs inside buildings or out on the walkways. The half-million people on Singapore Island is swelling to a million just as the Japanese turn their attention to bombing the city. The aerodromes that were their targets have nearly all been destroyed.

It would be safer for Marie to leave the colony, but where would she go? Home to Britain and another full-scale war, or to halfway houses like Australia, South Africa, or India, to live among strangers? Like many wives she feels that if she leaves, she would be deserting her husband. No man of fighting age is allowed an exit permit, not when the defensive lines are crumbling one by one down Malaya – the Slim River, the towns of Gemas and Segamat.

The Japanese barrel through them in their tanks. Their troops are dressed in long trousers tucked into waterproof boots, whereas British and Allied soldiers wear tropical shorts that expose them to the merciless thorns and insects of the jungle. Their thick, woollen socks get soaked in the many streams they have to cross, and take a long time to dry in the humidity.

In the middle of January, the Japanese reach the small district of Muar. Muar is only 120 kilometres from Singapore. A savage battle is fought by the Australians and the Indians, to no avail. Very few people know it, but the Battle of Singapore is lost.[5]

As January draws to a close, the Japanese bomb Kallang Airport incessantly. It has the last useable airstrip left on the island and the last fighter squadron. Its runway is pitted with craters.[6] Virtue and Fanny's move from nearby Geylang has been fully vindicated.

'You were so right to come here,' Liang tells his sisters. He is in Tiong Bahru to ask for their help. 'I haven't been so lucky. I've been on the waiting list for a flat in Tiong Bahru for weeks, but nothing's happening.'

'No one wants to leave,' Virtue agrees. 'The word's gone out that the buildings here are stronger than anywhere else.'

She notices the lines of anxiety on her younger brother's face. Her heart goes out to him.

'We can't wait any more.' A note of desperation breaks into Liang's voice. He reminds himself to keep calm. 'The children are frightened by the bombing in Kallang. And what's to stop the Japanese pilots from making a mistake or even deliberately letting bombs fall on Geylang?' He pauses. 'Can we stay with you? It will only be for a little while. Once the Japanese are satisfied they've destroyed Kallang, they'll leave the area alone and we can move back.'

'Of course you must stay with us!' Fanny and Virtue are unanimous in their agreement.

The sisters' fourth-floor flat in New Cemetery has three small bedrooms, a living room, kitchen and bathroom, but is the size of a modern one-bedroom apartment. It must now fit seven adults, two boys aged eight and three, and an infant. It is crowded, but Bernard and his younger brother Leonard seem happy enough in this confined space. Between air raids, they climb through the windows of the living room on to the flat roof of the apartment below. It juts out under their unit to form a level area where they can safely play. A concrete parapet prevents them falling over.

The news is filtering down that the Japanese decapitate those they capture, whether Gurkha, Indian, British or Australian. Or they use them, live, for bayonet practice. This is what it means to fight an enemy that has signed, but not ratified, the Geneva Convention of 1929.[7]

When Marie goes to work, the Army Intelligence officers who share her building look increasingly drawn. On 30 January, the rumour blows round Broadcasting House like a sigh: 'We can't hold.'

Marie reports this to her husband when she gets home. He turns pale. He asks for her passport. He disappears. He returns and puts her in a car. He speaks only to instruct. She is to board a troopship waiting by the dock. Soldiers will be guarding the gangway.

They are British, and this is not the time to open the gates that hold back a flood of inchoate emotions. Their farewell is brief, even abrupt, though Marie turns round for one last look as her car drives off. Her husband is standing very still, watching. She will hear later, on her voyage to South Africa, that Singapore has fallen and that there has been no evacuation of its men.[8]

The British can't hold the Malay Peninsula. The final withdrawal across the narrow Straits of Johore to Singapore Island is ordered. On the very last day in January, the British blow up a gap of 70 feet in the mile-long Causeway that joins Johore to Singapore. They know that, ultimately, this will be insufficient to stop the enemy following.[9]

The Japanese enter the town of Johore and are literally next door. They command the pipes that supply the colony with water.[10] They are so close that, from the tower of the local Sultan's palace, they have only to use a pair of binoculars to spy on Singapore.

Virtue and Fanny try to comfort the girls though they are frightened themselves. They tell each other that help from Britain is on its way.

Fanny has heard that Nyong and her family are moving

out of their house on Cantonment Road. It is so close to Keppel Harbour, it shakes when bombs fall on the docks. Tiong Bahru is not far from Cantonment Road. Fanny gets in touch before Nyong leaves.

It seems a lifetime ago when they were in Changi, chatting to the background swash of an incoming tide. How could they have known then what their future would be now? Their world has changed. They are two friends who can meet only briefly, with no ease in their hearts.

Fanny has done a lot of thinking. There is something she wants to give Nyong. They have talked about this before, but Nyong is still shocked when Fanny hands it over. Fanny says: 'It's only in case you need it.'

Cheng-Wah is becoming reticent, which Fanny takes to be an ominous sign. His contacts at the Kuomintang tell him things that he does not want his sisters or his wife to hear.

Fanny reads the newspapers compulsively in English and Chinese. The enemy is like a giant snake that slides on its belly through the Malay Peninsula: silently, methodically. It mesmerizes with the deadly ooze of its progress. It is suddenly very near. Its eyes do not blink, but its forked tongue flickers.

34

The Japanese film themselves as they bomb my home island, as flat and compliant as a dartboard on its back. I found the footage on YouTube. Giant bullets land and explode in clusters of 9, 15, 20, countless.[1] Singapore's anti-aircraft guns were running out of ammunition by February 1942. Therefore, Japanese planes could mass unimpeded in their formations every day, as many as eighty in a group.[2] They appear nonchalant.

Peter and his sisters run to the single air-raid shelter in Tiong Bahru. Virtue and Fanny stay behind with baby Eunice. The shelter is overcrowded and hot, an impossible place with an infant – if you can actually get in. But when the blasts start and Eunice cries, the neighbours in their block are terrified the Japanese pilots can hear her. (Their ridiculous fears so exasperated Virtue that sometimes, my mother said, she would take Eunice up with her on to the roof deck of their building to shout in Cantonese at the planes overhead: 'If you can hear us, kill us!')

The word 'siege' is still censored from the newspapers.[3] But ordinary people are not fools. Stockpiling is intense.

Virtue and Fanny walk with Violet and Florence to the shops in Tiong Bahru to see what they can buy, fighting the crowds. Baby Eunice is passed among them. She is eleven months old and growing heavy. When they get to the store, they find that prices go up on the whim of the shopkeeper and that lavatory paper has run out. Luckily, Virtue hoards old newspapers, so there is plenty to cut up into squares to use.

Clutching rice and salt, the women make their way slowly back with the baby, stepping carefully over Asian refugees from Malaya who lie in their dirty clothes on the arcaded pavements. An acrid whiff fouls the air of Tiong Bahru: the smell of disintegration. There is nowhere for these people to wash. They use the open drains as their latrines.[4]

It is possible, just, to hang on to the myth of invincibility. Lieutenant-General Percival has told a press conference: 'Our task is to hold this fortress until help can come – as assuredly it will come.'[5] The plan is for Singapore to sit out another couple of months. A delivery of tanks (finally!) is expected in March.

Therefore, on this little island, they still believe that they are safe. You can survive a siege. Just look at the Maltese.

The British decide that their best defence would be to retreat to a last redoubt in tiny Singapore, around the centre of the city in the south. On 6 February, they abandon their naval base in the north of which they had been so proud. They set alight its oil dumps to send a thick plume of dark smoke rushing into the sky like a distress signal. They move residents inland from the north coast. A million people are confined to 70 square kilometres of the town.

At last, the Governor casts aside his reservations over arming the Chinese. His men hastily train Kuomintang and Communist volunteers, who were eager from the start to fight the Japanese. Now they are given Bren machine guns or old hunting rifles and knives.[6] And told: Good luck.

The Japanese are commanded by a superb leader, Yamashita. He sends advance units down along the Malayan coast in collapsible rafts[7] to outflank the British, to fool them into thinking they are outnumbered when they are not. [8] In this way, his men have harried the British all the way south.

His soldiers are quickly filling the breach that the British blasted in the Causeway between Johore and Singapore, but he is too impatient to wait even for that. Yamashita wants to send his troops across the sea by raft. They will leave Johore's southwestern coast to land on the opposite shore in Singapore. As the Japanese assemble, they are watched secretly by Australian reconnaissance troops stationed on the opposite, northwestern bank. The Australian scouts warn British command but their reports are dismissed: this Japanese activity is a feint. Instead, Percival dispatches troops to the northeast, to wait on the wrong side.

The Japanese arrive on the northwest coast of Singapore on 8 February 1942, in the night. They have only three Australian battalions to resist them. The Japanese break through. Yamashita joins them the following night.[9]

Everyone in Japan has heard of Yamashita now. They call him the 'Tiger of Malaya'. When he visited Hitler and Goering in Berlin in early 1941,[10] Goering had predicted that a Malayan campaign would require eighteen months.[11] Yamashita has done it in two. The Tiger is about to take Singapore in his teeth.[12]

It is usually with little enthusiasm that I visit the British National Archives at Kew. The building is somewhat brutalist, quite on its own, facing man-made water. The whole effect is meant to convey calm. It is calm, but in the way a crematorium might be calm.

Inside, there isn't the SOAS Library's untidy but energetic sprawl of students. Men and women of a certain age go about their business quietly. Professional researchers? Their self-containment is sepulchral. (Our breathing must slow down to keep pace with the records of people mostly dead.) It feels intimidating at first, but even someone as inexperienced as I am at mining the buried resources at Kew can find something startling there on old onion skin or the yellowing pages of ruled paper.

Fires burn uncontrolled on the streets of Singapore in February. Japanese bombs rain down several times a day. Broken pipes gush precious water on to the streets but workers won't turn up to make repairs. They will simply be fodder for the Japanese pilots. There is nowhere they can hide during a raid. There are no bomb shelters.

Governor Sir Shenton Thomas cables the Secretary of State for the Colonies on 9 February: 'Position during the last few days rather better but the whole question one of morale in existing conditions.'[13] Ah, morale. Sir Shenton appears not to know that the Japanese landed on his island the night before. They are about to shell the heart of his city with long-range artillery. The shelling is worse than the bombing. Shells shriek out of nowhere without warning.

The enemy's constant pounding has made a material difference to the landscape of the town. Familiar buildings have disappeared, replaced by rubble. Hundreds (some say thousands) are killed every day by the Japanese raids.[14] Their corpses lie unburied and putrefying. The danger of disease on top of all the other horrors is not one to contemplate.

The very last British plane leaves Singapore on 11 February. The Netherlands Consul General has gone, 'apparently disappeared', without making arrangements 'to give visas even for the quota of 500 Chinese women and children whose entry into the Netherlands East Indies has been approved'.[15] The letter between the Foreign Office and the Colonial Office cannot hide its bitterness. These five hundred have nowhere to go and they are but a drop in the ocean of Singapore's hundreds of thousands of Chinese.

On 12 February, the British turn their guns on the forty-two oil tanks that supply the region. These are on Pulau Bukom island just off Singapore.[16] If this war requires a final, dramatic metaphor, here it is. Dense smoke billowing from the burning oil is continuous. It darkens the skies; it blackens the rain. To those susceptible to premonitions, it carries great disquiet.

There is a final bid to save the very last European women and children left on the island, but it is not easy getting them to the evacuating ships. Bicycles and cars have been requisitioned, and anyhow there is no petrol to spare. If you manage to stumble through the broken city with your children and luggage – side-stepping corpses and dodging Japanese pilots grown so confident, they fly low to machine-gun people[17] – it is only to arrive at the docks to scenes of dismaying chaos.

Families have to wrestle their way through impenetrable crowds to stand perilously close to the edge of the quay, waving handkerchiefs imploringly while the Japanese dive-bomb the very ships meant to rescue them, and strafe them in the crowd at the dockside.[18] For all their struggle to get this far, they could be killed trying to embark.

Still, at the point of departure there is hope, and it continues to be easier for Europeans to leave the island than for ordinary non-Europeans. The records show that decent, kind Sir Shenton tries his best to treat all races the same but the truth is, there are no ships to China, few to India, and visa restrictions everywhere else.

*

'Can we not at least get Violet and Florence out?' Virtue's voice is pleading – Virtue, who never pleads for anything.

'No, I'm afraid not.' Fanny struggles to keep her voice steady. 'There are very few passes for Java and they only go to well-connected people. Even if we had a chance, the visas are offered first to women with young children.' It breaks her heart that she must force Virtue to face their impasse. 'Baby Eunice was adopted in your name, Eldest Sister. Would you take her and leave both your grown daughters?'

Virtue is silent.

Visas are needed not only for the Dutch East Indies but for South Africa and Australia. The Governor had hoped Australia would accept five thousand Asians, mostly Chinese. So far it has agreed to take fifty Chinese and fifty Eurasians.[19]

India is a possibility, but only if Virtue can provide a letter of credit to prove that her daughters have money for rent and food for as long as they need.[20] Virtue and Fanny have no savings. It is the same whether you are Indian or Malay or Chinese. If you want to leave, you have to be rich.

But even if they could flee to Australia, why should the Japanese not reach them there? They had come all the way down to Singapore from China. Already, the white man has proved unequal to the supposedly squat and myopic Japanese.

Fanny is at her bedroom window. You can no longer see the sky in the day. A greasy fog hangs over everything, coating hair and skin with grime. When rain falls, it is sooty. Breathing is difficult. There is hardly any water.[21] Their flat smells, badly.

She hears that out there it is a sort of hell. Fires blaze constantly on the waterfront to turn night into day.[22] British and

Allied soldiers roam the streets in confusion. Gangs of deserters swig alcohol from bottles that they have looted. There is the rumour that some of these men rape[23] though they do not kill their victims afterwards. In Nanking, the women were nearly always killed.[24]

Fanny reads her Bible quietly. She moves and speaks as little as possible to conserve energy. If she is thinking of Nanking, she speaks of it to no one. She keeps it in her heart. She certainly cannot bear to discuss it with her sister.

35

The Chinese calendar is not lunar, but lunisolar: lunar months between new moons are deposited in a solar year between summer solstices. Inevitably, the two drift apart. Complex mathematical ratios are required periodically to synchronize them.[1] It is a science that has preoccupied the Chinese for millennia.

The calendar had its last great adjustment in the seventeenth century, initiated by Jesuits who were imprisoned and nearly put to death for their trouble – the German Schall and his Belgian counterpart Verbiest. Their astronomical expertise so aroused the jealousy of a Chinese rival that he proclaimed it better for their calendar to be wrong, than right with foreign help.

In 1942, Chinese New Year's Eve coincided with St Valentine's Day, a synchronism that would not recur again for sixty years.

The eve of their New Year is deeply important to the Chinese, who will travel huge distances to eat with their families, like Americans at Thanksgiving. Every family, rich or poor, tries to manage what to them would be a feast – ten of the finest courses that money can buy, or just a bowl of dumplings.

But Virtue is not planning anything special. She is too exhausted even to look at their depleted stores and think of what to cook. She no longer counts her sleepless nights with baby Eunice.

There are many pressing reasons to be unhappy on this Chinese New Year's Eve, but young Violet and Florence are upset because they cannot wash. They know that a festive dinner is out of the question but they would have liked at least to wash their hair. It seems a modest preparation for the New Year. They know it is impossible – there is no water pressure in the taps[2] and they haven't much stored water – but all the same it seems unfair.

Violet, who loves nice meals, would give up the idea of washing if they could have something to eat besides the usual cream crackers and tinned food. She wheedles: can't they steam a bit of rice with water that they have saved for emergencies? Can't Peter be sent off to find someone selling something fresh? It is hopeless to dream of fresh fish or meat of course, but a bit of ginger would be good, a quantity of something green would be wonderful, and a small bottle of soy sauce would be very heaven.

Florence rolls her eyes. Peter remonstrates, 'Vi, you are ridiculous.' Fanny says, 'If you were less greedy, you would be less hungry.'

They all turn to look at Fanny, surprised to hear her speak. She has been very quiet these past few days.

On the afternoon of the Chinese New Year's Eve that was also Valentine's Day, the transformation of a world continues. The Japanese are oblivious of a day so redolent with promise for both British and Chinese.

They arrive at the colony's British Military Hospital, set in splendid isolation among wide fields scarcely 5 kilometres from built-up Tiong Bahru. This hospital is the most modern outside Britain. It has 550 beds and specialist wards, though right now there are 900 patients and no nursing staff.[3] Nearly all the women were evacuated when the message got out that in Hong Kong, British nurses were raped repeatedly by Japanese soldiers.[4] (But the grip of fate is sometimes unrelenting, and many died when the boats on which they escaped were bombed near the Dutch East Indies. Those who survived the bombing were nearly all retrieved and executed by the Japanese.)[5]

The Japanese, who think that there are snipers at the hospital, begin their general slaughter. Doctors and patients are bayoneted or shot. A soldier under anaesthesia on the operating table is bayoneted.[6] No one outside the hospital knows a massacre is taking place.

As Valentine Day draws to a close, the Chinese prepare how they can for their New Year. It is delivered, unwanted, into the dark and troubled streets of Singapore, a dead city.[7] The silence is broken only by the sound of intermittent firing.

In better times, firecrackers would have exploded noisily from midnight till dawn and on and on for days, turning streets red with shreds of vermilion packaging inches thick on the ground. Now with martial law there is no chance of lighting firecrackers in the middle of the night, not that anyone has the desire to replicate the sound of gunfire.

Every Chinese in the colony would have pondered the question: what will this New Year bring? Those who read their astrological almanacs would know that this foundling year had a name, Black Water Horse, and a natal chart blighted by two elements opposed to each other: fire and water. The runes predicted traumatic change.

*

On Chinese New Year's Day, 15 February 1942, the War Council meets in Singapore's secure underground bunker at Fort Canning. Its commander-in-chief, Wavell, is in Java, which means that Lieutenant-General Percival is the most senior military officer in the room. He has before him the heads of the Allied British and Indian divisions.

They have just told him that the water supply on the island cannot be guaranteed for more than twenty-four hours, that they have nearly run out of petrol and anti-aircraft ammunition, and that the military has food left for only two days.

Misjudging the mood of his officers, or simply because he doesn't know how else to carry on, Percival asks: 'What do you all think is the best course now?'

The transcript from the War Council is electrifying to read.[8] The minutes taken down so assiduously that day fix Percival and the others like moths on a board in the fluorescent glare of posterity:

> *Lt Gen. Heath (Commanding Officer, Indian III Corps)*: In my opinion, there is only one possible course to adopt and that is to do what you ought to have done two days ago, namely surrender immediately ... to sacrifice countless lives because of a failure to appreciate the true situation is an act of extreme folly. We should surrender immediately.
>
> *Maj-Gen Gordon Bennett (Commanding Officer, 8th Australia Infantry Division)*: I agree with everything General Heath has just said.

Percival tries to echo his commander-in-chief's instruction from Java to fight on 'without consideration of what may happen to the civilian population', to which Heath replies: 'How can General Wavell command the battle from Java?'

257

It should have been a day of desperate fighting, hand-to-hand, through 'the ruins of Singapore city'.[9] Churchill had ordered it. Yamashita expected it – it was what he had feared. His supplies of ammunition were running out.

Yet Singapore falls not with a crash, the ostentation of empire, but with an embarrassed sigh. On the late afternoon of Chinese New Year's Day, Percival arrives to meet Yamashita at Ford Motor Factory in the suburbs of the town. One of his officers is carrying a white flag.

There is a YouTube video capturing the moment. Percival looks wan, but he strides with the oddly relaxed gait of a man who does not know what to expect. Yamashita approaches, saluting, and Percival almost smiles, politeness ingrained, when he takes Yamashita's extended hand.[10]

At 8.30 p.m. on the night of 15 February 1942, the surrender of the British becomes official. It is unconditional. For the first time in six weeks, there is no sound of bombing or gunfire.

The news starts to fly that the British have given up. 'Impossible!' Violet cries. 'They would never do that!' As there is nothing on the radio, hope emerges like a transgressive weed where it has no right to be, only to wilt in the long night as hearts falter: what if it is true?

There is incredulity and despair the next day when Sir Shenton Thomas makes his final broadcast as Governor of the Straits Settlements.[11]

Everything is changed in an instant. Singapore is now a Japanese colony and a Japanese flag is flying over City Hall. The island switches over to Japanese time, one and a half hours ahead. Singapore is no longer 'Singapore' but 'Syonan', named after the Emperor Syowa. Teachers will be expected to learn, and teach, in Japanese.

Violet and Florence are crying. The older women – Virtue, Fanny and Liang's wife – say nothing, but their faces cannot mask their dread. Liang and his nephew Peter keep switching the radio on and off in a nervous reflex but there is, of course, nothing. The Japanese have taken over the station.

On Tuesday 17 February, Sir Shenton Thomas is on the *padang* in front of City Hall with every European on the island to be inspected by the Japanese. There are the roughly fifty thousand British and Allied soldiers waiting to be marched off to prisoner-of-war camps.[12] There are the civilians of whom only Thomas's wife is absent, lying ill in an infirmary. They will not see each other again for three years.[13] Then Thomas leads his two thousand civilian countrymen and women to detention camps on the east of the island, before prison in Changi.[14] The British, former masters of Singapore, clutch their few belongings and set off on foot. The Asians who line the roads do not jeer as the Japanese expected. They are silent, overwhelmed.

There is sporadic looting by ordinary people of shops and each other's homes. The Japanese decapitate the looters and display their heads in public places as a warning to others. The looting stops immediately.

The island of Syonan turns quiet.

Then the Japanese officers let loose their men.

36

As if instructed by invisible telegraph, carried by the wind, everyone kept indoors after the Japanese takeover. This wasn't always enough. Soldiers entered homes at random to confiscate valuables or precious stocks of food. They took some men away; they beat up others. Most fathers knew to hide their daughters.[1]

Cheng-Wah would have tried to stop the stories from Nanking flooding back into his head, but there were too many and now they seemed only too portentous. Every man – Indian, Malay or Chinese – froze when they heard soldiers shouting in the streets.

With his blessing, Cheng-Wah's elder daughter Yin-Yue was now engaged to her first cousin Pak-Leong, his sister Orchid's son. Some very conservative Chinese still frowned upon such cousins marrying even though their surnames were different. Fanny had made her disapproval all too clear with her objections. But it was more important to Cheng-Wah that two good young people were so in love. Therefore, there was no sense in waiting. He had learned, in the past month, that what lies ahead is unpredictable. (Pak-Leong and Yin-Yue would go on to have two sons and several grandchildren in more than sixty-five years together. They died in their nineties, Yin-Yue three months after Pak-Leong.)

It had pleased Cheng-Wah that Pak-Leong had moved nearby with his family. Their flat in Tiong Bahru was at the quiet end of a street next to scrubland with an isolated electrical substation. Like everyone else, Pak-Leong and his family spent their days trying to attract as little attention as possible. There was little to do in the evenings except to wait it out in a dimly lit room, talking in low tones until they could give in at last to restless sleep. No one knew what to expect.

On one of those still evenings they heard the unmistakeable stamp of boots on the street outside their block and loud talking in Japanese, perhaps guards from the substation. All conversation ceased without anyone needing to raise fingers to lips. They held their breath. Luckily, the children were old enough to be quiet.

Then they heard someone climbing heavily and noisily up the stairs to their flat.

They had been preparing for, and dreading, this moment. Pak-Leong's stepmother melted into the bedroom with her girls – perhaps a useless place to hide, but there was nowhere else to go in their small flat.

There was loud knocking on their door. At first no one was able to move. Then Pak-Leong managed to stand up and walk to the door. He had seconds to compose himself before opening it. A flustered-looking soldier was outside. '*Guniang!*' he shouted in Mandarin Chinese to make himself understood. 'Young women!'

Pak-Leong held the door ajar, gesturing to his father and brothers. 'Only men here,' he managed to say when, to his horror, he saw out of the corner of his eye his half-sister, eleven years old, emerge quietly from the bedroom, overcome by curiosity, to crouch next to a bookcase. This was Hou-Seong, the youngest in the 1935 photograph. The soldier looked into the small living room, mercifully taking in only a father and his sons. He made a mental calculation that there were five of them to his one self. He was obliged to accept Pak-Leong's word. He left.

The tension in the room was palpable as each man waited to hear if the receding footsteps would stop and double back. What might the soldier do if he realized that Pak-Leong had lied?

In Fanny and Virtue's household, there were only two men to five women. And they had Eunice, not yet a year old, who could not understand their entreaties to hush. Each of them has had time for reflection, time to decide what they must do, how they will react, if the unspeakable becomes real.

Fanny has planned her escape. She has a quantity of rat poison, bought before it became impossible to buy things. She had given some to her friend Nyong, who was appalled.

'But the Japanese are never going to take over Singapore! The British would never surrender to the Japanese!'

Fanny had explained that it was only a contingency, to be there in the background as a safety net: 'If the very worst happens, and the Japanese behave as they did in Nanking, I would rather kill myself first. A woman can manage her fate even when it seems hopeless. Remember? I told you about the women who resisted rape, who were honoured by their emperor?'

'The dead women!' Nyong had said bitterly. 'Fanny, how can you think of yourself as a Christian? Christians don't take their own lives! It doesn't matter that it was honourable in China.'

Fanny had been thoughtful then, as she is now. She is caught in the remnant of a terrifying dream that cannot be shaken off. She had worried that dread might incapacitate her, which is why she has the poison ready, to be the safety net into which she can simply let herself fall. But now something makes her stop. She does nothing. Perhaps she cannot bear to abandon Virtue, Violet and Florence to what might happen. She looks for solace in her Bible, possibly from an enduring psalm:

He maketh me to lie down in green pastures . . .

She is strict with Violet and Florence. She keeps the young women away from the bedroom windows that look out on to the street in case they are spotted by Japanese soldiers.

One day passes, then another. It is almost intolerable to be completely confined to a cramped and stifling flat, unable to venture out, with no idea of what is happening or about to happen – whether a soldier will come to your home, or not. But Fanny's household escapes attention.

If horror were not absolute but relative, one could say that the rampage of those Japanese soldiers in Singapore was not on the same scale or as unrestrained as in Nanking. Their uncontrolled behaviour – drinking, looting, cases of rape[2] – seemed to peter out after three days,[3] by 20 February. Whereas in Nanking it had carried on for six weeks.[4]

Yamashita had lived in Bern and Vienna as a successful and sociable military attaché. He might have been conscious of the eyes of the wider world upon him.

Fanny and her family lived in the middle of a crowded residential street and it was becoming clear, at least in urban areas, that Yamashita's soldiers did not like their transgressions too visible.

But Yamashita was pragmatist enough to understand that with only about thirty thousand troops on an island of more than three hundred thousand male Chinese,[5] of whom the majority were adult, he had to act decisively to protect his position. More than a thousand of these Chinese had fought in the volunteer forces against his men, and had apparently fought fiercely despite being poorly armed. They could galvanize tens of thousands of others like them against his occupying troops.

Yamashita knew how to control this. He had seen it done before. In north China, after the Japanese Kwantung Army occupied Manchuria in 1931, instant execution without trial had been made law.[6] The Kwantung Army called this method of containment *genju shobun*, harsh disposal, or *genchi shobun*, disposal on the spot.[7] Anyone – even a woman or a child – could be killed on the decision of a single officer, without his consulting a superior. When Yamashita was chief of staff in north China from 1937 to 1938, this was his procedure for mopping up operations.[8]

Nanking had also provided a powerful precedent. Japanese troops had been heavily outnumbered in a city of six hundred thousand Chinese, of whom a significant number were soldiers. The Japanese executed enough soldiers and civilians there – two hundred thousand at least – to ensure compliance from the rest.[9]

Yamashita and his officers had understood, even before they arrived, what they had to do in Singapore if they occupied it.[10] They already had lists distilled from the local newspapers by former Japanese residents of Singapore. Over the years, the name of every Chinese believed to be anti-Japanese had been added: businessmen or teachers who supported trade bans against Japan, or who had spoken out against Japan's invasion of China.

Yamashita's starting point was China nationalists, whether Communist or right-wing Kuomintang. But soon it would be anybody.

37

The operation began untidily.

A general summons for registration was sent out and there was terrible confusion. Whole families turned up with food for several days, struggling to walk with their babies and children, pots and pans and portable stoves, to the few reporting centres on the island. Whole streets were jammed with what looked like refugees. They camped outdoors in the night.[1]

The Japanese learned to go from house to house to explain to each Chinese family that only their men were wanted for registration, a neutral word with a dangerous designation. Able-bodied men between the ages of eighteen and fifty.

For two weeks from 21 February to 4 March,[2] these men had the total attention of the Japanese.

Singapore was divided into four segments,[3] each with its own Kempeitai command. The Japanese military police had translators to help with their interviews and holding cells for those whom they wanted to interrogate further. They had tested methods to encourage loquaciousness, of which water-torture was only one.[4]

But as there were over a hundred thousand men to be processed and only two hundred members of the Kempeitai,[5] screening was later fanned out to satellite stations run by ordinary soldiers trained for battle, not administration. At these outposts, there were no interpreters and no holding cells. It was chaos – which could work to your favour, or not.

The Kempeitai had a screening centre in Tanjong Pagar

near Tiong Bahru, not far from Cantonment Road where the Law family had once lived.[6]

'We shouldn't be long,' Liang tells his sisters and his wife as he leaves with Peter. 'It's not far. I know exactly where to go. It's near the police station at Tanjong Pagar. The Japanese want our names, that's all,' he tries to reassure the women, 'to make sure we don't go forming resistance groups.'

Liang and Peter arrive at the centre to find hundreds and hundreds of men in a compound roughly fenced off with barbed wire and rope. Many have waited patiently for hours in the sun with no water. Some have stayed in their queues overnight without food. They all accept the humiliation of having to shuffle forwards in a squat down the line, waiting for their turn to be interviewed indoors.

Japanese guards shout roughly to the two men, indicating that they should sit on their heels like the others. They do as they are told.

What my uncle and great-uncle did not know was that, inside the building, every man was being appraised for execution. Because of the sheer number of Chinese men who had to be questioned, there was not always the chance of a meaningful interview with the officers. Life or death could be decided on whether you sported a tattoo (and might therefore be a gangster and troublemaker), whether you wore glasses (and were therefore bookish, likely to be a schoolteacher and loyal to China), or simply whether or not in your nervousness you seemed shifty.

Sometimes the assessments were informed by nothing more than the fleeting emotions of a hard-pressed officer interviewing thousands of strangers in the humid heat – a grumble of hunger, a passing irritation, how he liked your face.

It seemed innocuous: you were held back for further questioning or sent home with a square ink-stamp on your arm. It would only emerge later that if you were not sent home right away, you were killed.

As they wait on their haunches in the hot sun, Liang turns to Peter and says quietly in Cantonese, 'Nephew, I don't like this.'

Liang had been an interpreter for Police Special Branch in the former British colony, so he has an idea how things work. They have been moving forward slowly in a waddle, like ducks. There is something about their deliberate abasement that makes him uncomfortable. Why are the Japanese treating ordinary civilians reporting for a census in this way?

When eventually they find themselves next to a makeshift barrier with no soldiers in sight, Liang lifts up the rope and, acting on pure instinct, nods to Peter: 'Let's go.'

Fanny and Virtue are hugely relieved when their two men return. Peter and Liang lack the vital square stamp on their arm, but for the moment they are oblivious of its importance. They focus instead on worrying about Cheng-Wah, their eldest brother.

It was my uncle Bernard in Canada – Liang's son – who told me that his uncle Cheng-Wah was 'head of' the Singapore division of the Kuomintang, the Nationalist Party of China with which Japan was at war. This needed to be verified. Cheng-Wah was one of the colony's handful of Chinese to have had a higher education in China. He had been at college in Nanking at a time of historic change, when China had become a republic for the first time. He was a China patriot. He was therefore eminently qualified to be on the committee of the local Kuomintang. But *head*? It was not something that Cheng-Wah's daughter Yin-Yue ever mentioned to me. Bernard was still young when his uncle and his father died. Not every detail of his recollection may have been correct.

I looked for the names of Singapore's senior Kuomintang members in the National Archives at Kew. There were very few lists, and on them nothing that remotely resembled 'Law Cheng-Wah' or his art or style names. Could he have used an alias? There was no way that I could find out.

In any case, Cheng-Wah's standing in the local Kuomintang was probably immaterial because he already had the sort of profile that the Japanese were looking for. He ran his own Chinese school – everyone knew that teachers in Singapore's Chinese schools were loyal to China – and he supported the China Relief Fund which raised money to help China's fight-back against Japan.

Even his name was a giveaway. 'Cheng' was a generational name chosen by the clan but 'Wah', the name that his father picked for him, referred to their motherland. He could never forget his roots.

Despite all these clues available to the Japanese, Cheng-Wah was interviewed, discharged and sent home.

He restoreth my soul . . .

It is a miracle. His family is elated. Fanny and Virtue are overjoyed.

Before he set up his tiny school in Chinatown, Cheng-Wah taught at Yeung Ching, probably the most prestigious Chinese school of its day in Singapore. I wrote to the Yeung

Ching Alumni Association to confirm that my great-uncle was a teacher there. I received an enigmatic reply.

Dr Ho Nai-Kiong, then vice-president (now president) of the Alumni Association, emailed back to say that hardly any archival material existed. The school had merged with two others thirty years before and moved to entirely new premises with a different pupil enrolment.

Everything was lost during the changeover, though Dr Ho had a few photographs and articles collected privately over the years which might be helpful. However, mysteriously, he had first to ask if I had any record of Cheng-Wah's death, 'when and where and the mode of death', to be sure that we were not 'talking on different wavelengths'.

I do not know the 'mode' of Cheng-Wah's death, but I do know what happened after he was screened and cleared by the Japanese. He was arrested, probably later that same day.

The Japanese understood that their vetting was not foolproof, so they also offered bribes to informants. The husband of a family friend took soldiers to the bottom of Cheng-Wah's block of flats and pointed to his window: 'There. Up there.' A member of the Kuomintang, a China patriot, lived up there.

The Japanese soldiers who tramped up the stairs to the flat appeared reasonable, unwilling to haul someone off merely on hearsay. They were not impolite. They asked first, before searching the flat. They found a photograph of Cheng-Wah posing with a group of schoolchildren and the Chinese flag. There were postcards that he sold to support the war effort in China. These alone were enough to incriminate him.

As the soldiers talk among themselves, Cheng-Wah feels a weight descend upon him, the weight of anticipation, even before the lead soldier turns to him with a darkened expression while the men behind him look regretful.

Seven years before this moment, Cheng-Wah's daughter Yin-Yue had posed for a photograph in Hong Kong with her grandfather. She wore a silk cheongsam printed with what look like sprigs of blossom. Her short hair was combed to a neat side-parting. She had to one side her brother and, to the other, her cousin Pak-Leong with whom she was secretly in love. The complications of life were simple and sweet. Now she watches, frozen, as the soldiers indicate that they want to take her father away for further questioning.

Neither Cheng-Wah nor his family feels able to protest. They are a quiet, polite family not given to histrionics or the grand gesture. There is no time for his wife or children to hold him or to say goodbye. It is not seemly, anyway, for a Chinese couple to embrace in public, certainly not in front of these strangers.

Their small living room seems very crowded with the soldiers in addition to his family and, as the Japanese manoeuvre Cheng-Wah out of the flat, he can barely make out his wife in the moment when he turns his head at the door.

Yin-Yue moves, as if in a dream, with her mother to the bedroom window that overlooks the street to watch her father being marched away, a Japanese soldier on either side. He does not look up.

As his family heard no further news of him they hoped all through the years of the Occupation that he would return. He didn't.

I do not know the mode of Cheng-Wah's death but I can guess.

He would have been beaten, perhaps tortured for

information and a confession. Then Cheng-Wah was executed. He could have been bayoneted or beheaded near his cell but I believe that he was formally executed – by firing squad – for being a member of the Kuomintang in Singapore or for raising money for the China Relief Fund. This was how, the day after Cheng-Wah's arrest, an example was made of 'traitors': anyone suspected of being part of a resistance movement. The Japanese command wanted to project an image of widespread activism to justify what it intended to do next – to massacre Chinese men indiscriminately as Japan had done in Nanking, with the object of subduing a large and potentially hostile population.

A new routine began over the next fortnight. Chinese men were herded on to lorries and taken to isolated places, mostly beaches, where they were told to dig trenches and to stand by them. Then they were machine-gunned. Or they had their hands bound by wire and were ordered to walk into the sea – and then they were machine-gunned. Or they were taken out by boat and told to jump in the water, to be picked off with bullets.

Sometimes they were not even killed anywhere remote. There were mass executions on the beach by the Seaview Hotel where, only weeks before, the Trio Granados had played as carefree diners danced. At Tanjong Pagar wharf, half an hour's walk from Tiong Bahru, decapitations took place in such number that tides and currents were washing up headless bodies to its west near the Royal Singapore Yacht Club.[7]

The Chinese in Singapore have their own name for this period of their history. They call it Sook Ching – a purge or a cleansing.

The diary of a Japanese officer exists which suggests that

at least five thousand Chinese were executed during this time.[8] This figure does not tally with the number of human remains that continued to be found through the 1960s when thirty mass graves were exhumed. It is simply too low. Authoritative estimates put the total dead conservatively at fifty thousand[9] – anywhere between 15 and 25 per cent of adult Chinese men in Singapore between the ages of eighteen and fifty.[10]

The Sook Ching ended in Singapore after two weeks as the Japanese turned their sights back up the Malay Peninsula. Japanese troops worked their way northwards through all the villages and towns that they had conquered on their way down to victory in Singapore.

It was here, in the Malayan states of Johor, Malacca and Negri Sembilan, in remote areas beyond the watchful eyes of the world and their own top command, that some of the depravities seen in Nanking reportedly crept back in. By the time the Japanese reached Penang in April, they seemed to have completed another Sook Ching, with claims that another twenty-five thousand Chinese had been killed.[11]

When Fanny finds out that Cheng-Wah has been arrested, her descent from joy to dismay is vertiginous. Her brother had talked to her about the war in China. She knows what the Japanese do to men they do not trust. The dark hand of the enemy has reached into the bosom of her family and plucked out its heart.

She is numb until she looks back to the history of her father's homeland. Both her father and Cheng-Wah had taught her that it is her history too. She clings to it now, as to a post in surging flood water.

In imperial China, there was a protocol that you could

follow when you were desperate. Sometimes it was to protect what you believed in, when it was an act of determination, not of defeat.[12] Sometimes, it was simply to express anguish or regret.

One woman in Singapore still responds to these ideas. It is reflexive under threat. She cannot help it. Despite her modern education and her Christian faith, Fanny reaches into Chinese antiquity for a solution to her plight.

Thou preparest a table before me in the presence of mine enemies . . .

Their household retires for the night, burdened with the news of Cheng-Wah's arrest. Liang, his wife and their two sons go to their bedroom next to the kitchen, Violet and Florence go to theirs next to Fanny, Virtue and baby Eunice. Peter sleeps in the living room. Fanny lies down without changing her clothes which Virtue finds unremarkable. She expects Fanny to be restless tonight. When Fanny rouses much later, Virtue doesn't stir.

Fanny has a packet of rat poison concealed in her hand. She goes into the kitchen as quietly as she can to dissolve its powdered contents in a glass of water.[13] She might have sipped it, wondering with each sip if she should take the next; or she might have shut her eyes and swallowed all of it as quickly as she could. She might have filled the emptied glass with more water, rinsing her mouth. Then she slips into the living room, pausing briefly to check that Peter is in a young man's deep sleep.

Listening, to be sure that her entire family is completely stilled by slumber, she climbs on to a chair and out through the open window of their living room as her younger nephews had often done. On the terrace formed by the level roof of the apartment below, she finds a place to sit under a narrow overhang. It will provide some shelter the next day from the sun, if she lives that long. Then she waits.

Traditional Chinese believed that an unmarried woman contaminated the surroundings where she died. Even those families who embraced their sworn spinsters could not shake off this conviction. Better that she end her days not in the family home but somewhere like an outhouse. Fanny removed herself from the flat out of respect for ritual and love of her family.

Virtue is distraught the next morning when they see Fanny out on the terrace – an odd place for her – and she tells them that she has taken poison. There is little that they can do. The few British doctors and nurses who remain are in prison camps. Local clinics have closed.[14] Hospitals are now run by the Japanese for their troops. It has only been a week since the surrender of Singapore.

Fanny won't let her family near her. She thinks she may defile them. They have to hand her food and drink on a tray but she does not touch the food, though she allows herself some sips of water. Phosphorous in the rat poison has given her a powerful thirst. She is beginning to feel nauseous, but she has eaten so little in recent weeks that she brings up nothing when she retches.

Liang sends his wife and two sons to stay with his mother-in-law. It is not right that the boys should see their aunt in this state. Eunice remains in the flat, too little to be aware of what is happening though she whimpers for Virtue – Virtue has left her completely in Violet's and Florence's care.

Fanny's family is braced for her death when they make a discovery. It is one thing to poison yourself, another to actually die. A day passes. Still Fanny lingers. Now she has stomach cramps in addition to the nausea.

'How about camphor oil?' someone is asking, though not of Virtue, who is now unable to make any decision. Every Chinese household has camphor in its medicine chest, a pungent cure-all that drives away midges or dulls the pain of arthritis. It is also anti-spasmodic. If taken orally in very small amounts, it may stop the stomach heaving.

'Do you think she will try it?' Violet ventures.

'Ask her,' says Florence, who has taken over from their mother. She is as rational as Virtue, their mother's true heir.

It is agreed that if Fanny would allow anyone near her other than Virtue, it would be Violet. Violet is distressed, and nervous, but she climbs through the window on to the terrace with a bottle of camphorated oil. Will Fanny try some? It might ease her stomach pains. Fanny gives a weak nod to say 'yes'.

Violet thinks she sees regret in Fanny's eyes as she gently lifts her aunt's blouse to rub oil on to her stomach. Then Fanny opens her mouth for Violet to tilt in a little of the oil from a teaspoon. Her breath smells oddly of garlic from the poison.[15] Most of the oil spills out of Fanny's mouth and the effort she has to make to swallow is so great that Violet cannot bear to feed her more.

Miraculously, Fanny seems to get better.[16] The stomach cramps fade; so does the nausea. She even manages to eat a little.

But over the course of the third day the nausea returns and she tries, uncontrollably, to throw up. Now she reeks of camphor. Eunice told me decades later that her mother couldn't bear to have camphor near her. Virtue said it was the smell of Fanny dying and it was intolerable.

Fanny is in agony, that much is clear. She is prostrated by the pain and the discomfort. She is shaking and short of breath. She is in confusion, no longer aware that she needs water. Her skin has turned dark. Perhaps it is the sun that has such force at this time of year?

She moans, involuntarily. Then she is delirious. 'What is she saying?' Virtue begs, pitifully, but no one can understand Fanny. Virtue, always so strong, is completely reduced, undone by waiting while her sister struggles to die out on the roof terrace.

Mercifully, the incoherent outbursts begin to be separated by long periods of silence. Could the camphor finally be working? Liang says nothing. He thinks the original poison is paralysing her brain.

Another day finally ends. Now that her convulsions and groans have passed at last, her family falls into an exhausted sleep.

Fanny dies softly in the night, with those she loves oblivious though nearby, separated only by a wall. It is how a chaste spinster in classical China would have chosen to go, quietly and without fuss. She was not yet thirty-five.

38

It was Florence who found that Fanny had died when she looked out in the morning to check on her. She woke her mother and her uncle Liang. Although Virtue could have expected no other outcome, she was inconsolable.

Virtue, usually the one in charge of all practical things, could no longer be practical. Liang, Violet, Peter and Florence had to decide what to do with Fanny's body.

It was now 24 February, nine days since Singapore was taken by Japan. The people of the island were closely watched. There was intimation of worse to come. Only the day before, the Chinese printing presses were restarted by the Japanese to make an urgent announcement: the 'leader of the traitors' and others linked to the resistance movement against Japan had been executed by firing squad.[1] The arrests and summary executions took place over two days, the 21st and 22nd, when Cheng-Wah was taken away. If he were not already dead, he would have been among them.

The existence of these men was proof to the Japanese that 'a thousand rebels' had 'caused confusion'. Therefore, the announcement continued ominously, the executive had decided to bring the army back into the city where it would 'explore and adopt the same fighting strategies' – presumably as in war – to handle those residents of Singapore who had not managed to 'admit or regret their actions', whose conduct was 'evil'.[2]

The words 'disorder', 'enemy' and 'betrayal' are used

liberally to explain why the army must now control civilian life. The communiqué is vaguely worded but extremely disquieting to read. It would become clear only in retrospect that this was setting out the rationale for ethnic cleansing.

My family had its own immediate tragedy and a corpse to bury, but the Chinese community had shut down. All Chinese burial companies were closed. There was no one to deal with Fanny. Someone suggested that they bury her in the yard behind their block of flats (not so inappropriate perhaps in the New Cemetery of Tiong Bahru). Virtue manages to rise sufficiently out of her grief to reject this: there could be no worse ignominy for her beloved sister than to be interred in waste ground like a dog.

Fanny may have believed in ancestor worship but she also thought of herself as Christian and had attended church regularly when that was possible. Peter went to her pastor for advice. He was told that a Christian burial firm, the Casket Company, had remained open. The company was owned and run by a German-Eurasian family, the Hochstadts.

When Singapore was still a British colony, there were social hierarchies that were not crossed. The Casket Company served mainly Europeans or Eurasians. Wealthy and influential 'Asiatics' might have had the confidence to make use of its services but ordinary people did not. The Laws would never have got in touch with the Casket Company before the war. Now there was no choice. Peter would have to try.

To his relief, the man who answered the telephone agreed to bury Fanny. This would have been John Hochstadt, the company's founder. His son-in-law, the general manager, had become a Japanese prisoner of war. There was virtually no one left to help him apart from his wife and a teenage grandson.[3] Nearly all his workers had disappeared.

In those terrible days when all certainties had been removed, old Mr Hochstadt must have found some feeling for the poor Chinese lady whose Christian faith had proved insufficient, and who had felt compelled to take her own life. But as he was on his own he needed help with digging the grave, which would have to be at the more obscure paupers' end of the cemetery.

Mr Hochstadt arrives in Tiong Bahru in a hearse, with a coffin. Florence has washed Fanny and put her in clean clothes. She is very light. They put Fanny in the coffin with her bible.

For thou art with me; thy rod and thy staff they comfort me.

The coffin is carried with some difficulty down the narrow stairs from their apartment. Florence is holding up Virtue, whose body is racked by sobs. Violet, carrying baby Eunice, is crying uncontrollably.

Peter and his uncle Liang will bury Fanny. It is a serious risk to leave their flat. Neither man has the stamp to prove he has been vetted by the Japanese and the two know better than most that the Japanese can be unforgiving. But of course they go. It is what you do: you bury your little sister; you bury the aunt who brought you up.

They climb into the back of the hearse with the coffin and are concealed. The vehicle moves off slowly. As it approaches the first checkpoint, Japanese soldiers see that it carries the right pass and wave it through. It rumbles out of the city on to deserted suburban roads. Inside, every man is silent, preoccupied with his own thoughts.

The Bidadari Cemetery on Upper Aljunied Road is about 12 kilometres from Tiong Bahru in a quiet, wooded area northeast of the city. The hearse drives through the gates of the cemetery, framed on either side by stone pillars topped with scrolled capitals and lobed urns. The gestures of the European renaissance are all that remain of a deposed power.

Inside, the cemetery is deserted. After the bombing and shelling of the past two months and the turmoil of the Japanese takeover, this place feels curiously calm.

They wind through overgrown lawns dotted with *tembusu* trees whose creamy flowers yellow quickly, but keep their strong, sweet scent. They turn down an unpaved road away from the fields of marble crosses, the lofty angels, the occasional Madonna.

Finally, they stop in a place that feels secluded even here. The funeral director opens the back door of the hearse to let Peter and Liang out. He hands them each a spade and sets off on to a bare tract of land, beckoning them to follow. Peter and Liang dig a grave for Fanny's coffin in the place where he points. The earth is dry and compacted from a recent drought.[4]

When at last they finish and there is a brief pause, Peter looks around to fix the place in his mind.

They are in a shallow valley with a banyan growing nearby. The tree that is sacred to Hindus represents both death and immortality. Its brown aerial roots reach for the same ground into which Fanny is finally lowered. Her brother and her nephew cover her coffin with earth. Neither Liang nor Peter are Christian, so the undertaker says a brief prayer. Then he gives them a number for this pauper's grave.

39

'*Kura!*' is a Japanese word that Singapore's civilians would learn quickly to recognize and to dread. Roughly translated, it means, 'Come here!' In occupied Singapore it was nearly always threatening, even in the most innocuous of situations.

For instance, you might have bowed but not low enough. You could be kicked for this. Or the expression on your face was meek, but not meek enough. You could be struck with a rifle for this. Or perhaps there was some other, unintended transgression: you had a hat on but you forgot to remove it when you went past the Japanese sentry. On a very bad day, you might be bayoneted. Or shot.

It was the last thing that Fanny would have wanted but her suicide had put the men she loved in great danger.

The authorities had announced the previous day that they would be ruthless in preventing 'disorder' – whatever that meant. The Japanese needed few excuses to arrest a Chinese man. The safest place was presumably indoors, but Peter and Liang have had to venture out to bury her.

The funeral director's premises were on Lavender Street, not far from the cemetery. Tiong Bahru was another 8 kilometres beyond. He was not going to be able to take the two men home. There was a shortage of petrol and other people needed burying.

Liang and Peter climbed out slowly from the hearse, instinctively watchful. They needed to head southwest to Tiong Bahru and would have to walk through the town to get to a bridge over the Singapore River. Even then they would be only halfway home.

After getting out at Lavender Street, they could have carried on down Serangoon Road where most of the Indian immigrants lived. It was a vibrant area where Chettiars, the moneylenders, sat cross-legged in their bureaus next to shops selling garlands of gold and yellow marigolds, or curry mixes from mounds of saffron-coloured powder. There wouldn't have been many Japanese soldiers there. The Chinese, not the Indians, were their target. Liang and Peter would have been relatively inconspicuous on a street still busy in spite of the Occupation.

But as they left the inner suburbs to enter Singapore city, the military presence would have been greater. This was where the major bridges were located, going south across the river to the Chinese town.

Even in their ignorance of Chinese men being indiscriminately killed, Liang and Peter sensed that they were vulnerable – though they had no idea how bad the situation had become. The Japanese had occupied Singapore for little more than a week. No one knew that a massacre had begun. It was just off the starting blocks, yet to take its full stride. But it had begun.

Suddenly, they heard the word '*Kura!*' and, terrified, became aware that a Japanese soldier was shouting at them, his rifle already raised and aimed at them. They were under no illusion that, in their situation, they could expect the very worst.[1]

But in the next instant they heard another shout. The soldier whipped round immediately to face the road, standing rigidly to attention, his rifle held vertically in front of him. A staff car was approaching. The white flag flying above its fender was imprinted with a blood-red circle. A high-ranking official was inside, perhaps Yamashita himself.

The Imperial Japanese Army had a system of calculated cruelty to instil discipline in its men.[2] Retribution could be vicious if it was felt that soldiers were not showing sufficient respect to their officers. The Japanese military could as easily shoot one of its own as anyone else.

The two men did not wait to see what might happen. They took off. They ran, round a street corner, down one lane then another, onwards, hearts pounding. When Liang and Peter finally stopped, bent double, panting to catch their breath, their legs nearly gave way under them. They were certain that they had narrowly escaped death.

They could not risk another encounter with the Japanese but the main bridges were likely to be watched. They were already tired from the hours spent digging a 6-foot-deep trench in hard soil, and they were emotionally worn-out from burying Fanny. Now they faced a dash to safety against great odds. They would constantly have to weigh the risk of going down quiet streets, where they would be visible, against the danger of busier roads where there could be soldiers.

I cannot remember what they did next. Children do not listen carefully to the stories that grown men and women tell, and when we are grown too and think to ask, they are gone.

My uncle and great-uncle could have worked westwards along the north bank of the Singapore River, which would take them out of the heavily patrolled town centre to where they might find a bridge without a sentry. They would have to be quick: these detours would extend their journey, but time was not on their side. Once the curfew started at sunset, they would be in even greater jeopardy. The Japanese military probably thought nothing of shooting wanderers in the back.

But they could not let their anxiety cripple them. They had to press on.

Somehow – somehow! – they crossed the Singapore River to reach its southern bank. They then had another 4 kilometres to walk when they could not let their guard down for an instant, not even after they entered the outskirts of Tiong Bahru for the final trek. The sky was hazy – the fires around the island were only gradually burning out – but the afternoon sun shone through.

They made it back.

Epilogue

No one had wanted to talk to me about my great-aunt Fanny. None of her nieces and nephews, not even my mother, had much to say about her beyond how she died: she had poisoned herself and the poison took longer than expected to work through.

Everyone accepted that she killed herself because she was afraid of being raped and losing everything she considered dignified about herself. There was quiet regret at the mistiming and the waste. She could not have known it, but she had ended her life just as the danger for women had passed, when Japanese soldiers were turning their attention to Chinese men.

Nobody said that Fanny's suicide had anything to do with Cheng-Wah's arrest. In fact, no one mentioned Cheng-Wah and Fanny in the same breath, almost as if brother and sister never knew each other, certainly as if their tragedies had taken place months or even years apart.

It was only after I started a timeline on my family that I realized how closely their deaths followed one another's. When I matched the day that Yin-Yue said her father was taken away with when Fanny took the poison – worked back from the date of death on her tombstone – it was the same day.

This offered an entirely different reason for Fanny's suicide: not anxiety for herself but anguish at Cheng-Wah's arrest and certain execution. This was not an idea that her nieces and nephews ever considered. The concept of the righteous or loyal suicide had vanished in a mere generation.[1] It was the sort of thing that happened a long time ago in China, not something that happened in the present, in a former British colony, in your own family. Or it may simply have been too painful to think of Cheng-Wah's tragedy precipitating Fanny's.

As a result, Fanny's suicide stirred up not feelings of pity or respect but of embarrassment. There had been no imminent threat. She had been needlessly hasty. Could she even have valued her chastity too much?

'Virginity!' her nephew Pak-Leong had exclaimed dismissively when we talked about Fanny more than sixty years later: 'All she worried about was her virginity!' As if he were disappointed that she could be so afraid of being violated and murdered, though he had never forgotten his own palpable fear the night that a Japanese soldier had entered his flat.

The way that Fanny died obscured everything else about her. She had exceptional resolve and courage and she was prescient in understanding the power of education for women. She had sacrificed everything to transform the lives of her sister's children and therefore of their descendants. But no one had time to reflect on this after her burial.

Peter and Liang were still in grave danger, not yet cleared by the Japanese military. Peter took his fate in both hands to go to a registration centre for vetting. He knew by then that there was an even chance he would not return, but he was not prepared to hide. What might have saved him was Fanny's certainty that his education should be in English. The Japanese were far more suspicious of men who had gone to Chinese schools.

Liang, on the other hand, hid for nearly all the three and a half years of the Japanese Occupation. He knew that his former links with British Special Branch would condemn him. But the Kempeitai caught up with him in the end. He was arrested and tortured, freed only on the intercession of a Chinese friend trusted by the Japanese.

He never fully recovered from his injuries. He was already malnourished from the food shortages of the Occupation. He died in the chaotic months following Japan's surrender and the return of the British to Singapore in September 1945. Only Virtue and Florence were by his side. Virtue had heard that her brother was dying in one of Sago Lane's desolate funeral houses. She found him, just in time.

Orchid had long gone, Cheng-Wah was executed by the Japanese, and Fanny had taken her own life. By the end of the Second World War, only Virtue was left of all her father's children.

Like other people, my family had to move on. New calamities had taken the place of earlier misfortunes. It seemed easiest for most of the family to forget Fanny, who had died in a way that made her uncomfortable to remember. Some of my cousins have never even heard of her, which was what had worried her most. She had agonized over being lost from the family narrative after she died.

She was Christian and yet hostage to Chinese superstition. She believed not in a Christian but a Chinese afterlife where if you were a woman, and single, and forgotten after your death, you were cast into a purgatory of lost souls. Only Virtue understood the depth of this fear. It was why she had asked to be buried with Fanny after her own death twenty-one years later. She knew that then, when her children visited her grave, they would be visiting Fanny's too.

*

A final, unexpected gift. After completing my manuscript, looking for photographs for the book, I wrote to my cousin John Law in Canada to see if he could find the picture that his father Bernard had copied to me in an email before he died in 2018 – the one from early 1931, where his grandfather (my great-grandfather) looked so strong and commanding.

John said that his sister Jacqueline was now in charge of their father's picture archive. Jacqueline went patiently through two boxes of old photographs to make a selection. She posted the high-resolution scans to me on a memory card with a note that said, 'I don't always know who's who.'

There was one photograph that I had never seen before: Fanny wrapped in a dark fur coat, leaning over her father. Law's appearance is somewhere between his robust self in 1931 and the frail, dying man of 1935. Fanny appears confident, protective. She is hunched over her father like a watchful raven ready to spread her wings to defy anything that could hurt him. There they are: the interpreter and his daughter. There is an easiness and an intimacy between them that reaches out of the photograph to fold me in. I feel for the first time a measure of this woman, her inner strength, her loyalty, her passion.

I sometimes catch myself thinking that if Fanny hadn't swallowed that poison, I might have known her. But of course I couldn't have. If she had lived, my mother Violet wouldn't have married, and if eventually Fanny had died of old age, Violet would have been past childbearing. She was only ten years younger than her aunt, after all.

Violet married ten years after Fanny's death when she was thirty-five years old, about the same age as Fanny when she died. One day a friend had said to her, 'Vi, you can't always do what your mother wants,' and she realized that she could no longer ignore her longing to have her own child. No wonder Virtue never smiled at me.

I never knew my great-aunt Fanny and yet I feel bound to her. It was because of Fanny that my mother had an education and a career in the civil service. It counted for everything after my father died unexpectedly when I was ten, leaving us unprovided for. It meant that my mother could support us. When my grandmother Virtue left her husband Chang and took their children with her, no one was sure what would become of them. Chang himself struggled to provide for his second family by his concubine. His eldest granddaughter from this family grew up to be a 'sing-song girl', groomed for concubinage. The road between indigence and respectability is slippery, and many fall.

If not for Fanny, who would I be now?

Probably not a writer in south London! Now that our boys have grown up and become independent, we've moved from our cold, north-facing house to a small flat that is warm and light, near streets as crowded and noisy as any in Asia. It has a wide view of Victorian rooftops and chimneys, and the odd steeple. It never feels grey, even on a grey day. Sometimes I actually find our south-facing balcony too sunny. Imagine.

I arrived in a new country in early middle age knowing that I might never again live where I was born. The loneliness was hard at first but the years spent putting together this story gave me permission to stay close, emotionally, to the places I had left. While I recovered the past – the history of my antecedents – I could bond with the present. Many of the strangers at the school gate are now close friends.

Britain is where our sons grew up and where they call

home. Raised on shepherd's pie and spaghetti bolognaise, their favourite type of takeaway is Indian, especially chicken tikka masala, and they always order 'crispy aromatic duck' in a Chinese restaurant, a dish known only in Britain where the unhappy fowl is irradiated to cinders and served with a kind of pancake. I have done my job. I have brought them up to be British.

As for me, it would be hard now to leave forever the smell of damp leaves underfoot in autumn or the sight of dark sloes ripened in their thorny banks, or those clear cold winter days when one forgets the need for spring.

And I would miss these island people, devoted to their gardens and their DIY. The British are fair-minded on the whole, kind and polite, partial to a laugh and a cup of tea. They don't like to be too earnest. They do like a quiz. They think that a walk will cure anything. I'm beginning to believe that it will.

Where I lived when I grew up, street vendors sold spicy noodles and ice scraped off blocks to shape into snowballs covered in green and red syrup. The bustle of those early years can never be removed. I have learned that what formed us remains with us. History is alive. We are constantly the sum not only of all that we've experienced but of those who came before us. The genes of our ancestors are in us. They instruct us to pass on what is best of us. Perhaps they even communicate long-dormant hopes to us? How else to explain why, though my mother never talked about her unless I asked, I seem to have written a remembrance of Fanny?

Fanny left few traces of herself. There is her copy of Emerson's essays, a volume of short stories by Conrad, and her delicate gold watch that I inherited from my mother. Its case is etched with four stars, a minute diamond in each. Its bracelet of narrow gold links is so small that it could now, in our time of relative peace and plenty, only fit a child.

My grandmother Virtue died in 1963 when she was sixty-nine years old. For a while, the two sisters lay together under a marble bible and a cross with the inscriptions entirely in English, even Virtue's Chinese name *Mong-Han* – my grandmother, who couldn't speak or read English.

But the grave that they shared is gone. The Bidadari Cemetery in Singapore is no more, dug up to make way for an underground reservoir and blocks of flats. Only photographs and a few old things remain of these two women.

And this story. It may not be what they envisaged or expected but it is as heartfelt as any ceremony at their grave. I hope it returns Fanny to her place in the family narrative, which both sisters wanted more than anything else.

Fanny need no longer drift, unclaimed, like a cloud. She has a home. She is safe.

For the rest of us, however ordinary or disappointing we judge our lives to be, if we could ever come back – long after we must be forgotten – it may surprise us to find that we are still remembered, and who it is that remembers us.

Notes

Chapter 1

1 Albert Kawasi (2003), *Xinhui*, www.legacy1.net: 'The name *Xinhui [Sun Wui]* first appeared in AD 420 when *Xinhui Quon* which initially contained three and later increased to twelve counties was established.' (Last accessed 03/02/2021.)

2 Qihao Weng (2007), 'A historical perspective of river basin management in the Pearl River Delta of China', *Journal of Environmental Management*, Vol. 85, No. 4, pp. 1048–62.

3 Robert Marks (2004), 'Robert Marks on the Pearl River Delta', *Environmental History*, Vol. 9, Iss. 2, pp. 296–9; and Robert B. Marks (1998) *Tigers, Rice, Silk and Silt* (Cambridge University Press), p. 81.

4 Susan Mann (2005), 'Women in East Asia: China, Japan and Korea', in *Women's History in Global Perspective*, Vol. 2, ed. Bonnie G. Smith (Urbana, Ill: University of Illinois Press), p. 56.

5 Janice Stockard (1989), *Daughters of the Canton Delta: Marriage Patterns and Economic Strategies in South China, 1860–1930* (Stanford University Press).

6 Andre Gunder Frank (1998), *ReORIENT: Global Economy in the Asian Age* (Berkeley, Calif: University of California Press), p. 174.

7 *Qing China's Internal Crisis: Land Shortage, Famine, Rural Poverty*, Asia for Educators (Columbia University), at http://afe.easia. columbia.edu/special/china_1750_demographic.htm, accessed 06/02/2021.

8 Stephen Platt (2012), *Autumn in the Heavenly Kingdom: China, the West, and the Epic Story of the Taiping Civil War* (New York: Alfred A. Knopf), p. 359.

9 Weng, 'A historical perspective of river basin management'.

10 Brian Fagan (2000), *Little Ice Age: How Climate Made History 1300–1850* (New York: Basic Books).

11 Zhang De'er (1992, 'The Little Ice Age in China', in *New Data Challenges in Our Information Age*, ed. P. S. Glaeser and Michael T. L. Millward (CODATA), p. B-68.

12 *Qing China's Internal Crisis*. These provinces are now known as Shanxi, Henan, Shandong, Hebei and Shaanxi.

13 *The Famine in China: Illustrations by a native artist with a translation of the Chinese text* (1878), trans. James Legge (London: C. Kegan Paul & Co).

14 *The Famine in China.*

15 Paul Richard Bohr (1972), *Famine in China and the Missionary: Timothy Richard as Relief Administrator and Advocate of National Reform, 1876–1884* (East Asian Research Center, Harvard University, Cambridge, MA). Kiangsu is now spelt Jiangsu.

16 Kathryn Edgerton-Tarpley (2008), *Tears from Iron: Cultural Responses to Famine in Nineteenth-Century China* (Berkeley, Calif; London: University of California Press).

17 Bohr, *Famine in China and the Missionary.*

18 *The Analectic Magazine*, Vol. 12 (July–December 1818. Philadelphia: Moses Thomas), p. 343. Also P. J. Rivers (2004), 'Monsoon Rhythms and Trade Patterns: Ancient Times East of Suez', *Journal of the Malaysian Branch of the Royal Asiatic Society*, Vol. 77, No. 2 (287), pp. 59–93.

Chapter 3

1 Reuters (22 March 2007), *Chronology – Who banned slavery when?* at https://www.reuters.com/article/uk-slavery/chronology-

who-banned-slavery-when-idUSL1561464920070322. (Last accessed 08/12/2021.)

2 Persia Crawford Campbell (1923), *Chinese Coolie Emigration to Countries within the British Empire* (London: P. S. King and Son).

3 Robert J. Plowman (2001), 'The Voyage of the "Coolie" Ship Kate Hooper, October 3, 1857–March 26, 1858', *Prologue Magazine*, Summer, Vol. 33, No. 2 (U.S. National Archives and Records Administration), at https://www.archives.gov/pub lications/prologue/2001/summer/coolie-ship-kate-hooper-1.html.

4 Rudolph Ng (2014), 'The Chinese Commission to Cuba (1874): Reexamining International Relations in the Nineteenth Century from a Transcultural Perspective', *The Journal of Transcultural Studies*, Vol. 5, No. 2 at http://nbn-resolving.de/urn:nbn:de:bsz:16-ts-130092.

5 W. Pember Reeves, in Persia Crawford Campbell (1923), *Chinese Coolie Emigration to Countries within the British Empire* (London: P. S. King and Son), p. viii.

6 'The maritime rhythms of the Indian Ocean monsoon' (2014), *Shipwrecks and Submerged Worlds* (Centre for Maritime Archaeology, University of Southampton), at http://moocs. southampton.ac.uk/shipwrecks/2014/10/02maritime-rhythms-indian/ocean/monsoon/.

7 John S. Bastin (2009), *Letters and books of Sir Stamford Raffles and Lady Raffles: The Tang Holdings Collection of autograph letters and books of Sir Stamford Raffles and Lady Raffles* (Singapore: Editions Didier Millet), p. 256.

8 Cheryl-Ann Low (2004), 'Singapore from the 14th to 19th Century' in *Early Singapore 1300s–1819: Evidence in Maps, Text and Artefacts*, eds. John N. Miksic and Cheryl-Ann Low Mei Gek (Singapore: Singapore History Museum).

9 Abd Allah Ibn Abd Al-Qadir (1955), *The Hikayat Abdullah*, trans. A. H. Hill (Singapore: Malaya Publishing House), p. 156.

10 Saw Swee-Hock (2007), *The Population of Singapore*, 2nd edn (Singapore: Institute of Southeast Asian Studies), p. 9: in 1881 the population was 137,722.

11 The 1876 report of a Commission of Enquiry appointed by then Singapore governor Sir William Jervois to look into Chinese immigrants.

12 Campbell, *Chinese Coolie Emigration*. Also Yen Ching-hwang (2013), 'Chinese Coolie Emigration, 1845–74', in *Routledge Handbook of the Chinese Diaspora*, ed. Tan Chee-Beng (Abingdon: Routledge), p. 82 – the death toll on a coolie ship could sometimes be over 30 per cent.

13 Arnold J. Meagher (2008), *The Coolie Trade: The Traffic in Chinese Laborers to Latin America 1847–1874* (Philadelphia, Pa: Xlibris), p. 188.

14 Yen Ching-hwang (1986), *A Social History of the Chinese in Singapore and Malaya, 1800–1911* (Oxford University Press), p. 151.

15 F. W. Burbidge (1880), *The Gardens of the Sun* (London: John Murray).

16 Isabella L. Bird (1883), *The Golden Chersonese and the Way Thither* (New York: G. P. Putnam's Sons).

17 Leung Yuen-sang (1988), 'The Economic Life of the Chinese in late-nineteenth century Singapore', in *Early Chinese Immigrant Societies: Case Studies from North America and British Southeast Asia*, ed. Lee Lai-To (Singapore: Heinemann Asia).

Chapter 5

1 Thomas Taylor Meadows (1856), *The Chinese and their Rebellions* (London: Smith, Elder and Co.; digitally printed 2015,

Cambridge University Press), p. 48; the road to Guangzhou over the Meiling Pass is said to have been opened in the Tang dynasty in AD 713: Michael Dillon (1992) 'Transport and Marketing in the Development of the Jingdezhen Porcelain Industry during the Ming and Qing Dynasties', *Journal of the Economic and Social History of the Orient*, Vol. 35, No. 3, p. 281.

Chapter 6

1 Ichisada Miyazaki (1976), *China's Examination Hell: The Civil Service Examinations of Imperial China*, trans. Conrad Schirokauer (New York: John Weatherhill, Inc.).

2 Joseph Needham (2004), *Science and Civilisation in China Volume 7, Part 2: General Conclusions and Reflections* (Cambridge University Press), p. 8: 'There was at first a semblance of landed property securely held by individual families, but this institution never developed in Chinese history in a way comparable with feudal fief tenures of the West, since Chinese society did not retain the system of primogeniture. Hence all landed estates had to be parcelled out at each demise of the head of the family.'

3 'Traditional Society and Culture' (1987) in *China: A Country Study*, eds. Robert L. Worden, Andrea Matles Savada and Ronald E. Dolan (Washington, DC: GPO for the Library of Congress).

4 Miyazaki, *China's Examination Hell*, p. 16.

5 Ibid.

6 Frank Ching (1988), *Ancestors: 900 Years in the Life of a Chinese Family* (London: Harrap), p. 129.

7 Oral History Interviews, National Archives of Singapore.

8 Ibid.

9 Ying Bai (2019), 'Farewell to Confucianism: The Modernizing Effect of Dismantling China's Imperial Examination System', *Journal of Development Economics*, Vol. 141: 102382.

10 David Curtis Wright (2011), *The History of China* (Santa Barbara, Calif: Greenwood, an imprint of ABC-CLIO, LLC), p. 300.

Chapter 7

1 C. Tan and K. Fujita (2014), 'Building Construction of Pre-war Shophouses in George Town Observed Through a Renovation Case Study', *Journal of Asian Architecture and Building Engineering*, Vol. 13 (1), pp. 195–202.

2 J. A. Bethune Cook (1907), *Sunny Singapore, an account of the place and its people, with a sketch of the results of missionary work* (London: Elliot Stock), p. 33.

3 Felix Chia (1994), *The Babas Revisited* (Singapore: Heinemann Asia), p. 20.

4 Leung Yuen-sang (1988), 'The Economic Life of the Chinese in late-nineteenth-century Singapore', in *Early Chinese Immigrant Societies: Case Studies from North America and British Southeast Asia*, ed. Lee Lai-To (Singapore: Heinemann Asia).

5 *The Singapore and Straits Directory for 1883*; for an interesting account of early education in Singapore, see also Yap Kwang Tan, Hong Kheng Chow and Christine Goh (2008), *Examinations in Singapore: Change and Continuity, 1891–2007* (Singapore; Hackensack, NJ: World Scientific).

6 Lim Peng Han (2008), 'English Schools and School Libraries before the Second World War: A Singapore Perspective', *Singapore Journal of Library and Information Management*, Vol. 37.

7 Vina Jie-Min Prasad and Jaime Koh (2014), 'Raffles Institution' (Singapore Infopedia), at https://eresources.nlb.gov.sg/infopedia/articles/SIP_17_2004-12-21.html. (Last accessed 08/12/2021.) The school's name was changed from Singapore Institution to Raffles Institution some time in 1868.

8 Isabella L. Bird (1883), *The Golden Chersonese and the Way Thither* (New York: G. P. Putnam's Sons).

9 Aruna Reena Singh (1995), *A Journey Through Singapore: Travellers' Impressions of a By-gone Time* (Singapore: Landmark Books), p. 194.

Chapter 8

1 Saw Swee-Hock (2007), *The Population of Singapore*, 2nd edn (Singapore: Institute of Southeast Asian Studies), Table 3.1, p. 29.

2 *Report on the census of the Straits Settlements* (5 April 1891), at http://www.sabrizain.org/malaya/library/straitscensus.pdf, p. 43 of the report. There were 35,000 Malays, 16,000 Indians and 5,000 Europeans to the more than 100,000 Chinese. (Last accessed 08/12/2021.)

3 Felix Chia (1994), *The Babas Revisited* (Singapore: Heinemann Asia).

4 Vernon Cornelius-Takahama (2018), 'Mount Sophia' (Singapore Infopedia), at https://eresources.nlb.gov.sg/infopedia/articles/SIP_482_2004-12-27.html, accessed 18/02/2021.

5 You chose a new name when your status or your ambition changed: Frank Ching (1988), *Ancestors: 900 Years in the Life of a Chinese Family* (London: Harrap), p. 42.

6 R. N. Jackson (1966), *Pickering: Protector of Chinese* (Oxford University Press), p. 59.

7 William Alexander Pickering (1898), *Pioneering in Formosa: Recollections of adventures among mandarins, wreckers, & head-hunting savages* (London: Hurst & Blackett).

8 In 1871, 40,000 of the 55,000 Chinese in Singapore were gang members. See C. B. Buckley (1902), *An Anecdotal History of Old Times in Singapore,* Vol. 1 (Singapore: Fraser and Neave), p. 213; and Saw, *Population,* 2nd edn, Table 3.1, p. 29.

9 Jackson, *Pickering,* p. 50, referencing article by Pickering in October 1876 for *Fraser's Magazine.*

10 S. Y. Ng (1961), 'The Chinese Protectorate in Singapore, 1877–1900', in *Journal of Southeast Asian History,* Vol. 2, No. 1, pp. 76–99.

11 Jackson, *Pickering,* p.106, quoting *Singapore Free Press and Mercantile Advertiser* (18 July 1887).

Chapter 9

1 Duncan France (2014), 'History of Chinese People in New Zealand – Helen Wong and Bill Wilmott', *New Zealand China Friendship Society,* at https://nzchinasociety.org.nz/helen-wong-and-the-history-of-chinese-people-in-new-zealand/.

Chapter 10

1 Modern History Sourcebook (Fordham University): *Qian Long: Letter to George III, 1793,* at https://sourcebooks.fordham.edu/mod/1793qianlong.asp, accessed 06/02/2021.

2 Zheng Yangwen (2005), *The Social Life of Opium in China* (Cambridge University Press), p. 11.

3 Zheng, *Social Life of Opium,* p. 46.

4 World Drug Report (2008), *A Century of International Drug Control,* p. 173, at https://www.unodc.org/documents/wdr/ WDR_2008/WDR2008_100years_drug_control_origins.pdf, accessed 04/05/2021.

5 Alfred W. McCoy (2000), 'From Free Trade to Prohibition: A Critical History of the Modern Asian Opium Trade', *Fordham Urban Law Journal,* Vol. 28, No. 1, Art. 4, p. 319–20, at https:// ir.lawnet.fordham.edu/ulj/vol28/iss1/4, accessed 29/04/2021.

6 McCoy, 'From Free Trade to Prohibition', *Fordham Urban Law Journal,* Vol. 28, No. 1, Art. 4, p. 320.

7 Ibid.

8 Zheng, *Social Life of Opium.*

9 Mitchell Chan (2019), 'Rule of Law and China's Unequal Treaties: Conceptions of the Rule of Law and Its Role in Chinese International Law and Diplomatic Relations in the Early Twentieth Century', *Penn History Review,* Vol. 25, Iss. 2, Art. 2, p. 27; and *The Unequal Treaties, Bulletin No. 5* (1927, The American Committee for Fair Play in China) available at https://digitalrepository.trincoll.edu/cgi/viewcontent. cgi?article=1007&context=moore, accessed 06/02/2021.

10 Louis G. Perez (1998), *The History of Japan* (Westport, Conn; London: Greenwood Press), pp.73–4.

11 *Contemporary Japan: A Teaching Workbook, Japan Answers the Challenge of the Western World,* Asia for Educators (Columbia University), at http://afe.easia.columbia.edu/special/japan_ 1750_meiji.htm, accessed 06/02/2021.

12 Wang Po Hou (AD 960), *Three Character Classic,* trans. Chiang Ker Chiu (1941, Singapore: Chung Hwa Mandarin Institution), p. 7, accessed through https://archive.org/details/TheThree-CharacterClassic/page/n7/mode/2up 03/05/2021.

13 Bernd Martin and Peter Wetzler (1990), 'The German Role in the Modernization of Japan – the Pitfall of Blind

Acculturation', *Oriens Extremus*, Vol. 33, No. 1 (Wiesbaden: Harrossowitz Verlag), p. 81, accessed through JSTOR 04/05/2021; and John Curtis Perry (1966), 'Great Britain and the Emergence of Japan as a Naval Power', *Monumenta Nipponica*, Vol. 21, No. 3/4 (Tokyo: Sophia University), p. 311, accessed through JSTOR 04/05/2021.

14 S. C. M. Paine (2003), *The Sino-Japanese War of 1894–1895: Perceptions, Power and Primacy* (Cambridge University Press), p. 181.

15 Collection of Japanese and Chinese prints depicting the Sino-Japanese War of 1894–1895, the British Library, London.

16 The Chinese were presented as 'sub-human' in at least one print. Benjamin Elman (2013), 'The "Rise" of Japan and the "Fall" of China after 1895', in *The Chinese Chameleon Revisited: From the Jesuits to Zhang Yimou*, ed. Zheng Yangwen (Cambridge Scholars Publishing), pp. 150–1.

17 Nicolas Schillinger (2016), *The Body and Military Masculinity in Late Qing and Early Republican China: The Art of Governing Soldiers* (Lanham, Md: Lexington Books), p. 3.

18 The warships that Japan won from China were state of the art and advanced the Japanese fleet. See Elman, 'The "Rise" of Japan and the "Fall" of China', in *Chinese Chameleon*, pp. 160–1.

19 Pekka Korhonen (2013), 'Leaving Asia? The Meaning of Datsu-A and Japan's Modern History', *The Asia-Pacific Journal*, Vol. 11, Iss. 50, No. 1: refers to Maruyama Masao, who points out that after Japan's victory in the first Sino-Japanese War, feelings of superiority over China emerged in Japan.

20 Dwight Kwok (2009), *A Translation of Datsu-A Ron: Decoding a Pre-war Japanese Nationalistic Theory*, MA thesis, University of Toronto, p. 48.

Chapter 11

1 Leung Yuen-sang (1988) 'The Economic Life of the Chinese in late-nineteenth-century Singapore', in *Early Chinese Immigrant Societies: Case Studies from North America and British Southeast Asia*, ed. Lee Lai-To (Singapore: Heinemann Asia).

2 Felix Chia (1994), *The Babas Revisited* (Singapore: Heinemann Asia), Ch. 4.

3 Joyce Ee (1961), 'Chinese Migration to Singapore, 1896–1941', *Journal of Southeast Asian History*, Vol. 2, Iss. 1, p. 33.

4 R. N. Jackson (1965), *Pickering: Protector of Chinese* (Oxford University Press), p. 93.

5 'Sun Yat-Sen and the Role of Japan' (1970), *Taiwan Today*, at https://taiwantoday.tw/news.php?unit=29,45&post=36812, accessed 04/05/2021.

6 'Miyazaki Toten', at http://www.bekkoame.ne.jp/~gensei/ten/etoten.html, accessed 07/02/2021.

7 Andrew Melville Pooley (1920), *Japan's Foreign Policies* (Reprint London: Forgotten Books, 2013), pp. 57–58.

8 Michael Mukunthan, 'Sun Yat Sen' (Singapore Infopedia), at https://eresources.nlb.gov.sg/infopedia/articles/SIP_845__2009-01-07.html, accessed 25/8/2021.

9 Ian Nish (2002), 'The First Anglo-Japanese Alliance Treaty', in *Anglo-Japanese Alliance Symposium*, Discussion Paper No. IS/02/432 (London: Suntory and Toyota International Centres for Economics and Related Disciplines with the Japan Society), p. 13.

Chapter 12

1 J. H. Drabble (1967), 'The Plantation Rubber Industry in Malaya up to 1922', *Journal of the Malaysian Branch of the Royal Asiatic Society*, Vol. 40, No. 1 (211), pp. 54–5.

2 Owen Rutter (1922), *British North Borneo: An Account of its History, Resources and Native Tribes* (Edinburgh: Constable and Co. Ltd), pp. 174-175.

3 *Singapore: A Country Study* (1991), ed. Barbara Leitch LePoer (Washington, DC: Library of Congress), p. 65; see also W. W. Willoughby (1925), *Opium as an International Problem: The Geneva Conferences* (Baltimore, Md: The Johns Hopkins Press).

4 Col. J. R. H. Hutchison of Glasgow, Central (16 June 1947), motion on 'British Firms, Borneo (Taxation)', *Hansard*, at https://api.parliament.uk/historic-hansard/commons/1947/jun/16/british-firms-borneo-taxation, accessed 07/02/2021.

5 Ichisada Miyazaki (1976), *China's Examination Hell: The Civil Service Examinations of Imperial China*, trans. Conrad Schirokauer (New York: John Weatherhill, Inc.).

6 Emma Woo Louie (1998), *Chinese American Names: Tradition and Transition* (Jefferson, NC: McFarland & Company, Inc.), p. 51.

7 Jonathan Clements, *Confucius: A Biography* (Stroud: Sutton Publishing, © Muramasa Industries 2004), pp. 85–100.

8 *I Ching or Book of Changes*, 3rd edn (1968), trans. Richard Wilhelm and Cary F. Baynes (London: Routledge & Kegan Paul), Hexagram 13 commentary on p. 59.

9 Lee Sheng Yi (1974), *The Monetary and Banking Development of Singapore and Malaysia* (Singapore University Press), p. 25, describes the great rubber boom of 1908–13 with its very high prices, high profits and extensive planting of rubber in Malaya.

10 Tze-Ling Li (2007), 'A Study of Ethnic Influence on the Facades of Colonial Shophouses in Singapore: A Case Study of Telok Ayer in Chinatown', *Journal of Asian Architecture and Building Engineering* (6:1, 41–8, DOI: 10.3130/jaabe.6.41), p. 44 for shophouse style in the 1880s.

11 Ma Mingde (2014), 'Tang Hualong in the 1911 Revolution' in *China: How the Empire Fell,* ed. Joseph W. Esherick and C. X. George Wei (London; New York: Routledge), pp. 147–8.

Chapter 13

1 Wilt L. Idema (2010), *The Butterfly Lovers* (Indianapolis, Ind: Hackett Publishing Company, Inc.), Introduction p. xiii.

2 'Fair, Fair, Cry the Ospreys' in *The Book of Songs: The Ancient Chinese Classic of Poetry* (1996), trans. Arthur Waley (New York: Grove Press), p. 5.

3 Chunming Gao (2010), *Chinese Dress and Adornment Through the Ages* (London: CYPI Press).

4 Idema, *Butterfly Lovers*, Introduction p. xviii.

Chapter 14

1 Edwin A. Brown (2007), *Indiscreet Memories: 1901 Through the Eyes of a Colonial Englishman* (Singapore: Monsoon Books), p. 47.

2 Prof. David R. Woodward (2014), 'The Middle East During World War One', *BBC History*, at http://www.bbc.co.uk/history/worldwars/wwone/middle_east_01.shtml, accessed 08/02/2021.

3 C. S. Hew (2001), 'Ancient Chinese orchid cultivation: A fresh look at an age-old practice', *Scientia Horticulturae* (87,1–2): 1–10

(ScholarBank@NUS Repository at https://doi.org/10.1016/
S0304-4238(00)00137-0), accessed 08/02/2021.

4 Shakila Yacob (2008), *The United States and the Malaysian Economy* (London; New York: Routledge), p.118: 'In addition, by 1921, a large stock of American makes, including ... the Studebaker, was available in Singapore.'

5 Owen Rutter (2001), 'The State of North Borneo', in *South East Asia, Colonial History: Empire-building during the Nineteenth Century*, ed. Paul H. Kratoska (London; New York: Routledge), p.285.

6 W. W. Willoughby (1925), *Opium as an International Problem: The Geneva Conferences* (Baltimore, Md: The Johns Hopkins Press): in Borneo, consumption of opium increased 27 per cent from 1914 to 1916.

7 W. H. Treacher (1891), *British Borneo: Sketches of Brunai, Sarawak, Labuan, and North Borneo* (Singapore Government print department).

8 D. J. M. Tate (1988), *Rajah Brooke's Borneo* (Hong Kong: John Nicholson Ltd), pp. 89–90.

9 Ada Pryer (1893), *A Decade in Borneo* (London: Hutchinson).

10 Edwin J. Clapp (1915), *Economic Aspects of the War* (Yale University Press), accessed through Brigham Young University's online library at https://net.lib.byu.edu/~rdh7/wwi/comment/Clapp/Clapp5.htm. In Ch. 11, 'The Export Situation', Clapp writes: 'In nine months ending May 31, 1915, we ... exported $30,000,000 of commercial automobiles, which is $29,000,000 more than in the previous year.' (Last accessed 08/12/2021.)

11 Choo Eng Kang (1975), *The Singapore Trade Depression, 1920–22* (National University of Singapore).

12 Weijing Lu (2008), *True to Her Word: The Faithful Maiden Cult in Late Imperial China* (Stanford University Press), p. 134.

Chapter 15

1 About 700 girls according to Tan Liok Ee (2003), 'A Century of Change', in *Asian Migrants and Education: The Tensions of Education in Immigrant Societies and among Migrant Groups*, ed. Michael W. Charney, Brenda S. A. Yeoh and Tong Chee Kiong (Dordrecht: Kluwer Academic Publishers).

2 'Leong Seng Ngian and family (Bukit Brown)' (2012), Rojak Librarian, at https://mymindisrojak.blogspot.com/2012/11/leong-seng-ngian-and-family-bukit-brown.html. (Last accessed 17/09/21.)

3 Jingdezhen in Pinyin as it is known today.

4 C. G. Kwa, J. Teo, D. Ang and J. Yoong (2015), 'Lee Choo Neo' in *Great Peranakans: Fifty Remarkable Lives*, ed. Alan Chong (Singapore: Asian Civilizations Museum).

5 Frank Ching (1988), *Ancestors: 900 Years in the Life of a Chinese Family* (London: Harrap), p. 390.

Chapter 16

1 縛跤

2 Jack Barbalet (2017), *Confucianism and the Chinese Self: Re-examining Max Weber's China* (Singapore: Palgrave Macmillan: Springer Singapore), p. 119; and Kenneth Gaw (1988), *Superior Servants: Legendary Cantonese Amahs of the Far East* (Oxford University Press), p. 43.

3 James Thayer Addison (1924), 'The Modern Chinese Cult of Ancestors', *The Journal of Religion*, Vol. 4, No. 5, p. 497 (The University of Chicago Press Journals), at https://www.journals.uchicago.edu/doi/10.1086/480458, accessed 18/02/2021.

4 Rubie S. Watson (1994), 'Girls' Houses and Working Women: Expressive Culture from the Pearl River Delta 1900–41', in *Women and Chinese Patriarchy: Submission, Servitude, and Escape*, ed. Maria Jaschok and Suzanne Miers (Hong Kong University Press), pp 28–9.

5 Janice Stockard (1989) called this 'delayed transfer marriage' in *Daughters of the Canton Delta: Marriage Patterns and Economic Strategies in South China, 1860–1930* (Stanford University Press).

6 Tomoko Shiroyama (2008), *China During the Great Depression: Market, State, and the World Economy, 1929–1937* (Harvard University Asia Center).

7 Stockard, in *Daughters of the Canton Delta*, calls this 'compensation marriage'.

8 Stockard, in *Daughters of the Canton Delta*, refers to this as 'bride-initiated spirit marriage'.

9 Julie Sherman (2003), *Silk in China Circa 1840: The Introduction of the Worldwide System to China's Silk Industry* (The Northampton Silk Project, Smith College, Northampton, MA) http://www.smith.edu/hsc/silk/papers/sherman.html

10 Julie Sherman, *Silk in China circa 1840*.

11 Ziling Ye (2008), 'Zishu Nu: Dutiful Daughters of the Guangdong Delta', *Intersections: Gender and Sexuality in Asia and the Pacific*, Iss. 17.

12 Stockard, *Daughters of the Canton Delta*.

13 Ibid.

14 Ibid. Sometimes a whole group of girls would commit suicide if one of them was forced to marry.

Chapter 17

1 'Memories, Gems and Sentiments: 100 Years of Methodist Girls' School' (1877, Singapore: Methodist Girls School), pp. 5–6: the school's white and blue uniform was introduced in 1922, worn with white stockings.

2 Earnest Lau (2008), *From Mission to Church: The Evolution of the Methodist Church in Singapore and Malaysia: 1885–1976* (Singapore: Genesis Books), p. 15.

3 Claire G. Jones (2009), *Femininity, Mathematics and Science, 1880–1914* (Palgrave Macmillan), p. 19: in 1886, William Withers Moore's presidential address to the British Medical Association touched on *anorexia scholastica* in women, prompting calls for protective legislation.

4 C. Mary Turnbull (2002), 'The Malayan Connection', in *An Impossible Dream: Hong Kong University from Foundation to Reestablishment, 1910–1950*, ed. Chan Lau Kit-Ching and Peter Cunich (Oxford University Press), p. 106.

5 Turnbull, 'Malayan Connection', in *Impossible Dream*, ed. Chan Lau and Cunich, p. 108.

6 *An Impossible Dream: Hong Kong University from Foundation to Reestablishment, 1910–1950*, ed. Chan Lau Kit-Ching and Peter Cunich (Oxford University Press).

7 Peter Cunich (2012), *A History of the University of Hong Kong, Volume 1, 1911–1945* (Hong Kong University Press).

Chapter 18

1 Sir William Brunyate's inauguration speech in 1921, *University of Hong Kong: The First 50 Years 1911–1961* (1962), ed. Brian Harrison (Hong Kong University Press), p. 127.

2 Many thanks to Dr Peter Cunich, Associate Professor, Department of History, University of Hong Kong, for this information.

3 Staci Ford (2002), 'Women, Gender and HKU', in *An Impossible Dream: Hong Kong University from Foundation to Re-establishment, 1910–1950*, ed. Chan Lau Kit-Ching and Peter Cunich (Oxford University Press), p. 135.

4 Charles Poor Kindleberger (1973), *The World in Depression 1929–1939* (Munich: Deutscher Taschenbuch Verlag), p.137.

5 Steve Tsang (2007), *A Modern History of Hong Kong: 1841–1997* (London: I.B. Tauris and Co), p. 108.

6 Kenneth Gaw (1988), *Superior Servants: Legendary Cantonese Amahs of the Far East* (Oxford University Press), p. 45.

7 Janice G. Raymond (2001), *A Passion for Friends: Toward a Philosophy of Female Affection* (North Melbourne, Vic: Spinifex Press), p. 124.

8 Majorie Topley (1975), 'Marriage Resistance in Rural Kwangtung' in *Women in Chinese Society*, ed. Margery Wolf, Roxane Witke and Emily Martin (Stanford University Press), p. 83.

9 Gaw, *Superior Servants*; Janice Stockard (1989), *Daughters of the Canton Delta: Marriage Patterns and Economic Strategies in South China, 1860–1930* (Stanford University Press).

10 Gaw, *Superior Servants*, p. 45.

11 Stockard, *Daughters of the Canton Delta*, p. 74.

12 Ibid.

Chapter 19

1 *Report on the Census of the Colony of Hong Kong* (1931) as quoted in the Hong Kong Legislative Council minutes of meeting on

27 October 1932, p. 8 (or p. 221 at http://www.legco.gov.hk/1932/h321027.pdf, accessed 11/02/2021).

2 Irene Cheng (1962), 'Women Students and Graduates', in *University of Hong Kong: The First 50 Years,* ed. Brian Harrison (Hong Kong University Press), p. 150.

3 Dr Peter Cunich.

4 Cheng, 'Women Students and Graduates', in *University of Hong Kong*, ed. Harrison, p. 151.

5 Vera Schwarcz (1986), *The Chinese Enlightenment: Intellectuals and the Legacy of the May Fourth Movement of 1919* (Berkeley, Calif: University of California Press), p. 284.

6 Schwarcz, *Chinese Enlightenment*, p. 107, citing Daoist lawyer Wu Yu's 1917 article, 'The Family System as the Basis of Despotism'.

7 Thomas Edward La Fargue (1973), *China and the World War* (New York: Howard Fertig).

8 United Nations Office on Drugs and Crime (1953), 'Illicit Traffic in Opium', *Bulletin on Narcotics* (Iss. 3).

9 W. W. Willoughby (1925), *Opium as an International Problem: The Geneva Conferences* (Baltimore, Md: The Johns Hopkins Press), p. 444.

10 Bai Gao (1997), *Economic Ideology and Japanese Industrial Policy: Developmentalism from 1931 to 1965* (Cambridge University Press), p. 72.

11 Sandra Wilson (2002), *The Manchurian Crisis and Japanese Society, 1931–3* (London; New York: Routledge), p. 174.

12 Miriam Lynn Kingsberg (2009), *The Poppy and the Acacia: Opium and Imperialism in Japanese Dairen and the Kwantung Leased Territory, 1905–1945* (dissertation, University of California, Berkeley), p. 3.

13 Kingsberg, *The Poppy and the Acacia*, p. 6.

14 *The Newest Link in the Principal Highway round the World* (1915), a pamphlet on the South Manchuria Railway; and Henry W. Kinney (1928), *Modern Manchuria and the South Manchuria Railway Company* (Japan Advertiser Press), p. 44.

15 Donald A. Jordan (2001), *China's Trial by Fire: The Shanghai War of 1932* (Ann Arbor, Mich: University of Michigan Press), p. 11.

Chapter 20

1 Henrique de Senna Fernandes (2004), *The Bewitching Braid*, trans. David Brookshaw (Hong Kong University Press), p. 150.

2 Donald A. Jordan (2001), *China's Trial by Fire: The Shanghai War of 1932* (Ann Arbor, Mich: University of Michigan Press), p. 63.

3 Harold R. Isaacs (1985), *Re-encounters in China: Notes of a Journey in a Time Capsule* (Armonk, NY; London: M. E. Sharpe, Inc.), p. 14.

4 James Z. Gao (2009), *Historical Dictionary of Modern China (1800–1949)* (Lanham, Md: Scarecrow Press), p. 171.

5 Edgar Snow (1934), *Far Eastern Front: The Sino-Japanese War of 1931–33* (London: Jarrolds), p. 212.

6 Arnaud Doglia (2011), 'Japanese mass violence and its victims in the Fifteen Years War (1931–45)', in *Online Encyclopedia of Mass Violence*, http://www.massviolence.org/Japanese-mass-violence-and-its-victims-in-the-Fifteen-Years, accessed 12/02/2021.

7 Hiroko Sherwin (2015), *Japan's WWII Legacy* (London: Quartet Books), p. 188.

8 Ben Bernanke and Harold James (1991), 'The Gold Standard, Deflation, and Financial Crisis in the Great Depression: An International Comparison', in *Financial Markets and Financial Crises*, ed. R. Glenn Hubbard (University of Chicago Press), p. 37.

9 Loh Kah Seng (2006), 'Records and Voices of Social History: The Case of the Great Depression in Singapore', *Southeast Asian Studies*, Vol. 44, No.1, Table 1, p. 34.

Chapter 21

1 Ralph Waldo Emerson (1841), *Essays: First Series* [online] *1996–2021 EmersonCentral.com*, at http://www.emersoncentral.com/selfreliance.htm, accessed 13/02/2021.

2 Loh Kah Seng (2006), 'Beyond Rubber Prices: Negotiating the Great Depression in Singapore', *South East Asia Research*, Vol. 14, No. 1: 634 bankruptcies in 1929, 1,004 in 1932.

3 Loh Kah Seng, 'Beyond Rubber Prices'.

4 John G. Butcher (1979), *The British in Malaya, 1880–1941: The Social History of a European Community in Colonial South-east Asia* (Oxford University Press), p. 143.

5 Butcher, *British in Malaya*, p. 132.

6 Ibid.

7 Loh Kah Seng (2006), 'Records and Voices of Social History: The Case of the Great Depression in Singapore', *Southeast Asian Studies*, Vol. 44, No. 1 (Kyoto University), p. 46.

8 Hu Wen (2004), *To Forge a Strong and Wealthy China? The Buy-Chinese Products Movement in Singapore 1905–1937*, thesis, National University of Singapore, p. 47.

9 C. Mary Turnbull (1977), *A History of Singapore 1819–1975* (Oxford University Press), p. 135.

10 C. F. Yong and R. B. McKenna (1990), *The Kuomintang Movement in British Malaya, 1912–1949* (Singapore University Press), p. 64. Also Hu, *To Forge a Strong and Wealthy China?*

11 The National Archives (Kew), *FCO 141/19947*: 'In February 1930 ... Sir Cecil Clementi had a meeting with 17 local

Kuomintang leaders at which he forbade the holding of Kuomintang meetings, collection of subscriptions, enrolment of members or publication of propaganda. All branches were unlawful and must be dissolved forthwith although an individual might be a member of the Tang.'

12 'Heong Jo' means 'Orchard'.

Chapter 22

1 Loh Kah Seng (2006), 'Records and Voices of Social History: The Case of the Great Depression in Singapore', *Southeast Asian Studies*, Vol. 44, No. 1 (Kyoto University), p. 36.

2 Tony Latter (2004), *Hong Kong's Exchange Rate Regimes in the Twentieth Century* (University of Hong Kong and Hong Kong Institute for Monetary Research), p. 19.

Chapter 23

1 Albert Galvany (2012), 'Death and Ritual Wailing in Early China: Around the Funeral of Lao Dan', *Asia Major*, 3rd Series, 25.2, pp. 15–42.

Chapter 24

1 Richard J. Smethurst (2007), *From Foot Soldier to Finance Minister: Takahashi Korekiyo, Japan's Keynes* (Cambridge, Mass: Harvard University Asia Center), p. 238.

2 Smethurst, *Foot Soldier*, p. 263.

3 Hugh Byas (1942), *Government by Assassination* (New York: Alfred A. Knopf).

4 E. R. Dickover (1936), *Report and telegram from the Chargé in Japan to the Secretary of State Oct 1ˢᵗ and 2ⁿᵈ* (Office of the Historian: Foreign Relations of the United States Diplomatic Papers, The Far East, Vol. 4), p. 368; R. S. Chaurasia (2004), *History of Modern China* (New Delhi: Atlantic Publishers and Distributors), p. 190.

Chapter 25

1 Faizah bte Zakaria (2016), *Sembawang Naval Base* (Singapore Infopedia), at https://eresources.nlb.gov.sg/infopedia/art icles/SIP_1820_2011-07-19.html, accessed 14/02/2021.

2 A Correspondent (April 1938), 'Peaceful Singapore' *British Malaya Vols. 12–13, 1937–39* (Association of British Malaya).

3 Andrew Field (2004), *Royal Navy Strategy in the Far East 1919–1939: Preparing for War against Japan* (London; New York: Frank Cass), p. 104.

4 The Washington Naval Conference resulted in the Four Power and Five Power Treaties of end 1921 and early 1922; see Jon Christopher Scully (2011), *From Alliance to Enmity: Anglo-Japanese Relations, 1930 to 1939,* MPhil thesis, University of Birmingham, p. 22.

5 Nicholas Roosevelt (June 1929), 'The Strategy of Singapore', *British Malaya* (Association of British Malaya), p. 55.

6 Edwin P. Hoyt (1993), *Three Military Leaders: Heihachiro Togo, Isoroku Yamamoto, Tomoyuki Yamashita* (Tokyo; London: Kodansha International), p. 129. See also General Matsui's testimony to the International Military Tribunal Tokyo in

Callum MacDonald (1999), '"Kill All, Burn All, Loot All":
The Nanking Massacre of December 1937 and Japanese
Policy in China' in *The Massacre in History*, eds. Mark Levene
and Penny Roberts (New York; Oxford: Berghahn Books),
p. 233.

7 MacDonald, '"Kill All, Burn All, Loot All"', in *The Massacre in
History*, ed. Levene and Roberts, p.228.

8 Ibid., p.226.

9 'Cable Was Suppressed by Japan: Tells of Outrages in Nanking' (5 February 1938), *Singapore Free Press and Mercantile
Advertiser*, p. 2, at http://eresources.nlb.gov.sg/newspapers/
Digitised/Article/singfreepressb19380205-1.2.17.aspx,
accessed 14/02/2021.

10 MacDonald, '"Kill All, Burn All, Loot All"', in *The Massacre in
History*, ed. Levene and Roberts, p. 240.

11 'More Atrocities in Nanking: Mass Murder, Rape & Bayonet-
ting' (29 January 1938), *Singapore Free Press and Mercantile
Advertiser*, p.1, at https://eresources.nlb.gov.sg/newspapers/
Digitised/Article/singfreepressb19380129-1.2.5, accessed
14/02/2021.

12 Hiroko Sherwin (2016), *Japan's World War II Legacy: Interviews
with Japanese Survivors* (London: Quartet Books), pp. 25–6.

13 *Substantive and Procedural Aspects of International Criminal Law:
The Experience of International and National Law Courts* (2000),
ed. Gabrielle Kirk McDonald and Olivia Swaak-Goldman,
Vol. 2, Pt 1 (The Hague; London; Boston: Kluwer Law International), p. 779.

14 Ibid.

15 Shi Young and James Yin (1997), *The Rape of Nanking: An
Undeniable History in Photographs* (Chicago, Ill: Innovative Publishing Group), p. 188. Also *China News Digest*.

16 'Japanese Atrocities Alleged' (28 December 1937), *Straits Times*, p. 9, at https://eresources.nlb.gov.sg/newspapers/Digitised/Article/straitstimes19371228-1.2.31, accessed 14/02/2021.

Chapter 26

1 Siyen Fei (2012), 'Writing for Justice: An Activist Beginning of the Cult of Female Chastity in Late Imperial China', *The Journal of Asian Studies*, Vol. 71, No. 4, p. 1008.

2 Susan Mann (1987), 'Widows in the Kinship, Class, and Community Structures of Qing Dynasty China', *The Journal of Asian Studies*, Vol. 46, No. 1, p. 43.

3 Weijing Lu (2008), *True to Her Word: The Faithful Maiden Cult in Late Imperial China* (Stanford University Press), p.7 and pp. 89–90.

4 Lu, *True to Her Word*, p. 68.

5 Ibid., p. 143.

Chapter 27

1 'Leong Seng Ngian and family (Bukit Brown)' (2012), Rojak Librarian: this article on the Leong family tomb includes information on Leong's son-in-law Ng Seng Choy, at https://mymindisrojak.blogspot.com/2012/11/leong-seng-ngian-and-family-bukit-brown.html, accessed 15/02/2021.

2 Reports from General Chiang Kai-Shek's conference with international press in Chungking (11 February 1939), as conveyed by the Chargé in China (Peck) to the Secretary of State: 'Southward advance of Japanese expansionist

movement: Hainan and the Spratly Islands' (Office of the Historian: Foreign Relations of the United States Diplomatic Papers, The Far East, Vol. 3), p. 106, at https://history.state.gov/historicaldocuments/frus1939v03/comp2, accessed 15/02/2021.

3 *British Malaya* (October 1939, Association of British Malaya).

4 John H. Drabble (1991), *Malayan Rubber: The Interwar Years* (Basingstoke: Macmillan Academic and Professional), p. 24.

5 R. C. H. McKie (1942), *This was Singapore* (Sydney; London: Angus & Robertson).

6 Ilsa Sharp (1981), *There Is Only One Raffles: The Story of a Grand Hotel* (London: Souvenir Press), quoting Ian Morrison.

7 *British Malaya* (April 1939, Association of British Malaya).

8 'Shakespearean Recital by Marie Ney' (24 April 1940), *Singapore Free Press and Mercantile Advertiser*, p. 2, at https://eresources.nlb.gov.sg/newspapers/digitised/issue/singfreepressb194 00424-1, accessed 15/02/2021.

Chapter 28

1 My mother told me that she was in a rickshaw – there were still nearly 4,000 of these in use in the colony in 1940. It was the Japanese who reintroduced trishaws to Singapore during their occupation of the island. See Bonny Tan, 'Rickshaw', at eresources.nlb.gov.sg/infopedia/articles. (Last accessed 09/12/2021.)

2 Janice Stockard (1989), *Daughters of the Canton Delta: Marriage Patterns and Economic Strategies in South China, 1860–1930* (Stanford University Press).

Chapter 29

1 'Amusements Hit' (5 December 1941), *Malaya Tribune*, p. 5, at eresources.nlb.gov.sg/newspapers, accessed 06/09/2021.

2 'Australian Troops Arrive in Thousands' (19 February 1941), *Malaya Tribune*, p. 3, at eresources.nlb.gov.sg/newspapers, accessed 06/09/2021.

3 C. Mary Turnbull (1977), *A History of Singapore 1819–1975* (Oxford University Press), p.169.

4 Ayako Hotta-Lister (2002), 'The Anglo-Japanese Alliance of 1911', in *Anglo-Japanese Alliance Symposium*, Discussion Paper No. IS/02/432 (Suntory and Toyota International Centres for Economics and Related Disciplines with the Japan Society, London), p. 43, quoting Sir Edward Grey, British Foreign Secretary at the time of negotiations for the third treaty.

5 Louis G. Morton (1987), 'Japan's Decision for War', in *Command Decisions,* ed. Kent Roberts Greenfield (Center of Military History, United States Army, Washington DC), pp. 99–124.

6 Sachiko Murakami (1981), *Japan's Thrust into French Indochina, 1940–1945* (New York University).

7 Turnbull, *A History of Singapore*, p. 168.

8 'Amusements Hit', *Malaya Tribune*.

9 Ilsa Sharp (1981), *There Is Only One Raffles: The Story of a Grand Hotel* (London: Souvenir Press).

10 Ibid.; and R. C. H. McKie (1942), *This was Singapore* (Sydney; London: Angus & Robertson).

11 Sharp, *Only One Raffles.*

12 Denis Russell-Roberts (1966), *Spotlight on Singapore* (London: Tandem Books Ltd).

13 Ibid.

14 'Japan's Dilemma' (23 June 1941), *Malaya Tribune*, p. 3, at eresources.nlb.gov.sg/newspapers, accessed 06/09/2021.

15 Barry Gough (2007), 'Prince of Wales and Repulse: Churchill's "Veiled Threat" Reconsidered' in *International Churchill Conference Vancouver*, available through the International Churchill Society at https://winstonchurchill.org/publications/finest-hour/finest-hour-139/prince-of-wales-and-repulse-churchills-veiled-threat-reconsidered/, accessed 13/02/2021.

16 Morton, 'Japan's Decision', p. 104.

17 Ibid., p. 105.

18 'Japan & Her Next Move' (17 September 1941), *Singapore Free Press and Mercantile Advertiser*, p. 4.

19 Brian P. Farrell (2005), *The Defence and Fall of Singapore 1940–1942* (Stroud: Tempus), p. 342.

20 Brian Montgomery (1984), *Shenton of Singapore: Governor and Prisoner of War* (London: L. Cooper in association with Secker & Warburg) p. 77.

21 Diana Cooper (1964), *Trumpets from the Steep* (Harmondsworth: Penguin Books), p. 589.

22 Cooper, *Trumpets*, p. 592.

Chapter 30

1 'State of Emergency in Singapore' (2 December 1941), *Sydney Morning Herald*, p. 1, at http://trove.nla.gov.au/ndp/del/article/17776751, accessed 16/02/2021.

2 *British Malaya* (September 1939, Association of British Malaya). These clichés were repeated throughout 1941.

3 *British Malaya*, (December 1939, Association of British Malaya). Throughout 1940 and 1941, no air-raid shelters were built and when Japanese pilots bombed Singapore before dawn on 8 December 1941, the street lights were on.

4 'State of Emergency in Singapore' (2 December 1941), *Sydney Morning Herald*, p. 1, at http://trove.nla.gov.au/ndp/del/article/17776751, accessed 16/02/2021.

5 'Australia Takes Vital War Decisions' (6 December 1941), *The Courier-Mail* (Brisbane), p. 1, at https://trove.nla.gov.au/newspaper/article/41953178, accessed 16/02/2021.

6 Harrison Foreman (15 May 1941), 'News report direct from Singapore' for NBC, *Gordon Skene Sound Collection*, at https://pastdaily.com/2017/05/15/may-15-1941-reinforcements-singapore/, accessed 16/02/2021.

7 C. Mary Turnbull (1977), *A History of Singapore 1819–1975* (Oxford University Press), p. 169.

8 *British Malaya* (April 1939, Association of British Malaya).

9 Kevin Tan (2008), *Marshall of Singapore: A Biography* (Singapore: Institute of Southeast Asian Studies).

10 Kevin Tan, *Marshall of Singapore*.

11 Diana Cooper (1964), *Trumpets from the Steep* (Harmondsworth: Penguin Books), p.613.

12 Diana Cooper, *Trumpets from the Steep*.

13 William H. Bartsch (2003), *December 8, 1941: MacArthur's Pearl Harbor* (Texas A & M University Press), pp. 192–4.

14 Lance Olsen (2014), 'World War 2 – Did it begin at Pearl Harbor?', at https://hubpages.com/education/WWIIDiditbeginatPearlHarbor, accessed 16/02/2021: Olsen explains that Kota Bharu is in the Eastern Hemisphere, 8 hours ahead of GMT, while Pearl Harbor is in the Western Hemisphere, 10 hours *behind* GMT. When the Japanese attacked Kota Bharu at 00:25 Malayan local time on 8 December 1941, it was only 06:25 on 7 December 1941 in Hawaii. They subsequently bombed Pearl Harbor at 01:50 on 8 December 1941 Malayan local time, when it was 07:50 on 7 December 1941 Hawaiian local time.

15 Maj. Gen. S. Woodburn Kirby (1971), *Singapore: The Chain of Disaster* (London: Cassell and Co.), p. 14.

16 *Admiralty War Diaries of World War 2*, transcribed by Don Kindell: 'Eastern Theatre Operations, the diaries of Admiral Sir Geoffrey Layton, Commander-in-Chief, China Station, November 1941 to March 1942' (Naval-History.Net), at https://www.naval-history.net/xDKWD-EF1941ChinaStation.htm, accessed 16/02/2021.

17 'Eyewitness Account of Sinking' and 'Aerial Torpedoes Sank Prince of Wales, Repulse' (12 December 1941), *Singapore Free Press and Mercantile Advertiser*, pp. 1–2; available at https://ere sources.nlb.gov.sg/newspapers/Digitised/Article/singfreepressb19411212-1.2.5 and https://eresources.nlb.gov.sg/newspapers/Digitised/Article/singfreepressb19411212-1.2.12, accessed 16/02/2021. The journalist-survivors included Cecil Brown, correspondent of the Columbia Broadcasting System.

18 Barry Gough (2007), 'Prince of Wales and Repulse: Churchill's "Veiled Threat" Reconsidered' in *International Churchill Conference Vancouver*, available through the International Churchill Society at https://winstonchurchill.org/publications/finest-hour/finest-hour-139/prince-of-wales-and-repulse-churchills-veiled-threat-reconsidered.

19 'Eyewitness Account of Sinking' and 'Aerial Torpedoes Sank Prince of Wales, Repulse', *Singapore Free Press and Mercantile Advertiser*, pp. 1–2.

Chapter 31

1 John Grehan and Martin Mace (2015), *Disaster in the Far East 1940–1942 (Despatches from the Front)* (Pen and Sword Books

Ltd), Appendix M, Malaya (Air Chief Marshal Sir Robert Brooke-Popham's Despatch on Operations 17 October 1940 to 27 December 1941). His Order of the Day was issued on 8 December 1941.

2 *Britain at War* (1997), 'Chronology of Malaya: Northwestern Front' (14 December 1941), at http://www.britain-at-war.org.uk/WW2/Malaya_and_Singapore/html/body_chronology_of_malaya.htm, accessed 17/02/2021.

3 Mary H. Williams (1960), *Special Studies, Chronology, 1941–1945* (Washington, DC: Office of the Chief of Military History), 'Dec 14', p. 6.

4 'Forces Reorganized: "British Frontier in North Malaya Unbroken"' (11 December 1941), *Singapore Free Press and Mercantile Advertiser*, p. 1, at https://eresources.nlb.gov.sg/newspapers/Digitised/Article/singfreepressb19411211-1.2.8?ST=1&AT=advanced&K=badminton&KA=badminton&DF=&DT=24/12/1979&NPT=&L=&CTA=&P=676, accessed 17/02/2021.

5 Shakila Yacob (2008), *The United States and the Malaysian Economy* (London; New York: Routledge), p. 118: 'By the 1920s, it was possible to drive from Singapore to Bangkok, with the Malayan north-south highway being completed in 1922 and by September 1923, the Johore causeway linked Singapore to the Malay States.'

Chapter 32

1 'Civilians Leave Penang' (20 December 1941), *Singapore Free Press and Mercantile Advertiser*, p. 1, at https://eresources.nlb.gov.sg/newspapers/digitised/issue/singfreepressb19411220-1, accessed 17/02/2021.

2 Anthony Bevins (2011), 'Singapore files reveal bitter power struggle: Newly released papers contain evidence of a damaging personality clash in the colony before the Japanese invasion', *Independent*, at https://www.independent.co.uk/news/uk/politics/singapore-files-reveal-bitter-power-struggle-newly-released-papers-contain-evidence-of-a-damaging-personality-clash-in-the-colony-before-the-japanese-invasion-anthony-bevins-reports-1480816.html, accessed 17/02/2021.

3 Chua Ai Lin (2012), ''The Modern Magic Carpet': Wireless radio in interwar colonial Singapore', *Modern Asian Studies*, Vol. 46, No. 1 (Cambridge University Press), pp. 172, 181.

4 Ilsa Sharp (1981), *There Is Only One Raffles: The Story of a Grand Hotel* (London: Souvenir Press).

5 C. Mary Turnbull (1977), *A History of Singapore 1819–1975* (Oxford University Press), p. 174.

6 Brian Montgomery (1984) *Shenton of Singapore*: *Governor and Prisoner of War* (London: L. Cooper in association with Secker & Warburg).

7 'Malayan Paper Joins Cry for a War Council' (31 December 1941), *Chicago Tribune*, p. 2.

8 'Night Raid' (31 December 1941), *Singapore Free Press and Mercantile Advertiser*, p. 5, at https ://eresources.nlb.gov.sg/newspapers/digitised/issue/singfreepressb19411220-1, accessed 02/12/2021 ; 'British Declare Martial Law in Singapore Area' (30 December 1941), *AP*, at http://archives.chicagotribune.com/1941/12/31/page/2/article/british-declare-martial-law-in-singapore-area.

9 'Malaya Convoys: January 1942' (1962), *Australia in the War of 1939–1945*, Series 3 – Air, Vol. 1 – Royal Australian Air Force, 1939–1942, Ch. 16, from Australian War Memorial at https://s3-ap-southeast-2.amazonaws.com/awm-media/

collection/RCDIG1070487/document/5519770.PDF, accessed 17/02/2021.

Chapter 33

1 Outpost (1942), *Singapore Nightmare: A Story of the Evacuation and an Escape to Australia* (London: John Crowther).

2 Diana Cooper (1964), *Trumpets from the Steep* (Harmondsworth: Penguin Books), p. 614.

3 Maj. Gen. S. Woodburn Kirby (1971), *Singapore: The Chain of Disaster* (London: Cassell and Co.), p. 30.

4 C. Mary Turnbull (1977), *A History of Singapore 1819–1975* (Oxford University Press), p. 180.

5 Turnbull, *Singapore*, pp. 175–6.

6 Kenneth G. Wynn (1989), *Men of The Battle of Britain: A Biographical Dictionary of The Few: The pilots and aircrew from throughout the British Empire and her allies, who flew with the Royal Air Force, Fighter Command, between July 10 and October 31 1940* (Norwich: Gliddon), entry on John Noble Mackenzie; also Turnbull, Singapore, p. 179.

7 *Documents on the Tokyo International Military Tribunal: Charter, Indictment and Judgements* (2008) ed. Neil Boister and Robert Cryer (Oxford University Press), p. 1,373 – *Dissenting Opinion of the Member from India (Justice Pal)*; also Turnbull, *Singapore*, p. 196.

8 Marie Ney (October 1942), 'I Remember', *British Malaya* (Association of British Malaya), p. 61. Marie wrote her article after arriving in South Africa. Her husband was interned at Changi. He survived.

9 'The Battle of Singapore' (27 February 1948), a special supplement from dispatches by A. E. Percival, *Straits Times*, p. 13,

at https://eresources.nlb.gov.sg/newspapers/Digitised/Article/straitstimes19480227-1.2.89.6, accessed 17/02/2021.

10 Ibid. The water supply at Gunong Pulai in south Johore was captured by the Japanese on 27 January.

Chapter 34

1 '1942 The Taking of Singapore – Japanese Footage Only' from *Unknown World War 2 in Color* (Romano-Archives) on https://www.youtube.com/watch?v=s1u-GdEyfvQ, accessed 18/02/2021.

2 Alan Warren (2002), *Britain's Greatest Defeat: Singapore 1942* (London; New York: Hambledon Continuum), p. 204.

3 C. Mary Turnbull (1977), *A History of Singapore 1819–1975* (Oxford University Press), p. 179.

4 Lucy Lum (2008), *The Thorn of Lion City* (London; New York; Toronto; Sydney; New Delhi: Harper Perennial), p. 83.

5 C. Mary Turnbull (1977), *A History of Singapore 1819–1975* (Oxford University Press), p. 182.

6 Alex Chow (2014), 'Dalforce' (Singapore Infopedia), at https://eresources.nlb.gov.sg/infopedia/articles/SIP_765_2005-02-01.html, accessed 18/02/2021.

7 Masanobu Tsuji (1997), *Japan's Greatest Victory: Britain's Worst Defeat*, ed. H. V. Howe, trans. Margaret E. Lake (Staplehurst: Spellmount), p. 93.

8 John Deane Potter (1963), *A Soldier Must Hang: The Biography of an Oriental General* (London: F. Muller), p. 200.

9 Turnbull, *Singapore*, p. 183.

10 Edwin P. Hoyt (2001), *Japan's War: The Great Pacific Conflict* (New York: Cooper Square Press edn), pp. 198–200.

11 Hoyt, *Japan's War*, p. 229.

12 Henry P. Frei (2004). *Guns of February: Japanese Soldiers' Views of the Malayan Campaign and the Fall of Singapore 1941–42* (Singapore: NUS Press), p. 76; and Bill Yenne (2014), *The Imperial Japanese Army: The Invincible Years 1941–42* (Oxford: Osprey Publishing), p. 64.

13 Telegram from Sir Shenton Thomas to Secretary of State for the Colonies (9 February 1942), The National Archives (Kew), *FCO 141/19947*.

14 Turnbull, *Singapore*, p. 184.

15 Letter from Ashley Clark (Foreign Office) to G. E. J. Gent of the Colonial Office (7 February 1942), The National Archives (Kew), *CO 273/669/14*.

16 Vernon Cornelius-Takahama and Janice Loo (2016), 'Pulau Bukom' (Singapore Infopedia), at https://eresources.nlb.gov.sg/infopedia/articles/SIP_922_2005-01-19.html, accessed 18/02/2021.

17 J. G. Farrell (1979), *Singapore Grip* (Glasgow: Fontana/Collins), p. 508; and Mary Harris (2012), 'The Fall of Singapore February 15th 1942: What happened to the women and children?', COFEPOW (Children of Far East Prisoners of War), at https://www.cofepow.org.uk/armed-forces-stories-list/mary-harris-talk, accessed 18/02/2021.

18 Frank Man, 'The Fall and Evacuation of Singapore', p. 2, at http://www.manfamily.org/wp-content/uploads/2017/10/Frank-Mans-Singapore-Evacuation.pdf. (Last accessed 08/12/2021.)

19 Colin Smith (2005), *Singapore Burning: Heroism and Surrender in World War II* (London: Viking), p. 432.

20 Farrell, *Singapore Grip*, p. 444.

21 'The Battle of Singapore' (27 February 1948), *Straits Times*, p. 13; also Turnbull, *Singapore*, p. 185.

22 Man, 'Fall and Evacuation of Singapore', p. 3.

23 Anthony Bevins (2011), 'Incompetence that led to fall of Singapore', *Independent*, at https://www.independent.co.uk/news/uk/incompetence-that-led-to-fall-of-singapore-1477824.html, accessed 18/02/2021.

24 *Substantive and Procedural Aspects of International Criminal Law: The Experience of International and National Law Courts* (2000), ed. Gabrielle Kirk McDonald and Olivia Swaak-Goldman, Vol. 2, Pt 1 (The Hague; London; Boston: Kluwer Law International), p. 779.

Chapter 35

1 Helmer Aslaksen (2002), 'When is Chinese New Year?', *Griffith Observer*, Vol. 66, No.2, pp. 2–17.

2 'The Battle of Singapore' (27 February 1948), *Straits Times*, p. 13.

3 Phyllis Wee (2016), 'British Military Hospital' (Singapore Infopedia), at https://eresources.nlb.gov.sg/infopedia/articles/SIP_568_2005-01-24.html, accessed 27/02/2021.

4 'English Nurses Raped By Japanese Soldiers' (27 October 1945), *The Mirror* (Perth, WA), p. 1, at https://trove.nla.gov.au/newspaper/article/76017527, accessed 16/02/2021.

5 'The Bangka Island Massacre (1942): Sister Vivian Bullwinkels Story' [online] www.pacificwar.org.au, at https://www.pacificwar.org.au/JapWarCrimes/TenWarCrimes/Banka_Massacre.html, accessed 18/02/2021.

6 Irene Lim, 'Alexandra Hospital Massacre' (Singapore Infopedia), at https://eresources.nlb.gov.sg/infopedia/articles/SIP_2014-04-07_090735.html, accessed 21/09/21.

7 Lee Kip Lee (1995), *Amber Sands: A Boyhood Memoir* (Singapore: Federal Publications), p. 117.

8 Lee Geok Boi (1992), *Syonan: Singapore under the Japanese 1942–1945* (Singapore Heritage Society), p. 35.

9 C. Mary Turnbull (1977), *A History of Singapore 1819–1975* (Oxford University Press), p. 176.

10 'The Fall of Singapore' (2017), Australian Broadcasting Corporationonhttps://www.youtube.com/watch?v=sIB7hbrZj7c, accessed 19/02/2021.

11 'The Fall of Singapore – Sequence of Events, Annex B', National Archives of Singapore, at https://www.nas.gov.sg/archivesonline/data/pdfdoc/20120209002/annex_b_media_release_-_battle_for_singapore_(timeline).pdf, accessed 19/02/2021.

12 About 50,000 to begin with, mainly at Selerang Camp, then several thousand very quickly moved on to Burma, Sumatra or Thailand. *Prisoners of War of the Japanese 1939-1945,* Forces War Records at https://www.forces-war-records.co.uk/prisoners-of-war-of-the-japanese-1939-1945; see also Turnbull, *Singapore*, p. 181.

13 Brian Montgomery (1984), *Shenton of Singapore: Governor and Prisoner of War* (London: L. Cooper in association with Secker & Warburg), p. 148.

14 Changi Prison, National Heritage Board.

Chapter 36

1 Cheong Suk-wai (2019), *The Sound of Memories: The Recordings from The Oral History Centre* (National Archives of Singapore), p. 75.

2 Ibid.

3 Henry P. Frei (2004), *Guns of February: Japanese Soldiers' Views of the Malayan Campaign and the Fall of Singapore 1941–42* (Singapore: NUS Press), p. 147.

4 Callum MacDonald (1999), '"Kill All, Burn All, Loot All": The Nanking Massacre of December 1937 and Japanese Policy in China' in *The Massacre in History,* ed. Mark Levene and Penny Roberts (New York; Oxford: Berghahn Books), p.223.

5 An estimate worked from tables provided in Saw Swee-Hock (2007), *The Population of Singapore,* 2nd edn (Singapore: Institute of Southeast Asian Studies), Table 3.1, and Table 3.2, p. 29 and p. 32. The census of 1947 counted 387,318 men.

6 Hirofumi Hayashi (2009), 'The Battle of Singapore, the Massacre of Chinese and Understanding of the Issue in Postwar Japan', *The Asia-Pacific Journal,* Vol. 7, Iss. 28, No. 4. Yamashita and some of his officers in Singapore had served in northern China with the Kwantung Army when *genju shobun* had become accepted practice.

7 Ibid.

8 Ibid.

9 At least 200,000 people were killed. See Iris Chang (1997), *The Rape of Nanking* (New York: Basic Books), p. 100. The BBC reported in 'Scarred by history: The Rape of Nanjing' (11 April 2005): 'Based on estimates made by historians and charity organisations in the city at the time, between 250,000 and 300,000 people were killed, many of them women and children', at http://news.bbc.co.uk/1/hi/world/asia-pacific/223038.stm, accessed 19/02/2021.

10 Hayashi, 'Battle of Singapore'.

Chapter 37

1 Lee Geok Boi (1992), *Syonan: Singapore under the Japanese 1942–1945* (Singapore Heritage Society); Lim Choo Sye (interviewed

by Low Lay Leng), 'Japanese Occupation of Singapore', Accession number 000330, Reel/Disk 2 of 16, National Archives of Singapore, pp. 9–10.

2 Stephanie Ho (2013), 'Operation Sook Ching' (Singapore Infopedia), at https://eresources.nlb.gov.sg/infopedia/art icles/SIP_40_2005-01-24.html, accessed 20/02/2021; and Hirofumi Hayashi (2009), 'The Battle of Singapore, the Massacre of Chinese and Understanding of the Issue in Postwar Japan', *The Asia-Pacific Journal*, Vol. 7, Iss. 28, No. 4.

3 Hayashi, 'Battle of Singapore'.

4 H. Wong (2017), 'Kempeitai' (Singapore Infopedia), at https://eresources.nlb.gov.sg/infopedia/articles/SIP_ 79_2005-02-02.html, accessed 20/02/2021.

5 C. Mary Turnbull (1977), *A History of Singapore 1819–1975* (Oxford University Press), p. 193.

6 H. Wong, 'Kempeitai'; and Henry P. Frei, (2004), *Guns of February: Japanese Soldiers' Views of the Malayan Campaign and the Fall of Singapore 1941–42* (Singapore: NUS Press), p. 149.

7 H. Sidhu (1991), *The Bamboo Fortress: True Singapore War Stories* (Singapore: Native Publications).

8 Hayashi, 'Battle of Singapore'.

9 Transcript of interview given on 6 July 2009 by Lee Kuan Yew (then Singapore's Minister Mentor) to Mark Jacobson for the January 2010 edition of *National Geographic*: Mr Lee said that 'verifiable numbers' for the Sook Ching massacre 'would be about 50,000' even though estimates 'go up to about 90,000'. Available at https://www.nas.gov.sg/archivesonline/data/ pdfdoc/20100104007.htm, accessed 20/02/2021. See also Kevin Blackburn (2000), 'The Collective Memory of the Sook Ching Massacre and the Creation of the Civilian War Memorial of Singapore', *Journal of the Malaysian Branch of the Royal Asiatic Society*, Vol. 73, No. 2, p. 73.

10 There was a census in 1931 and another in 1947 but none in-between. There were 261,000 Chinese men in 1931, and 387,318 Chinese men in 1947. My rough estimate of 300,000 Chinese men in Singapore in 1942 is worked from tables provided in Saw Swee-Hock (2007), *The Population of Singapore*, 2nd edn (Singapore: Institute of Southeast Asian Studies), Table 3.1 and Table 3.2, p. 29 and p. 32. How many of these were between the ages 18 and 50 would determine the percentage massacred.

Sex ratios of Chinese men to women in population statistics also offer a clue even if imperfect. Even factoring in the greater migration of Chinese women into Singapore through the 1930s, still the ratio of Chinese men to women fell sharply after the war, from 1,656 Chinese men to 1,000 Chinese women in 1931 to 1,132 men to 1,000 women in 1947.

11 The Chinese post-war press claimed that 25,000 Chinese civilians were massacred in the state of Johore alone – Kevin Blackburn and Karl Hack (2012), *War Memory and the Making of Modern Malaysia and Singapore* (Singapore: NUS Press), p. 140.

12 J. M. Pierre (22 March 2015), 'Culturally sanctioned suicide: Euthanasia, seppuku, and terrorist martyrdom', *World Journal of Psychiatry*, 5(1): 4–14, at https://www.ncbi.nlm.nih.gov/pmc/articles/PMC4369548/, accessed 20/02/2021.

13 Jai Prakash Soni, et al. (2020), 'A fatal case of multi-organ failure in acute yellow phosphorous poisoning', introduction in *Autopsy Case Reports* at https://core.ac.uk/download/pdf/287196506.pdf, accessed 01/03/2021.

14 Private clinics and dispensaries only reopened in March: see C. Mary Turnbull (1977), *A History of Singapore 1819–1975* (Oxford University Press), p.192.

15 Robert E. Gosselin, Harold C. Hodge and Roger P. Smith (1984), *Clinical Toxicology of Commercial Products,* 5th edn (Baltimore, Md: Williams and Wilkins).

16 Robert E. Gosselin et al., *Clinical Toxicology.*

Chapter 38

1 *Zhao Nan Ri Bao* (23 February 1942), National Library of Singapore, trans. from microfilm by Chua Yilin.

2 Ibid.

3 According to Herman Hochstadt, whose grandfather was John Hochstadt, his cousin Guy Webb was living with their grandfather at the time. Guy's mother and brothers were in Australia, while his father Carlo had become a Japanese prisoner of war. Guy did help out in the company but he was only in his teens. (Email from Herman R. Hochstadt to Teresa Lim, 06/01/2016). It seems unlikely to me, given the danger of the time, that John Hochstadt would have sent his young grandson out on his own to organize a burial.

4 'The Battle of Singapore', from dispatches by Lieut. Gen. A. E. Percival, formerly General Officer Commanding Malaya (27 February 1948), *Straits Times*, p. 13.

Chapter 39

1 Rudy Mosbergen (2007), *In the grip of a crisis: the experiences of a teenager during the Japanese occupation of Singapore, 1942–45* (Singapore: Rudy Mosbergen).

2 Edwin P. Hoyt (1993), *Three Military Leaders: Heihachiro Togo, Isoroku Yamamoto, Tomoyuki Yamashita* (Tokyo, London: Kodansha International).

Epilogue

1 J. M. Pierre (22 March 2015), 'Culturally sanctioned suicide: Euthanasia, seppuku, and terrorist martyrdom', *World Journal of Psychiatry*, 5(1): 4–14, at https://www.ncbi.nlm.nih.gov/pmc/articles/PMC4369548/, accessed 24/05/2021: In China, as in Japan, suicide was sometimes culturally sanctioned and considered an act of volition affirming a life rooted in ideals of loyalty, duty or honour, especially during periods of patriotic nationalism.

Acknowledgements

My enormous thanks to the National Heritage Board of Singapore for the grant that made it possible to translate our Law genealogy into English.

I am much indebted to the people who provided me with crucial pieces of this family jigsaw: Dr Peter Cunich of the University of Hong Kong History Department and Dr Ho Nai-Kiong of the Yangzheng (Yeung Ching) Alumni were generous in sharing time and information with me, even though I was just a name on an email; Tang Wee-Kit kindly linked me up with the indispensable Mazelan Anuar at the National Library of Singapore; and I found young Fanny only with the help of the Methodist Girls' School Alumnae Association's Mrs Anna Tham (former principal of the school) and Barbara Chee Yeo (former president of the alumnae).

My heartfelt appreciation to my sprawling Singapore family, for their stories and pictures: it was a privilege to know my late uncle Bernard Law, the late Lye Pak-Leong and his wife Lye Yin-Yue, and to still be in touch with the sole surviving member of the photograph from 1935, Lye Hou-Seong – even though she is over 90 years old, we are in touch through WhatsApp. I am also obligated to my cousins Linda Neo and Susan Tsang for their insights, and to John Law and his wife Li Zhang, Jacqueline Law, Freida Neo, and Eunice Yap. Each of you added colour to the canvas.

I am especially beholden to those friends who read my manuscript from start to finish – some of them twice! – and gave me their invaluable comments: Amanda Godfree,

Ed Brumby, Suzy Frith, and Simon Frith. Amanda kept me going through my first major re-write and, among her many talents, turned out also to be an exact but always tactful editor.

But if not for Suzy Frith and a fateful walk we shared on Gara Rock in Devon, Fanny's story may never have been published. Suzy asked to read the manuscript because her neighbour and friend, a literary agent, was interested in stories about strong women.

Rowan Lawton of The Soho Agency turned out to be a formidable advocate. She connected me with Ariel Pakier, an editor committed to coaxing out the best possible book from her writers. I am deeply grateful to them both for their advice, dynamism, vision, and support. Ariel is also assisted by a great team at Penguin Michael Joseph that includes Gaby Young, Rachael Sharples, Emma Henderson, Paula Flanagan, and the meticulous Richenda Todd.

Thanks are due also to everyone – friends and strangers – who provided contacts, or short translations, or information: Dr Chan Lau Kit-Ching; Christa Tam; Lee Huay-Leng (Chinese Media Group Singapore); Chua Yi-Lin who found a Chinese newspaper from 1942 with the critical Japanese announcement on the execution of 'rebels', and Prof Koh Keng We of the Nanyang Technological University who recommended her help; and to Mr Herman Hochstadt, distinguished former civil servant, for the story of his grandfather, and the Eurasian Association of Singapore who put me in touch with him. Thanks, too, to Heather Addison, Wong Chun-Wai, Dr Dianne Lim, Devan Janadas, Richard Lee, Angela Sheng, and Anna McCormick.

Not least, I am grateful to the men and women who run the British Library, the SOAS Library, the National Archives at Kew and in Singapore, and those everywhere who maintain their precious archives and the wonderful World Wide Web – thank you for looking after the nameless thousands who pass through your portals.

But without my husband, Nick – who believed in me and whose support has been unwavering – and without my late mother, Violet, whose reminiscences have proved remarkably correct, I could not have written this book.

He just wanted a decent book to read ...

Not too much to ask, is it? It was in 1935 when Allen Lane, Managing Director of Bodley Head Publishers, stood on a platform at Exeter railway station looking for something good to read on his journey back to London. His choice was limited to popular magazines and poor-quality paperbacks – the same choice faced every day by the vast majority of readers, few of whom could afford hardbacks. Lane's disappointment and subsequent anger at the range of books generally available led him to found a company – and change the world.

'We believed in the existence in this country of a vast reading public for intelligent books at a low price, and staked everything on it'
Sir Allen Lane, 1902–1970, founder of Penguin Books

The quality paperback had arrived – and not just in bookshops. Lane was adamant that his Penguins should appear in chain stores and tobacconists, and should cost no more than a packet of cigarettes.

Reading habits (and cigarette prices) have changed since 1935, but Penguin still believes in publishing the best books for everybody to enjoy. We still believe that good design costs no more than bad design, and we still believe that quality books published passionately and responsibly make the world a better place.

So wherever you see the little bird – whether it's on a piece of prize-winning literary fiction or a celebrity autobiography, political tour de force or historical masterpiece, a serial-killer thriller, reference book, world classic or a piece of pure escapism – you can bet that it represents the very best that the genre has to offer.

Whatever you like to read – trust Penguin.